A Voyage Across the Americas
The Journey of Henri de Büren
1852-1853

ADAPTATION BY

Jean-François de Buren

EDITED BY

August Cosentino

EDITIONS DE PENTHES

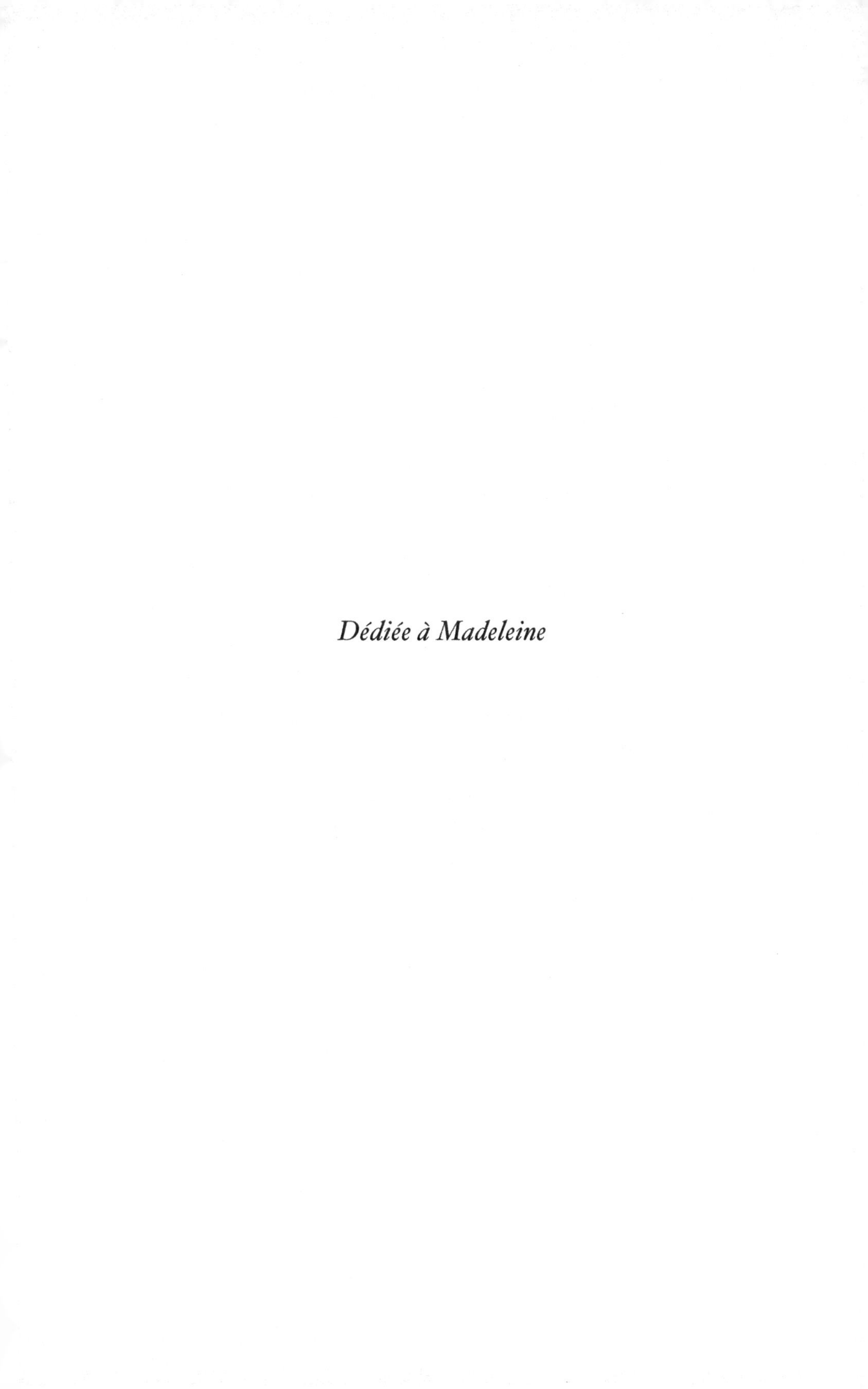

Dédiée à Madeleine

Contents

Preface iii

Acknowledgements vii

Introduction I

Letters 7

    Aboard the Niagara 9

    Boston II

    New York I3

    Niagara I8

    Aboard the Fanny Spurhawk 26

    Aboard the Empire Estate 28

    Philadelphia 32

    New Orleans 40

    Havana 47

    Mexico City 53

    Panama City 83

    Lima 91

    Moyobamba I02

Illustrations & Drawings III

Journal – Voyage on the Amazon I27

    Havana I29

    Santiago I33

    Contumazá I37

    Tambo I42

    Cajamarca I43

    The Poianka hacienda I53

    Celendín I55

    Tambo Viejo I57

    Chachapoyas I65

    Moyobamba I93

Tambo de Era *230*

Tambo de Roque *234*

Rio de San Miguel *236*

Chasuta *241*

Between Lagunas and Nauta *247*

Between Nauta and Loreto *252*

Loreto *258*

Aboard the Marajo *265*

Barra do Rio Negro *277*

Aboard the Marajo *280*

Pará *289*

The Lost Album 295

Glossary 303

Name Index 305

Preface

In 2007, while looking through old books in an armoire at my parents' home north of San Francisco, I stumbled upon a tattered journal. A flood of memories returned to me. It was the same journal I remembered holding as a boy. As before, I didn't know the journal's provenance, but upon seeing it again I was intrigued anew. A watercolor on the first page showed the sun glistening off the surface of a blue sea, a small vessel gently rocking as it made its way to port. Mid-morning sunlight illuminated an imposing fort and lighthouse crowned by the Spanish colors. Below in elegant cursive was the word "Havane."

Who had written this first-hand dispatch from 19th-century Cuba? As I thumbed through the journal, more locations jumped from the yellowing pages: Lima, Trujillo, Cajamarca, Iquitos, and Santarém. I felt compelled to read it in its entirety and hoped it would have a compelling story to tell. I would not be disappointed.

The journal had been penned by my great-great-grandfather, Henri de Büren (1825-1909), a Swiss nobleman, botanist, explorer, and artist. His writings, which include the journal along with letters home that I found months later, chronicle not just a voyage to Cuba and the Amazon, but also a two-year journey through the Americas of the 1850s. His first-hand accounts of Boston, New York, Washington, D.C., New Orleans, and Mexico City mention important Swiss expatriates and scientific figures, discuss race and society, and marvel at the diversity of the natural world.

The following work is the result of a dedication to researching and sharing that story, one that has been a true labor of love for six years. What started originally as a translation of a travel memoir has over time, become something more.

In 2009, I had a very important meeting with Anselm & Emmanuelle Zurfluh of the Editions de Penthes, the publishing arm of the Museum of the Swiss Abroad in Geneva. After a delightful lunch and a tour of the museum, the Zurfluhs expressed interest in publishing Henri's journal and letters. Anselm told me at that meeting, almost prophetically, "It will take about four years before all is said and done, you know, these sorts of projects take time." Four years, I thought to myself. You must be joking!

The initial intention was for the French transcription and translated English to sit together in a companion volume. The work was initially translated from French by Hervé Boblet, and Emmanuelle worked on the French transcription, deciphering handwriting and 19th-century turns of phrase with great skill—this adaptation would not have been be possible without them.

Over time, however, I felt that I wanted something different for Henri's narrative. In re-reading the translation with fresh eyes, I felt certain small edits could make the work better. I also came to feel that having the French and English side-by-side would transform the work into a far more academic exercise which might limit the overall appeal of the work.

I have gone to great pains to make sure my ancestor's voice remained intact as I refined his original language. The intention was not to make the work modern, but simply more approachable, edits were stylistic as opposed to contextual.

The adaptation includes punctuation, absent from the hand-written source materials; correct spelling of place names (if found today) as they were most likely written phonetically; localized metaphors; and the largest liberty taken was the usage of synonyms for overused terms (i.e., picturesque, beautiful, miserable, etc.)

There is one key element that I did not alter, and over which I agonized for a considerable time. That element pertains to his social commentary—on race, specifically. In the end, I realized that if I changed those sections to make myself feel more at ease I would be taking the slippery slope to historical revisionism and thus taint the project as a whole, so they remain.

I would also be remiss if I didn't mention the format of the work in some detail. As expressed earlier, Henri's journal was found first followed by his letters. They are presented here as I found them, as two parts. That said, there are two small items of potential confusion that I would like to address.

The first concerns the letters. While the letters were unified in one volume by his sister, they were not all addressed to her. They were written to many people in Henri's life; his mother and father, his sister, and his aunt and uncle. The letter salutations (when present) give a hint to the recipient, but not always.

The second potential source of confusion is the overlapping narrative and location of the letters and journal. If Henri had never gone on the expedition across Peru and Brazil (something that was not part of his original plan), I doubt there would have been a journal at all. He seemed to come around to the idea of the journal later on, as there are no entries from the U.S. and Canada, and while he wrote a small entry from Cuba, he only returned to it in earnest in Peru. The letters were for others, the journal was to capture his own thoughts and feelings. The following chart highlights the countries covered between the letters and the journal.

Countries Visited	Letters	Journal
United States	x	
Canada	x	
Cuba	x	x
Mexico	x	
Panama	x	
Peru	x	x
Brazil		x

Four years later after that momentous meeting in Geneva, and six years from when I started this project, Henri's entire work will finally see the light of day. The journey to publication has been like his voyage—countless twists and turns, an uncertain fate, and a deeply satisfying conclusion.

Jean-François de Buren

Novato, California
October 3rd, 2013

Acknowledgements

This work would simply not have been possible without the help of countless friends and family. The assistance provided has been in many forms; from financial assistance for translation costs and research trips, to historically relevant articles, to advice, to emotional support.

A deeply heartfelt thank you to: Anselm Zurfluh, Emmanuelle Zurfluh, Hervé Boblet, August Cosentino, Bénédict de Tscharner, Tim Omarzu, George Scharffenberger, Marie Arana, Peter Schibli, Jessica Dacey, Dr. James Hanken, Judy Warnement, Susan Schoelwer, Hilda Birchmeier, Wal Baur, Christophe Dufour, Eduardo Salazar, Daniel Ritière, Beth Zurbuchen, Jeff Kwaterski, Norma Garza, Evan Bloom, Natasha Proietto, Caterina Pierre, Milko Vuille, Carlos Leal, Christophe Vauthey, Shari Yantra Marcacci, Salomé Bryant Gysi, Gary Shapiro, Claudia Deutsch, Hadi Barkat, Francis Tapon, Vernon Goins, Vasco Dones, Dave Shaver, Von Babasin, Paul Obleas, Agota Jonas, Ian Nyquist, Jaison Starkes, Ashleigh Young, Margaret & Robert Turley, the Thalmann family, the Carter family, the Bardet family, the Gay family, the extended de Buren/von Büren/van Buren family around the world, my parents François and Sharon, my incredibly loving wife Jeannie and last but not least my two amazing daughters Pascale and Noémie.

I would also like to thank the following institutions: Les Editions de Penthes, L'Institut des Suisses dans le Monde, Musée d'Ethnographie de Neuchâtel, Muséum d'Histoire Naturelle Neuchâtel, swissinfo, Harvard University Museum of Comparative Zoology, Harvard University Botany Library, and the American Antiquarian Society.

My biggest thanks however goes to Henri for keeping a record of his journey, and his parents for allowing him chase his dream.

ISBN: 978-2-940531-02-8

Printed in the United States

Published in partnership with:

Musée
des Suisses
dans le Monde

Editions de Penthes

Institut and Museum of the Swiss Abroad

18, Chemin de l'Impératrice

CH-1292 Pregny-Geneva

Switzerland

www.penthes.ch

Introduction

Henri de Büren was born in 1825 as one of five children, the only son of Swiss Baron Albert de Büren (1791-1873) and Baroness Catherine de Büren-Senarclens (1796-1857). He grew up at the castle of Vaumarcus (the home of the de Büren family since the mid-17th century), which overlooks Lake Neuchâtel in French-speaking Switzerland. He came from an ancient noble Swiss family that could trace its roots to the 12th century and to the small town of Büren on the Aare River in the Canton of Bern. Henri was a great lover of nature and a prolific artist. As his father before him, he received his botanical training at Albrecht Thaer's Agriculture School near Berlin. Upon his return from Prussia, he also received forestry training in Switzerland, a skill that was crucial to ensure the health of the vast wooded lands that surrounded the castle.

Henri was born into privilege and wealth and certainly did not want for much, but unlike his ancestors his aristocratic title was merely honorary. Social change and revolution finally came to Neuchâtel in 1831 when noble titles were abolished. Henri knew from the age of six that he would not be granted the same status his ancestors had enjoyed. How this affected him is unclear, but it was certainly one factor that propelled him to look beyond Europe's borders to find his own place in the world.

Like many of his day, Henri was deeply moved to travel to the Americas by Alexander von Humboldt's accounts of the flora and fauna of Latin America, and was also certainly intrigued by the customs and lifestyles of the indigenous peoples of the New World. Another source of attraction for Henri was an opportunity to visit many preeminent Neuchâtel scientists who had left Switzerland in the 1840s for the more welcoming scientific climate in the United

States. After a period of considerable persuasion, his father and mother relented and agreed to fund their only son's wanderlust.

Henri de Buren left Switzerland in 1852. He would not return for almost two years, with sporadic letters home the only contact with his family during that time. Henri spent his first six months traveling the United States and parts of Canada, before sailing to Havana. After a short stay in Cuba, he traveled to Mexico, where he spent four more months, then journeyed on to Panama and then Lima. From Lima he had originally intended to go overland to Buenos Aires through Bolivia. However, due to political instability, he was instead persuaded to join a Peruvian expedition leading the first wave of German settlers to the town of Caballococha in Loreto state near the border with Brazil. He would travel with the expedition over the Cordilleras, finally making it to Loreto and then following the Amazon River to its mouth. His full journey across South America took him overland from Trujillo on the Pacific to the Brazilian state of Parà on the Atlantic, where he found a steamer back to Europe.

The first place Henri visited in 1852 was Boston, where he spent a fortnight, most of it at the home of his compatriot, Louis Agassiz. Agassiz was one of the most important scientists of his day, and knew Henri and his father well. For Henri, a young man in his late 20s, it would have been a significant honor to stay at the home of such a notable figure. The relationship seems to have been respectful and supportive: "During a captivating conversation, thanks to the spirit and scientific knowledge of these gentlemen, Mr. Agassiz let me know that he owned a beautiful forest herbarium. Imagine how interested I was! ... I could not resist asking Mr. Agassiz to allow me to go through his herbarium, which will be a precious guide for the rest of my journey."

Henri was a botanist first and foremost, so his biggest thrill in Boston was the time he spent with the preeminent American botanist, Asa Gray. "He is first and foremost (as you well know) a botanical genius, still young and extremely healthy and at the same time a charming gentleman in all respects, which signifies a lot to me. He gave me about fifty forest plants that he picked himself while we were walking in the botanical garden, even climbing the trees to find nicest examples."

After Boston, Henri traveled to Albany, marveled at Lake George ("the most beautiful sight that I have seen in America"), and toured Montreal before heading to New York. In a letter from New York he speaks of the palpable excitement of new discoveries while also still feeling close to his loved ones: "Not a single day passes when, among the activities and the thousand new sensations that my long and interesting journey produces, I do not address you in my thoughts, and steal from this unceasing whirlwind of new events that continually surround me a few moments that I spend softly and quietly with you in my heart."

While in New York, Henri took in Barnum's American Museum. P.T. Barnum, later of circus fame, operated a museum that was part concert hall, part zoo, and part freak show. For Henri, Barnum's museum represented the merging of the scientific and the fanciful—a very American creation: "Our science at home is liberal; in America, it is totally different. The cities here are not willing to build monuments to science, or are doing it very imperfectly, but it is individuals ... who take care of the whole thing inspired by the immense curiosity the inhabitants of this country have."

While Henri was focused on scientific concerns he could not resist commenting on the social environment of his new surroundings as well. "To sum it up, with Americans, the head leads and trumps the heart. It is the head that dictates their laws and instructs them in their behavior. The industrial spirit transforms society by reducing all relationships between men to usefulness. There are noble passions that enrich the soul; money spoils and withers it."

Henri continued on through the U.S. for months, by stage-coach, steamer, and train. He left the United States in December of 1852 by steamer from Mobile heading for Havana. After a small time in Cuba, he moved on to a four-month stay in Mexico, where he traveled the country with a number of fellow European aristo-crats. The lengthiest part of his journal is dedicated to his voyage across the Cordilleras and down the Amazon with the first German emigrants to Peru.

A year after returning to Switzerland he would marry his cousin Madeleine Sillem (to whom this work is dedicated). Tragically she would die only six weeks into their marriage of typhoid. The entire family including Henri was utterly devastated.

Five years later he would marry for a second time, with another cousin, Natalie de Freudenreich. They would have nine children, three of whom were deaf and mute from birth.

Henri would become a Member of the Grand Council of Neuchâtel from 1856 to 1865 and President of the Agricultural Society of Neuchâtel from 1859 to 1885. He was also two-time president of the Agricultural Society of Romand (French-speaking) Switzerland.

Interestingly Henri did not make great mention of his journey; he never published any articles on the subject and donated the items he brought back from the new world to local Neuchâtel museums (among them a tufted Capuchin and a Mundurucú headdress).

In 1888 after much soul searching and surely many sleepless nights, Henri under the advisement of fellow family members decided to sell the Château of Vaumarcus, home of the de Büren family since the mid 17th century. He sold the castle in large part as he needed to find a home that was near special services for his deaf children, for whom he cared a great deal.

He would move his family to the country home of La Châtelaine, in the district of Aïre near Geneva, the former home of

Dr. Théodore Maunoir, co-founder of the International Committee of the Red Cross. Years later, in gratitude for donating land from Châtelaine to the local power utility, a street that borders the old manor home was named after Henri and can still be found today.

Apart from his writings, the other lasting legacy on Henri's voyage was his son's emigration to South America. When Henri sold the castle at the end of the 19th century, he gave one of his sons seed capital to start a new life for himself in the New World.

Philippe-Frédéric de Büren emigrated to Argentina in 1891 and his children were born there. Philippe-Frédéric's first-born son, Henry, named in honor of his grandfather, would later emigrate to California and settle in the United States. All of Henri de Büren's living descendants are now children of the Americas.

His journey provides a unique glimpse of the pre-Civil War era. One that, through his lens, highlights scientific optimism, celebrates nature, explores social dynamics, and documents racial injustice. Henri was a man of his time for good and ill. His thoughts and observations on the 19th century open a larger window into the past, one that shows at times how far we have come and at others how far we still have to go.

< 6 >

Letters

ABOARD THE NIAGARA

June 22nd, 1852

By the time you receive this letter, I will be in the middle of the ocean, having started my long journey overseas, the success of which I know you will pray for; this is the reason I undertake it with so much confidence and hope.

The day after our arrival in Liverpool we headed to the boarding area at around two o'clock in the afternoon, where we met our fellow passengers. This was a rather important meeting since we will have to spend a couple of weeks together, destined to share the good and the bad sides, the advantages and the disadvantages of a sea voyage.

Although it is the smallest of the steamers that provide mail service between England and America, our ship, the Niagara, is nevertheless a respectable size, three times as big as the three steamships on Lake Geneva put together. It is also endowed with a very seaworthy aspect, with a length of two hundred feet, a width of fifty feet, and a six-hundred-horsepower engine. Underneath the lounge, which is rather beautiful, are our cabins—large enough so my tall comrade and I can share one with all our effects in comfort and with the ocean cradle gently rocking us to sleep—an excellent slumber.

Since the crossing is now over, I find myself more able to express my opinion about my fellow passengers. We were around thirty people in the first-class cabins, and only a few of them were in any way amicable or pleasant. Out of this category, there are three whom I shall remember gladly: a Mr. Oliver Middleton, and then a lady whose name I do not remember, but who is from Boston and, having learned that we would go west, very nicely wrote a letter of introduction to one of her acquaintances on our behalf. I should also mention Mr. Mazendorf, a native of Hamburg and a merchant in New Orleans, where he is returning.

Another character was Mr. Peabody, who was returning with his wife and daughter from a long trip to the Continent. Mr. Peabody had also visited Switzerland where he had admired the Schadau Castle and the Zielok[1] in Bern a great deal. He would have liked to play more of a role onboard but was not really able to, and was a bit hopeless in this respect. As well as this lot there were another two characters, one a rice planter from Carolina, who also happened to be a colonel in the militia and who was never without a large book under his arm (a beautiful edition of Wellington's dispatches), whom he considered, however, to have been rather a poor tactician! He seemed unable to say anything or speak without laughing—tilting his head back and running his hand through his hair—all at the same time.

The less playful of these two gentlemen was a tobacco planter from Virginia (a habitual smoker) but nevertheless agreeable and faithfully accompanied by his butler Don Juan Ferrera.

---

[1] *I assume he means the **Zytglogge**, the clock tower in Bern's old town and one of its most recognized symbols.*

Letter Two

BOSTON

June 28, 1852

I finished my last letter rather abruptly, having learned that in order for it to leave on the first ship it had to be mailed today.

Fortunately, we arrived in Boston on Friday morning: a very picturesque city indeed, built on the banks of a gulf, intertwined with peninsulas, islands, and bridges. It is not much by itself, considering that most of the buildings are (in my opinion) shacks, and therefore it looks neither big nor important but rather resembles a big village, despite its population of one hundred and forty thousand. Even Zurich looks like a much larger city and is certainly better paved. On the other hand, the countryside is beautiful, the greenery is magnificent, and its cottages, most of them built of wood with joists, are very charming, set among their trees.

We had dinner yesterday at Mr. Guyot's,[2] who greeted us perfectly and with whom we shall go for a walk later this afternoon and pay a visit to Mr. Agassiz[3]. I will give you more details on these two gentlemen in my next letter, which I am planning on sending to you from New York, where we shall probably go tomorrow.

The ocean voyage, during which I was only sick for two or three days, actually did me a great deal of good, but the twenty-degree

---

[2] ***Arnold Henry Guyot** (1807-1884), a Swiss-American geologist and geographer.*

[3] ***Jean Louis Rodolphe Agassiz** (1807-1873), a Swiss biologist, geologist, and physician. Henri knew both Arnold Guyot and Louis Agassiz before they left for America; it seems likely that the two may have even come to the castle of Vaumarcus, near Neuchâtel where Henri's father was a baron.*

heat that we are encountering now in Boston contrasts remarkably with the cold and hazy weather that accompanied us in England and during the crossing.

< 12 >

Letter Three

NEW YORK

July 11th, 1852

Not a single day passes when, among the activities and the thousand new sensations that my long and interesting journey produces, I do not address you in my thoughts, and steal from this unceasing whirlwind of new events that continually surround me a few moments that I spend softly and quietly with you in my heart; questioning you, listening to you, following you through the hours, the months, the seasons, trying to guess what impressions or events preoccupy you. Thus I immerse myself and I find repose among the memories of our family life. I also dream that some of your thoughts travel with me and I pursue my journey with greater strength, vitality, and confidence—regretting that you cannot actually participate in all the happy and interesting sensations that I feel in the New World. On the other hand, all the impressions are not of this same sort, since the life of a traveler is, like all other lives, a two-sided coin, a union of both flowers and thorns. Rest assured that the latter have not yet hurt me too deeply and that I would rather stop to gaze at these new flowers than grab their thorns.

You will have received by now (I suppose) the news of my happy arrival in Boston. I just have to tell you how I spent the two weeks between my two letters, a story which you will find interesting for all the pleasures and troubles that I encountered. As I told you, I have been, as has my friend, delightfully entertained by Mr. Guyot and his family. We had a very pleasant dinner, followed by a charming walk in the neighborhood.

On the following day, we had afternoon tea with Mr. Agassiz whom we visited in his laboratory. During a captivating conversation, thanks to the spirit and scientific knowledge of these gentlemen, Mr. Agassiz let me know that he owned a beautiful forest herbarium. Imagine how interested I was! My strong desire to acquaint myself with the rich forest flora of this country is both natural and taxing.

I could not resist asking Mr. Agassiz to allow me to go through his herbarium, which will be a precious guide for the rest of my journey. He granted his permission most graciously, insisting on my staying at his home for the duration of my study, authorizing and inviting me to keep all duplicates that might be of interest for you and me. You can imagine that this offer, made with the greatest generosity, touched and delighted me, but the hospitality I enjoyed during nine days at his home deserves as much gratitude, since it was as gracious and cordial as hospitality could ever be. This will not surprise you, coming from Mr. Agassiz, who has many amiable gifts and combines perfect kindness with the highest and deepest scientific knowledge.

Mrs. Agassiz is in every respect a charming wife, and their three children (although not her own) could not have a more tender mother. They are all well behaved and seem happy. The oldest girl, who looks a great deal like her father, is around fifteen years of age and rather pretty. The son, who is almost fourteen, and the youngest, Pauline, who is eleven, are fine, too. Surrounded by such a charming family, loved, well thought of, and having every ease and encouragement to focus on his science, Mr. Agassiz really has a charmed life. I am especially convinced of this, as he has not aged a day since the time when I last saw him in Neuchâtel.

Yet, despite the happiness he seems to enjoy in this country, he has not, I believe, really mixed wholeheartedly with the foreigners here. He is still completely attached to his native land and his fellow countrymen, whom he brings up quite regularly. During our time together he has often asked me to pass on his best compliments to you.

Torn between the urge of going through the whole herbarium, which is composed of about sixty large bundles, and the fear of indiscretion for overstaying my welcome, I reached my goal in nine days despite the heat that rose above thirty degrees. I kept for all the duplicates that I could take for us without feeling guilty. They represent two large bundles that Mr. de Graffenreid[4] will be kind enough to bring back to you when he returns to Europe.

I suppose that of all these plants, those from the Blue Mountains will interest you the most, considering the resemblance they bear to our alpine plants. I will, at the same time, send you Mr. Gray's manual, in order for you to determine the ones that aren't present, and correct the errors that I may have made in writing down the names of the others.

I visited Mr. Gray[5] who also greeted me most kindly. He is first and foremost (as you well know) a botanical genius, still young and extremely healthy and at the same time a charming gentleman in all respects, which signifies a lot to me. He gave me about fifty forest plants that he picked himself while we were walking in the botanical garden, even climbing the trees to find nicest examples.

The forest flora is immensely rich in this country, three times as rich as in ours, and the vegetation differs completely for trees from the same family and the same group. The tree that impressed me the most, because of the beauty of its stature and its leaves, is

---

[4] *François de Graffenreid was Henri's travel partner while in the United States, and a fellow Swiss aristocrat.*

[5] *Asa Gray (1810-1888) is considered the most important American botanist of the 19th century.*

the American Elm, whose branches bow with much more grace and much less melancholy than those of our most beautiful willows.

To name you some of the most remarkable ones, I would mention the Caryas,[6] five species of the Juglandaceae[7] family, then seven species of magnolias. The Gymnocladus Canadensis[8] has the most beautiful leaf of all the trees that belong to the leguminous family, from the same family as the Virgila Lutaia,[9] in which the branches bow in the same manner, with a magnificent flower that is, in my opinion, the most beautiful ornamental tree that you can see, then the Liriodendron,[10] the Sassafras, and the Nyssaceae.[11] Mr. Gray promised to give me all the seeds he could obtain.

You will probably remember reading in Mr. Lesquereux's[12] letters of the huge manufacture and trade of ice that is made in Boston and is valued at two to three million. All of America and a part of the West Indies, Calcutta, and Madras, receive their ice from Boston. For its own use, Boston consumes no less than fifty-seven-thousand tons per year, at a price of fourteen to fifteen cents per one hundred kilos.

Here, just as in Boston and Cambridge, people have their ice delivered in the morning, and the iceman comes as regularly as (and often simultaneously with) the milkman. Ice is a great and necessary comfort, when you find yourself at the same latitude as Lisbon and Madrid, and is widely available to the rich and well as the poor. In Boston, it will soon become impossible (because of a new law) to find a single glass of wine or beer to drink. Only those who will

---

[6] *Hickory*

[7] *Walnut Family*

[8] *Kentucky Coffeetree*

[9] *Name unknown and feel it may be in error.*

[10] *Tuliptree*

[11] *Flowering trees closely related to Dogwood.*

[12] **Charles Léo Lesquereux** *(1806-1889), Swiss bryologist and a pioneer of American paleobotany.*

be able to buy two hundred gallons at a time will have the right to drink. The law was accepted unanimously and in a smaller margin by the population of the state of Massachusetts; this very population who (I am sure) would collectively rise up if their ice was taken away for even one day.

It is close to Mr. Agassiz's mansion by the little lake of Fresh Pond—therefore very close to Cambridge—that this operation takes place on a large scale. This business, founded by shareholders, has seen (if I am not mistaken) the value of its shares triple in just a few years. It is in a large wooden warehouse with double doors, whose cracks are filled with sawdust so that the ice lasts. The ice arrives there and is piled up using a large machine which then loads the ice onto railroad cars, located below the warehouse. From there, it is transported to Boston.

Another rather surprising thing in this country is to see how houses travel. Mr. Agassiz, for example, had one containing his collections located on the banks of Fresh Pond Lake. He left for a two-month's excursion, and at the end of which he returned to see his house, only to find it gone! He asked about what had become of it and he was shown it not three hundred feet away, totally intact, not a single jar of his inside broken.

Also, not far from Cambridge, they managed to move a house over a cemetery without harming a single monument. You will have to tell anyone who doesn't believe you that it is true that most houses are built out of wood or bricks, and in a way that is very different from what we are used to back home. The transport takes place by a system of logs pulled by one or two horses. Very often, the houses are still occupied, and the locals continue to eat or sleep as though nothing was happening.

Excuse my scribbles, dear Father, but my ink is full of things that stop my quill and impede my calligraphic intentions.

Farewell

Letter Four

NIAGARA

August 5th, 1852

Thank you so much, dear Aunt, for your good and excellent letter. It is the first one in the New World, in this foreign land, to bring me news of all of you. I enjoy hearing from those who bind me to our good and old Europe, in order to have me love my country and appreciate more my home, as well as the happiness to have a family such as mine. My journey through the United States has nonetheless been great. This is because in this country, the minds, the way of life, the social relationships, and the public institutions are all brand new to me. They inspire in me, if not always admiration, at least great interest in their aspects, sometimes practical, sometimes superficial, almost always the result of financial calculation, and very rarely the fruit of sensibility or philanthropy.

To sum it up, with Americans, the head leads and trumps the heart. It is the head that dictates their laws and instructs them in their behavior. The industrial spirit transforms society by reducing all relationships between men to usefulness. There are noble passions that enrich the soul; money spoils and withers it. It seems that greed is blowing a harmful wind upon America, which, when it latches onto what is moral within man, destroys genius and smothers enthusiasm perhaps down to the bottom of the heart, in order to drain the source of noble inspiration and generous impulses.

If I turn my eyes and my thoughts away for a moment from the populace, I always lay them with pleasure on a nature which, although often uniform, still is of interest to me. Everything it offers is new to a European as far as sites, cultures, housing, trees, plants, and animals are concerned. The lines of nature are greater and more harmoniously integrated than in our countries and our largest plains. There are, as far as the eye can see, immense forests, separated sometimes by lakes, sometimes by rivers, always by settlers' farms, either alone or grouped four, five, or even ten together. Round about the towns and villages, the older farmlands, surrounded by fences similar to the ones you find around our mountain pastures, enjoy more light. The tree trunks that were there before the clearing have long since been removed. On the other hand, the newer farms that encroach little by little upon the forests—where the clearing has happened more recently—are littered with standing trunks of the old trees that have been first burned in order to remove them with greater ease. They stand to a height of four to five feet, black and smoking, until they rot.

The state of New York is mainly rich in cattle; therefore, fields and pastures play a big role. Other crops include potatoes, oats, corn, buckwheat, sometimes beans, rarely rye, and even more rarely, wheat. People never burn the land, and contrary to what the Americans say, it is very sandy.

Please consider, dear Aunt, the beginning of this letter only as a digression, since my intention is not to give you a course on American agriculture. I am consistently impatient to receive more news from you, which I hope will be soon, since you promised me (and I count on it) to write often. The thousands of miles that separate us burden me with a weight that each of your letters can lighten.

Since the letter that I sent you from New York, I have made a joyous and agreeable journey. After leaving the city, we cruised up the Hudson River, which is the first area that gave me an idea of how beautiful nature in America is. During the longest part of the trip,

I saw river banks lined with mountains, less elevated than our Jura Mountains, but much more picturesque and varied. The mountains are beautifully wooded from top to bottom, and their images are reflected in the rivers, which are as limpid as mirrors. The clearness of the water in America is an astonishing and admirable thing, one which I have already much regarded and contemplated. The waters at home are not in any way as calm, nor do they reflect this well the nature around them. Where does it come from? I am charmed and surprised even more—the banks covered with the most beautiful shade trees that let their branches gracefully fall in the water.

After disembarking in Albany, we stayed there for two days, without seeing anything remarkable—only piglets walking calmly on the streets, even on sidewalks. We then saw something even less interesting, a performance of Othello which gave me a sad idea of the American taste for theater (which does not surprise me, by the way) given the fact that Yankees do not generally have any taste— they are too entrenched in daily life to appreciate it or acquire it.

From Albany, we went to the high-end spas at Saratoga, the American Baden-Baden. There we found many members of American high society, stuff shirted, sprucing up, making themselves as big as their safes, accompanied by their beautiful wives and one or two young women. There was a multitude of elegant people, German music and—to serve from nine hundred to one thousand table guests—the nicest range of Negroes one has ever seen. The surroundings, with the exception of a small lake six miles away, and four square slopes planted as a park around the source, are totally insignificant, even impractical for a stroll.

From there, we headed towards Lake George, on the banks of which we stayed for a few days in Caldwell. This lake is still the most beautiful sight that I have seen in America and is especially charming, given its numerous islands. With a width of twenty miles at its greatest point and a length of thirty miles, there are three hundred and sixty lakes, all of which differ in size, shape, and foliage. There are deciduous trees here, evergreens there, nice rocks and formations, surrounded by wild grass and bathing in waters even clearer and more transparent than the Hudson.

Add to this an admirable harmony of colors and a superb sunset, and it will not be difficult for you to believe me when I tell you that I felt touched by gratefulness at the sight of such a magnificent spectacle. I think that I would have given a year or two of my life to reproduce it with fidelity, but all this was only, as the Germans say, a "frommer münch".[13] I had to comfort myself by sketching small sepia of the view which I later completed at home, yet it is as far away from reality as we are from each other. We left our charming location—where I would love all of us to spend a few months in the summer—to travel to Montreal.

We traveled by water for the most part. Leaving from one end of Lake George, we crossed it in its entirety which brought us in view of sites even more picturesque than those of Caldwell, but alas, we moved at the speed of an American steamboat, too rapidly for me to draw anything. From this lake, we went on to Lake Champlain, which in my opinion does not deserve its illustrious reputation. Besides a few islands, its banks are flat and monotonous and do not offer anything worthy of great interest.

We disembarked at Grosse Pointe around six o'clock at night and we followed the Saint Lawrence River by rail, continuing by steamboat to Montreal from the opposite bank, which we reached at ten o'clock at night. Although the great fire of Montreal had happened fifteen days before our arrival, the smoke still hung in the air. The fire burned between eight and nine hundred houses, a great number of which (naturally the poorest ones) were not insured. From my window where I could embrace the biggest part of the

---

[13] *Literally a pious monk. It refers more informally to a sacred moment.*

city, it was a sad but grandiose spectacle. The fire must have been intense since only portions of walls were still standing. It was a poor man cooking his bacon who started the fire.

I was pleased to see Montreal. Like our good European cities, its stone houses have a charming appearance—far from being characteristic in American cities. We saw a very nice review of an infantry regiment and an English artillery battery, whose presentation, performance, and visual aspect were praiseworthy. We also climbed the Royal Mountain (hence in French, Mont Réal), and from the summit one can enjoy a beautiful view: the city of Montreal at one's feet, the Saint Lawrence River with its islands, and an immense plain covered in farms and villages further away. In the far distance, mounds of beautiful shapes and forms rise isolated from one another in the mist.

After four days, during which I sketched two drawings and dried some plants, we traveled first by steamship through Blydenburgh, Kingston, and Cape Vincent, and then by railroad to Watertown. There, we took a small carriage to bring us to Alpina, around thirty miles away. The road, most of the time made of planks, was good up to Lewisburg but was less so for the six miles that remained until Alpina—during which we were jolted like never before. As for the driver, he was so tired of it that he swore he would never be fooled again, but like the raven[14] it was a little too late.

We were curious and impatient to make the acquaintance of Alpina, and drawing a conclusion from the road that led us there, I was expecting a rustic but comfortable log cabin, but that is not what we found. Leaving the forest, we caught a glimpse, around a hundred feet away, of a house sitting on a rise and lit by the moon... a very pretty house which would not dishonor New York's surroundings, nor those of Boston. We were therefore very nicely

---

[14] *Reference to **Jean de la Fontaine**'s fable, Le Corbeau et le Renard.*

surprised to see that the hosts we were about to visit were so well accommodated. Imagine an almost square area of about twenty acres, sometimes with scattered clearings, with stumps of trees that had to give way for farming, or big rocks of more or less considerable sizes and elevations. All of this was traversed by a creek running at the bottom of a ravine that split the square throughout its length and on top of which are located, facing each other, the master house with its outbuildings and the village composed of a dozen wooden houses looking more or less comfortable. These large woods that squeeze you on all sides, these clearings in their youth, these beautiful white rocks that appear all around and seem to fight nature—all of this gives Alpina an excessively wild aspect that I personally appreciate. This is first because I am a landscape lover, and secondly, because of an attraction and an empathy that coexists between me and this kind of nature that—without being able to really define it—inevitably captivates me.

Upon arriving in Alpina, we did not find either of the Freudenreich[15] gentlemen—the father having left the day before for Harrisville in order to visit acquaintances, the son having left only a few hours ago to survey his forest, work he carries out while lodging at a nearby farm. We were therefore very disappointed, but very nicely greeted by Mr. Pahud, Mr. Freudenreich's business secretary, who took us inside the master house and showed us to our rooms after supper.

I was pleasantly surprised at the first room I entered. I found myself back in Switzerland, surrounded by paintings which were for me old friends: "The Return of the Swiss Soldier," which hangs at home above the living room couch, several paintings by Freudenberger,[16] a view of Bremgarten, and underneath all of them

---

[15] *A Swiss nobleman who ran a business concern in Alpina. He was also a distant cousin of Henri's as his mother was also from the* **de Freudenreich** *family.*

[16] **Sigmund Freudenberger** *(1745-1801), Swiss painter who is most known for his scenes of rural Bernese life.*

I slept as well as possible and woke up, not in the Switzerland of my dreams, but rather in Alpina on a beautiful morning.

After meeting with some settlers established here, among them Mr. Braillard, a native of Gorgier, I made sure to keep the promise that I had made to our friend Major Freudenreich to draw a view of Alpina. After dinner, Mr. Pahud proposed that we take a small excursion on Lake Bonaparte, which is for the most part located inside the limits of Alpina and is only a quarter of an hour away from the house. I had the great pleasure of discovering this charming little lake, surrounded as it is by wooded hills, dotted with several pretty islands, favorable to hunting and fishing, and propitious to navigation. It must be counted as one of the foremost treasures of Alpina.

While we were briskly cleaving through the waters—thanks to our sails and a nice breeze—I saw in the distance a small boat that was sailing near the opposite bank, maneuvered by someone whom I promptly recognized as Mr. Freudenreich, who was returning from Harrisville. After hailing him and being recognized in turn, we greeted him on board, shook hands, and welcomed each other.

The next day, his son, who had been told of our arrival, returned and I had the pleasure of spending time with him—from Tuesday until the following Monday. We naturally talked a great deal about Bern and Switzerland. We went for a few hikes around the lake and its surroundings, hunted deer twice, and I gathered plants for my father and completed two drawings for the major that are better in devotion than in execution.

When we left the settlement, Graffenreid and I separated for a few days, he to visit acquaintances in another direction, I to Niagara where he is supposed to meet with me tomorrow. I took advantage of the time to do some drawings and to write you this letter, the length of which I hope will satisfy you. At this moment, I drink to the famous Niagara, the largest falls in the world. I will not give you a description as it would take too long to achieve—it is one of the great spectacles of nature that defy the power of words. It is magnificent, truly magnificent, but I admit that my imagination had greater expectations, and if there is material to astonish an American, there is not enough to surprise a Swiss. Despite the difficulty of the subject, I sketched two drawings which will give you a better idea than anything I could tell you, although in artistic terms, they are rather weak.

Since I am convinced that Graffenreid will bring me the expected letters that we asked Mr. Colomb to send to the various stops of our trip, I keep this piece of paper to acknowledge receipt of them. Here comes Graffenreid, but without letters. Coming from you, I find it really disappointing, since three to four steamers have arrived since we left New York. Be kind enough to repair this immense oversight with an immense deluge of correspondence.

Letter Five

ABOARD THE FANNY SPURHAWK

September 28th, 1852

I thank you with all my heart for having the courtesy to answer me promptly. When I found myself an entire month (as it happened lately) without news from you, I was nearly dying with impatience and worry. I received your letters in Highland. We recently spent more than three weeks there; Graffenreid spent it with his cousins, and I with Mr. Bandelier[17] who is established in this town as a farmer as well as a businessman. I also spent time sketching, walking around the town, and visiting former countrymen who are now established in Highland, most of them as farmers. Highland is in Illinois, but only thirty miles east of St. Louis. It is a little town of about a thousand inhabitants located on a small mount, which gives it its name. It is surrounded by hills extending all the way to the end of the prairie, which we had to cross for nine days to arrive here.

The town, founded in the Thirties, has since then and especially in the last few years, encountered rapid growth but will never become (as far as I can tell) a very large city. Its surroundings look too new and have too much of the uniformity typical of American cities. Its setting is too monotonous for a painter to call it picturesque and to give a landscape artist any desire to sketch it.

---

[17] *This is the same farm that **Adolph Bandelier**, the noted anthropologist of the desert Southwest grew up on. Henri surely met the young Adolph, and it is impossible to know, but his example may have helped inspire Bandelier to explore the Americas for himself when he became an adult.*

The person I had the greatest pleasure of meeting there was Mr. Bandelier. He and his wife were both being extremely kind, obliging, and hospitable to me during my stay—I will treasure excellent memories of them. Mr. Bandelier's farm bears the name Mary Hill, named after Mrs. Bandelier, and is located on a rather wooded hill planted with peach trees. There is a very pretty garden in front of the house, full of shade trees and well cultivated, despite the presence of weeds. The house is a former farm that Mr. Bandelier has transformed nicely. I made a small drawing of it for their parents in Bern, which seemed to please them.

I also had the great pleasure of being introduced to Mr. Warmouth, who comes from Alsace and who, after having traveled for a long time in America, ended up settling here and now owns a farm five miles away from Highland. He maintains two houses: one, his home, where he lives alone; the other, his workshop. He takes care of his garden, milks his cows, and cooks by himself. I spent three very agreeable days with him, because in him I found resources, as well as an elevated, religious, and cultivated spirit. I also met in Highland with one of my former companions from Colombier, the young Guyot, who was at the chancellery at the time of Mr. Faverger. Generally, Swiss nationals followed by Southern Germans are most dominant in Highland and its surroundings.

Letter Six

ABOARD THE EMPIRE ESTATE

September, 1852

You see, dear Father, that a few days has passed before I was able to continue this letter, but Graffenreid, who is as regulated as his books, has decided to embark on October 29th, having given his cousins more time than he had planned for, which obliged us to hasten our journey. Therefore, from Highland up to here, it was more like a whirlwind, since we traveled eight hundred leagues in thirteen days, Graffenreid having spent time in Saint Louis, Cincinnati, Baltimore, Washington, and Philadelphia, and I having visited Saint Louis, Cincinnati, and Columbus, Ohio.

In order to give you in a few words an idea of America as I understand it to this point, I will tell you that in summary:

America is a great country for: the poor man who has no more bread a home; the man who has a large family and little wealth, and who wants to give his children a stable and comfortable future; celebrities whose possessions bring richness to the country they live in; those who want to become rich doing business; and for all those skilled people: carpenters, cabinet makers, masons, cobblers, tailors, and more generally all craftsmen; those who want to hoard money; those who hate the courts and nobility; for all women who dream of emancipation; young people who do not like studies and serious occupations; the child who wants to flee paternal authority; those parents who do not like to worry about their children; and for those, most of all, who love money for the sake of it.

America is a sorry country for: the man who enjoys a home of honest leisure; those who likes to use wealth for noble ends; those who are attached to family and society; those who are friends of arts, either admiring them or cultivating them; and the one who respects order and those who represent it, such as policemen, soldiers, etc. It is sad for the farmer who does not want to spend his life raising corn and the one who neither likes temperance making laws nor whiskey. It is sad for the one who likes to dine in more than five minutes and does not pile everything onto one plate including seven different vegetables, two kinds of meat, one or two desserts, as well as a few salads. It is sad for one who can appreciate good taste in objects and manners; for the poor man whose house has burned down and who can only rebuild it by borrowing at a ten per cent rate; for the foreigner who falls into the hands of a German doing the commerce of the immigrants, or of an American knowing the mortgage business well. It is a sad for the scientist who likes to follow up with science (except burglary)[18] and for one who does not like to see religion spoiled by camp meetings.[19] It is sad for the one who likes to see gracious women, well-mannered children, and polite gentlemen; for one, finally, who likes to relax from his work by elevating his heart and spirit either by admiring, reading, or having a conversation.

My plans are to spend this month in New York to learn Spanish—I do not want to head south before I know enough to stay out of trouble. I settled down in a rather expensive hotel, the Pelerin. I could not find any others since everything is terribly expensive here and I would not want to stay in a house that would be improper. I find myself among French and Spaniards, all of them very polite and good company.

---

[18] *This meaning for me is obscure. I believe he is talking about the theft of scientific ideas.*

[19] *I assume he is referring to tent revivals here.*

From New York, I am thinking about leaving at the beginning of November to visit the cities of Philadelphia, Baltimore, and Washington. From there I would go on to Charleston, in Carolina, where I hope to meet with Mr. Agassiz, who told me of his intention to winter there. From Charleston, I will head to New Orleans through Mobile, where I am planning to arrive around November 20. I will only stop there for a short period and will then embark on a ship to Havana to stay a fortnight, maybe longer.

If I proceed inland, I will probably have to turn around and go back to New Orleans, in order to head towards Veracruz, Mexico, where I hope to arrive at the end of December. From there I will proceed to Mexico City, where I should be at the very start of the year. I will spend January there as well as February and March, and will leave (God willing) at the beginning of April to go to Jamaica, where they say the English and American steamships call at on their way to Brazil. If I travel during the months of April and May, I will get to Bahia or Rio by the beginning of June.

I will spend June, July, and August in Brazil, which are their winter months, and consequently the healthiest ones. I intended to leave Brazil at the beginning of September to be home around October or November and reunited in the shade of our towers.[20] As I said in my verses to you, which I read again and found rambling, that I have decided never to climb Parnassus[21] again, for if ever a guide could have brought me there successfully, it would have been the one that I had chosen.

Enclosed are seeds for Papa from Mr. Gray whom I visited, as well as Mr. Guyot and Mr. Agassiz, after having sent Graffenreid and Wurstenberger to Europe. I was only able to spend a day-and-a-half at Mr. Lesquereux's but I enjoyed it very much since he

---

[20] *A reference to Vaumarcus castle in Switzerland, home of the de Büren family.*

[21] *Reference to Mount Parnassus in Greece, the mythic home of the Muses, and known as the home of poetry, music, and learning.*

and his wife greeted me with the most cordial benevolence. I went with Mr. Lesquereux for a walk in the woods of Columbus where we found several interesting things. I also had the pleasure to see a magnificent northern deer in Mr. Sullivant's[22] park, as well as a beautiful buffalo.

---

[22] ***William Starling Sullivant*** *(1803-1873), noted U.S. bryologist*

Letter Seven

PHILADELPHIA

November 1st, 1852

If I am writing to you from here and not from anywhere else in America, it is because I wanted to salute and commemorate in a worthy way the beautiful name of Philadelphia which in Greek translates into friendship, or brotherly love. This I hope will inspire me to compose a letter that you have as much pleasure in reading as I have had in writing. I was hoping that the Niagara, which docked last week, would bring me letters, but it did not. I am very disappointed, since I will have to wait and be patient as I don't know where I will be in two weeks.

By telling you of my location, I am informing you that I have just begun my voyage south. I ask God to bless my current enterprise, as I know you do as well, so it can help to instruct me, improve me, elevate my soul, and make sure I always love, comprehend, and admire the Creator of all worlds and His marvels even more. I beseech you (as I do of my other sisters) to always accompany me with your prayers and to try as much as possible to calm and assuage Mother's worry about the idea of my faraway and lonesome journey. Calm her not only with human reasoning, but also by trying to make her feel that I am under God's safeguard, who will ensure that nothing will occur that is not for my own good. Whether the impression for me be hard or gentle, or the odds of my journey be hopeful or unfavorable, please make her understand that I want to see her again too much (as well as all of you) to allow me to voluntarily commit any kind of folly.

I left New York with some Spanish in my head, a very nice beginning, as my teacher says. Spanish is really a beautiful language and not too difficult for one who knows French and Latin. I hope that after three weeks in Havana, everything will be fine, and if not, at least sufficient.

I cannot tell you much about New York for the simple reason that I have not even seen what there is to see, since I stayed in a great deal in order to work. The most beautiful thing to see in New York is unquestionably its harbor. It is an immense meeting point of ships from around the world ships that surround the city with (as it seems) a forest of masts, since the harbor is built at the end of a long and narrow peninsula and only has one grand avenue, Broadway. This street, as well as several others that are parallel to it, although less important, is separated by a number of other streets that stretch from the Hudson River on one side of Manhattan Island to the East River on the other side. It is nothing more than the shrunken extremity of the arm of the sea that separates Long Island (the island which is to the east of New York) from the American continent.

Facing New York, you can find on one side Hoboken, New Jersey, and on the other side Brooklyn, and finally a little more south than the first, Jersey City. These three modern cities look like New York's suburbs with which they are linked by steam bridges called ferry boats, which leave each bank of the river every five minutes, transporting people and equipment. Adding to this incessant traffic are rowboats and watercrafts whose activity and trade are directly linked to New York, as well as the steamships that haul either large vessels or six boats on each side.

The thousands of vessels squeezed one against another and surrounding the city (as I said earlier) with a forest of masts, drop off their cargo on docks. The cargo consists of thousands of different products, ranging from gold from California, Chinese tea, and Havana tobacco, to Brazilian coffee, Indian ivory, English iron, and New Orleans cotton. Then debarking from these very same docks are the products that America exports to other continents, such as wood, corn, cotton, salted meat, and finally all other products from this hemisphere, of which New York is the most formidable warehouse. Imagine this immense business—and the movement that necessarily results from it: crowds of people busy rigging ships for departure and others moving the contents of the ships onto the docks. From the docks to the immense warehouses where these contents have to be stored, people give orders, all of them screaming, singing, or riding their horses, while hundreds of carts trot by on poor pavement. This should give you have an idea of a port like New York. You will trust then me when I tell you that it is one of the noisiest, and at the same time most interesting spectacles that you can see.

After this description which was as complicated as its subject, I am going to enter the city to tell you about the most interesting things I have seen in New York. I entertained, since my arrival, three ambitions: First, to see the first museum of science and natural history; then to visit New York's colorama and diorama which are the best representations of the fine arts; and finally to take a walk in Hoboken to have the most beautiful view of the area and to be able to take in the whole city from one vantage point These three ambitions have been met in a more or less satisfactory way.

When speaking of the Barnum[23] Museum in New York, it would be a mistake to compare them with our European museums, which

---

[23] *"P.T. Barnum's American Museum, located from 1841 to 1865 at the corner of Broadway and Ann Street in lower Manhattan, has been long recognized by historians as a pivotal institution in the development of nineteenth-century urban culture. In an urban culture characterized by increasing difference—in taste, in subject, and in audience—it was the first to combine sensational entertainment and gaudy display with instruction and moral uplift". - Overview from The Lost Museum*

are founded for the most part by cities or funded by individuals. Our science at home is liberal; in America, it is totally different. The cities here are not willing to build monuments to science, or are doing it very imperfectly, but it is the individuals selling, trafficking, speculating legally (as the ninety nine per cent of Americans do), who take care of the entire process, due to the immense curiosity the inhabitants of this country have, rather than for their love of science. Therefore, there is nothing less scientific than American museums. They are rather a collection of unclassified items tastefully arranged, and the Barnum Museum is a prime example.

You will find everything that could pique your curiosity, through rarity, oddness of shapes, and a more or less distant origin, but never through authenticity which Americans do not care about. This is especially true when it comes to animals. They purchase whatever is not too expensive but is spectacular, so that you ordinarily meet a lion, for example, with a bull to its right, a duck from the Carolinas, and to its left, in front or behind it, a rabbit, deer, or a moose. Barnum has all species; the Chinese especially show their rather national greatness. Various classes and ages are shown, from the carpenter up to the mandarin.

What interested me the most was neither a group of cardboard monkeys playing the violin, nor a little child in alabaster sleeping on top of roses, nor hundreds of daubs showing distinguished citizens, but rather the harmony that reigned in a large cage. A cage where all different kinds of animals coexisted peacefully, each with different habits and natures; two cats, three or four monkeys, white mice, bears, doves, eagles, owls, blackbirds, and many other animals whose names, I know, you won't remember. Interestingly, all of them live together on the best possible terms and I still have not figured out how it is possible for such a society to cohabitate. There is also a comedy troupe attached to the establishment, whose performances were much less interesting than the aforementioned cage.

The Barnum Museum is located on Broadway, which is to say, in the most exhilarating neighborhood in New York. It is housed in a large building at the corner on a square, all covered with painted fabric panels, like the ones you can see on the booths at a fair, with a balcony where each night a group of musicians play, expecting to attract the populace. As far as the colorama and the diorama are concerned, I was hoping to find the highest expression of fine arts in this city and I was satisfied.

Mr. Sattler[24] makes decidedly pretty things; the distortion of glass and lighting did not detract in any way from their merit. There were very pretty paintings from the Orient and the Austrian Alps, but nothing from Switzerland, which surprised me coming from an artist such as Mr. Sattler.

I went for a walk in Hoboken last Sunday, but the sun which was very promising when I stepped on the ferry dashed my hopes because just after disembarking all sunlight disappeared. After an hour's walk to the end of my hike (up to the mount that I wanted to climb in order to admire the spectacle of nature), the horizon suddenly found itself covered by such a thick fog that the best I could do was to go back to the ferry and then home, without enjoying the slightest pleasure walking along the Hudson River.

Before I leave New York, I have to tell you that Broadway is so busy and obstructed with carriages of all kinds, including buses and carts, that one has to wait for a long while before being able to cross it from sidewalk to sidewalk. The busy American is anything but polite and does not have a problem pushing and jostling people passing by, but is outraged when he himself is shoved. Coaches and buses also join this brutality. Not a day passes when they don't knock somebody over with more or less grave consequence and without ever trying to prevent the accident with a yell or a warning.

---

[24] **Hubert Sattler** *(1817-1904), Austrian landscape painter, and son of Johann Michael Sattler who was famous for the Sattler-Panoramas of Salzburg.*

I saw some, on the contrary, who seemed to be looking for such an encounter. Thus, people are now busy investigating a streetcar that, like the ones that already exist on other streets, could be pulled by horses, which, in my opinion, is not really nice, but you have to admit that this system would be very useful.

The road from New York to Philadelphia is nothing less than picturesque. A glimpse of a few timber planks boldly arranged over a river and at a rather great length can make you feel like you are riding in a balloon. This is what appeared to me as the most interesting moment of the four-hour trip. Although you cannot compare it to our beautiful European capitals, Philadelphia is nevertheless the best one I saw, as far as American cities are concerned. All its streets are parallel and intersect at square angles. Every other street is residential, where the rich live and keep to themselves more or less. The commercial streets are much more animated. The fashionable streets, which are to say noncommercial, are really beautiful. Almost all the houses have an elevated first floor built in white marble, as well as the staircase and window frames, whose blinds are painted in a lovely green. The remaining walls are tiled and usually jointed with black grout.

Additionally, the city displays very nice parks and promenades with beautiful trees and large walkways. All along the walkways are small seats which resemble our fruit seller chairs, but which are placed so distant from one another that it makes it difficult to converse. Given the haste of our journey and the lack of opportunities, I have not yet seen many American institutions, so I have decided not to leave Philadelphia before I could visit all the most interesting ones. I was anxious to do so, since this is what constitutes the best in America. If Philadelphia is the city where religion appears to be the most austere, there are not many others who practice it more assiduously. The Hospice for the Deaf and Mute; the House of Refuge; the Penitentiary; the House for the Poor; the Museum of

Arts; City Hall; the Athenaeum; Girard College; and the Hospice for the Blind are all places that I intend to visit. I am going to tell you now about what I have already seen. The day after my arrival, I was not able to see much since it was a day of great excitement– Election Day for the presidency of the United States.

On the second day, I went to Girard College which is still inside the city limits, although it is located three miles away from where I reside. A Frenchman living in this country donated two million dollars or ten million francs upon his death, in order to build and maintain a hospice for orphans. This Frenchman's name is Stephen Girard, who died in 1831. The hospice is Girard College, the most magnificent monument that humanity has ever dedicated to charity. No monarch, no powerful state, no rich philanthropist has, I believe, ever created anything so beautiful for such a purpose. It is housed in five buildings, all clad in white marble from top to bottom. The monument in the middle represents a Greek temple in all its rigor and style, like Diana's temple in Ephesus, measuring two hundred and eighteen feet long, by one hundred and sixty feet wide, by ninety-seven feet high. It is surrounded and supported by thirty-four columns with Corinthian capitals of a beautiful material and appearance.

This marble creation, as white as snow, conceived in gigantic and beautiful proportions, executed with care and peerless taste, is definitely the monument that left the greatest impression on me and will always leave me with potent memories and deep esteem. It is the only really beautiful monument I have seen in America that has the right to be proud in every respect. The other four buildings surround the main edifice and are actually the active part of the foundation, for it is there that the orphans are lodged, fed, and taught, and where the teachers reside. I have rarely seen so much luxury together with such cleanliness: from dormitories to dining rooms, everything is well maintained and a pleasure to see.

On the same morning, I was able to visit the U.S. Mint, a very interesting building, although very different from others I saw in the city. What is especially remarkable is the beauty of the steam machines that have replaced the old pendulum system. At the moment of my visit, the minters were melting a great quantity of gold from California (that I saw in its raw state) which is collected by gold miners and then melted into ingots with a value of six thousand dollars each. They are then beaten into strips that go through a circle punch, and on to another machine that stamps them. There is one machine for twenty dollar coins that stamps sixteen hundred dollars per minute.

The same night, I attended a concert and a few readings given by the blind. I have very rarely listened to music that touched me as much. The Home for the Blind has a beautiful exterior, but I could not venture inside to appreciate its details, since entry to it is not allowed to mere mortals like me. Today, I visited three more establishments (that is my daily number) finding that it is neither too much nor too little for an intelligence like mine, and I will stick to that number.

This morning, I went to the art museum, about which I will not say much, then to City Hall, from the top of which I enjoyed a breathtaking view of the entire city, and where I visited the room where the Declaration of Independence was signed. I also viewed a number of portraits; the one of William Penn, the founder of Pennsylvania, was the most remarkable among them. This afternoon, I was able to visit the Home for the Deaf and Mute, and as with the Home for the Blind. Instructing people about these establishments is done more or less by generalities and I have to say that I do not appreciate this system, since it prevents you from completely examining and judging the place in detail. Tomorrow, I will visit the House of Refuge and the Penitentiary.

Letter Eight

NEW ORLEANS

November 30th, 1852

Leaving Philadelphia, I covered almost fourteen hundred miles, sometimes by railroad, sometimes by steamboat, and for seventy miles, even by a stagecoach from another century. I traveled across Maryland, both Carolinas, Virginia, and the state of Alabama before I arrived in Mississippi, where I am right now.

From Philadelphia, I took the train to Baltimore—which the Americans call pompously "the city of monuments." It contains three remarkable examples: the monument to Washington, from the top of which one enjoys a beautiful view of the city; the Battle Monument, dedicated to the memory of a military victory; and the Armistead Monument, erected in memory of young Major Armistead for having valiantly defended Fort Henry, which protects the bay of Baltimore.

From Baltimore, I went to Washington, the capital of the United States, where I was able, not without some difficulty, to find my old friend François Pourtalès[25] who works for the Coast Guard and who greeted me very warmly. I went with him to the Capitol, where Congress holds its sessions. Despite its huge dimensions and its immense dome, the Capitol is in my opinion such a jumble and a hodge-podge of styles that it is impossible to consider the whole

---

[25] **Louis François de Pourtalès** *(1824-1880), Swiss-born American naturalist, and pupil of Louis Agassiz. He would work for the U.S. coastal survey for many years and would later become the custodian of the Harvard Museum of Comparative Zoology.*

thing a beautiful creation. The few paintings that decorate the dome are more interesting for their reference to historical figures than for their execution or color. The subjects they represent are the Declaration of Independence, Washington handing back his powers, and the surrender of a fortress by the English.

From Washington, I headed towards Virginia which I crossed in its eastern section, which is the least interesting. Most of the road crosses immense pine tree forests that are exploited for the sap and consequently look rather shabby. The soil is light and sandy, and the vegetation, for that reason, is not very vigorous or lush. The other part of the state is a land of hills, with corn, tobacco, and a small amount of grains. The soil is rather poor and would be appropriate for the breeding of sheep, if there were not such harsh changes in the climate, which would not be hospitable to the cultivation of many of our European products, like colza, beans, grapes, etc.

We went through Richmond, the capital of Virginia, which is picturesque. It overlooks a river dotted with a few small islands and is divided by daringly constructed bridges. The next day, we arrived at Wilmington's Harbor where we boarded a steamer to arrive the following day at Charleston, the capital of South Carolina.

I spent a few days there in the hope of meeting with Mr. Agassiz, who had the intention to spend the winter here, but to my disappointment, I left without being able to find him. I went to visit one of his acquaintances that I had met at his home last spring, a Doctor Holbrook, who greeted me very nicely as did as his ladies. One day, he lent me his carriage so I could go visit his country house a few miles outside Charleston. It is from here that I truly grasped well that I was approaching warmer lands. The vegetation is totally different from that of the North, as much for its vigor as for its variety. The trees, plants, crops, people, and dwellings are altogether different. The Sarosa Pine and the Swamp Pine, with their immense needles, replace the Weymouth Pine and the Rezida Pine. You can also see other species of oak trees, among them, the evergreen oak, known as Quercus Sempervirens. All the Liquidambar[26] shrubs are covered with a long gray moss which hangs from every branch, even from the highest ones, and which gives the forests a sad, but picturesque appearance.

The road from Charleston to Doctor Holbrook's country house is really very interesting, lined with large trees, especially oaks and pines, whose wide branches are covered with the same moss, presenting a beautiful interplay of shadow and light. Here, corn is slowly starting to be replaced by cotton, which is sold at the Charleston market. The cotton plant, which I will see in Cuba during the summer, only reaches the height of a small shrub, one and a half, two, maybe three feet high that you have to replant every year, since it does not tolerate winter well in these parts. Sweet potatoes are a big part of the culture in this area as well. This vegetable, which at first seems a little too sweet, deserves to be better known.

The houses, although simply constructed (built either of wood or bricks) are nevertheless, to my mind, more visually appealing and seem more comfortable than their northern counterparts, embellished by verandas shaded by beautiful trees. Horseback riding is very fashionable here, and there is not one instance when you do not see riders go by, who are less interesting than their horses. The Americans ride very poorly and without grace. They are either tilting forward, or rather folded in two, elbows sticking out, wearing a long worn riding coat, their hats either falling back on their neck or forward on their nose, without gloves and usually chewing tobacco. This is a rather accurate portrait of the average American rider.

Here, mules are beginning to take the place of horses, but are far more beautiful in this country than in ours: strong, tall, and well fed. They are charged with transporting cotton, which at this time

---

[26] *Sweetgum*

of year arrives in great quantities from all over the country in large bales weighing half a ton, compacted on site at the plantation with a large press, in order to reduce their volume.

Depending on the quality of the harvest, cotton sells at the market for between seven and eleven cents per pound, with the average price of one of these bales selling for forty dollars.

The black race thoroughly dominates in Charleston, since for every two whites, you can count three Negroes (slaves, of course) but well fed, strong, and vigorous, and for the most part they appear more happy than unhappy. They are by themselves too happy-go-lucky, too lazy, and too unintelligent to manage to do anything themselves. Their history, or rather the lack thereof, says it enough. On their own, they would not be able to cultivate anything or would do it poorly.

Whites, incapable of sustained work in such a climate, are on the other hand capable of directing the Negroes in their work in a useful manner for the Negroes' own interest, and without forcing them in any way with work or exhaustion. They feed them, lodge them, and instruct them much better than the Negroes could do themselves, even if they were free.

I am not saying that I am in favor of slavery, but only that through this system and its practices, as understood and applied in this country, there are many slaves who enjoy an easy upbringing. They have a quarter, a third (and more, depending on the season) of each day to themselves, during which they can, if they want to, work and make enough money to buy their freedom, which the owner never refuses. An immense plot of land will thus be satisfyingly and wisely cultivated: then a great quantity of first necessity products, such as cotton, sugar, coffee, for the trade and consumption of a great part of the world, something that the Negroes, left to themselves, and thanks to their natural apathy, would never achieve.

The free Negroes in the North differ a great deal from the slaves in the South, and if there is a slight difference, doesn't it come from that motivation, that forced training that inflicts upon them, willingly or unwillingly, their position among the white population, so active and entrepreneurial?

I left Charleston for Georgia, passing through two of its largest cities, Augusta and Atlanta, which offer nothing worth seeing, and simply look like every other American city. Georgia is a land that is undulating in the most regular, even monotonous way. You go up and down a hill just to go up and down another hill of similar height, unremittingly displaying the same alternatives between a plantation and a forest, a forest and a plantation.

The cotton plantations are always surrounded by a wooden fence, as are all plantations throughout America. You usually see a good master house, built of wood or brick, with a balcony and a veranda. Then scattered all over the plantation are the houses of the Negroes, sorts of chalets, or log houses, built like ours with super-posed beams, but looking much less comfortable. Often, you don't even have to step in to realize that they are poorly furnished and ugly, accessible to winds and rains, but this does not prevent their occupants to be, as I said earlier, robust or in good shape. They are indeed better fed than lodged, since Negroes each have a pound of bread a day, together with vegetables, and can take care of a cow, and also a dog, an animal they much care for.

In Atlanta, I met with a voyager who, like me, travels through America for his pleasure and his education. His name is Mr. Schnitzler, a Prussian, who after retiring from what would have been a success-ful business began at sixty years of age to travel the world. He knows all European countries, parts of Asia and Africa, and while having a house built in Bonn, came to tour America for a little while. He has mastered seven languages, and this definitely facilitates his passion for travel.

I decided to partner with him for the rest of his trip. After spending a day with him in Montgomery, the capital of the state of Alabama, we traveled down the river for fifty hours, during the first part of which we encountered a continuous storm, despite very cold temperatures. The boat often stopped to load up cotton to the point where, once we arrived in Mobile, it carried over fourteen hundred bales.

From Mobile, we left together on the Florida, an excellent steamship that dropped us off in New Orleans. Before I say anything about this city, I will tell you that we went back to Mobile, where we bought our tickets on board the Black Warrior,[27] which is set to leave tomorrow for Havana. From Cuba, Mr. Schnitzler expects to return home. Once in New Orleans, I experienced two great joys; the first was to find your good and excellent letter, the other to find my old friend Charles Pillichody, with whom I had the pleasure to reconnect with again.

I had seen after four days what was most interesting in New Orleans, especially its vast harbor and bustle, to which the Creole diversity—a great number of Negroes and mulattoes, carrying and loading up cotton—adds something very original, in addition to a sugar cane plantation, and finally Lake Ponchartrain, where the locals like to stroll. After all this, I gladly accepted Mr. Pillichody's offer to accompany him to the house in Mobile (a branch of Rham and Volz in New Orleans). These Rham and Volz gentlemen trade cotton, which is an innovative and lucrative business.

To give you an idea, I will tell you that they expect a harvest this year, in all the countries that produce cotton, of about two million five hundred thousand bales, roughly one million six hundred thousand of them going to the New Orleans market, the rest for

---

[27] *The steamer **Black Warrior** would later become famous in 1854 for an international incident during which it was seized for a brief time by the newly appointed governor of Cuba. It led many in the Southern United States to call for war with Spain.*

Charleston and Mobile. Since the bale is worth forty dollars, the total is one hundred million dollars, or five hundred million francs. For a trader who has ten thousand bales, it represents a profit of fifty thousand francs. I have to add that it is a very delicate business and that one cannot be totally skilled in it until after a few years' practice.

I like Mobile a great deal. We already went for two horseback rides around the city, which is very pretty, and yesterday we paid a visit to a tribe of Indians, who were camping outside the city. They are of the Chola tribe, but look so unhappy, so ugly, so dirty, and so poisoned by alcohol that I would find no pleasure whatsoever in describing them.

Dear Mother, I have to bid farewell for now

HAVANA

December 14th, 1852

At last, here I am in a country that through its nature, its poetry, its originality, its sky and land, its cities and its people, its morals and its physics, is willing to reward my journey. A country that will pay me in return for such a long and distant separation from my country, from my family and friends, that often puts me in such a deep loneliness that I really need something powerful, beautiful, and new in order to lighten its weight, to give me a relief that I rarely encountered during my journey across the United States.

Here I am now on this beautiful island of Cuba, in its magnificent and picturesque capital. Embarking from Mobile on Thursday, December 10th at noon, I arrived in Havana around seven o'clock Sunday morning, after two nights and one day of rather bad weather. The night before, at eight o'clock, Havana was in sight but since it is forbidden to enter the harbor after sunset, we were obliged to sway to and fro all night on a stormy sea.

We were indeed rewarded for the slight delay as I do not believe that there exist many other ports as beautiful and interesting as Havana's. The entrance to the harbor by itself is worth a trip and a crossing. Wider than two times the length of a vessel, it is protected on each side by forts. The one on the left, the Castel Del Morro, is extremely picturesque, and then once in the bay, you can still find on your left several forts that occupy the high ground. On your right, the city of Havana is a feast for the eyes, with its promenades that follow the water, and finally before you is the harbor with its vessels from all around the world: steamships, frigates, warships, trade ships, a quantity of small rowboats loaded with pineapples, oranges, and all sorts of other fruits, driven by brown-faced boatmen, Spanish in appearance. Finally, at the far end of the bay, other forts stand out in the distance, near the water factories surrounded by palm trees and serviced by Negroes.

If you wish to color the accompanied drawing[28] and turn it into a painting, imagine the greenery and the vegetation of these parts. Paint the forts using that yellow color that I have only seen, with such warm tones, in the paintings of our Riviera. Imagine the city, composed of houses of all colors: blue, red, most of all white, which is well adapted to the Moorish aspect that they all have. Separate them with the greenery of the palm trees and the other trees that you find inside the city. Post on all ships flags of all countries; give them that ivory color and those white hatches; paint all rowboats with different colors, let them sail in all directions, with or against the wind, with their white sails; load them up with oranges and other fruits; cover the whole painting with blue skies that only exist under these latitudes, and you will indeed have one of the most beautiful spectacles that nature can offer. My clumsy and unskilled hand cannot describe the subject correctly but I wanted to give you an idea of these magnificent views.

When I wrote in my letter about originality, I was thinking more of the general appearance of the city and of the bay, of its activity and its commerce, rather than of a detailed impression of its architecture, its buildings, and finally of the general look of the city which is very Spanish and reminds my travel companion, Mr. Schnitzler, of Seville, Granada, and other Spanish towns. You can imagine that all this is new for me and that if from time to time, I find something that reminds me of our good old Europe; I am even

---

[28] *He apparently enclosed a sketch.*

more charmed since I was getting tired of the flat and monotonous architecture of the United States.

As in all hot climate cities, the streets are very narrow and rarely paved. The houses have sometimes three, or more often two levels, including the ground floor. All apartments have extremely high ceilings, and the windows usually go from the floor to the ceiling, even at street level. The windows rarely have glass panes, but more commonly interior shades. They are insufficient to prevent thieves from walking in, but they are garnished with strong metallic bars on all floors. However, they do allow people walking on the sidewalks, comparatively as narrow as the street itself, to easily examine the living standards and people inside.

The Cuban carriage is always stationed at the entrance of the corridor; therefore it is the first thing that you can see upon walking in the house, since every honest Cuban has his own *volante*. The volante is an open carriage with two enormous wheels that are located in the rear and are as high as the carriage itself, with two long poles at the end of which a horse is harnessed, ridden by a Negro wearing a striped suit and hat, tall boots with spurs, and many silver buckles. The horse's mane is trimmed, and its artfully braided tails tied up on the side.

The Alameda, which is the most beautiful promenade in Havana, is busy every night with *Corso*, that is to say crowded with open carriages, mostly occupied by ladies who, I have to tell you, never go on foot. Most of the time, they ride by three, the *linda mina*, which is to say the prettiest sits in the middle, but since they are usually all good looking, they must often be embarrassed about whom to select as the most beautiful.

Together with this promenade, the Plaza de Armas is the nicest place in the city, which is shown at the top of my letter. In the background stands the governor's palace, and on the right, the administration building, both of them built with yellow stone that look very similar to those in Neuchâtel. In front of the Plaza Nueva, right in its center, stand beautiful palm trees surrounding a statue of Ferdinand VII, as well as other trees and shrubs with magnificent flowers and foliage. It is a charming picture in that it manages to gather, in a rather small space, tasteful architecture, along with exquisite plants and foliage. Every morning at seven o'clock, and every evening at eight o'clock, music is played on the square. Military bands give concerts in turn and play very well. It is unfortunate that they perform such complicated musical numbers. Military personnel, who are numerous in Havana, look well polished in their nice white uniforms, which are clean and bright. It is natural that the garrison is so strong right now, since the Americans do not hide their desire to make this city a part of their union. The garrison must be considerable at all times, given the number of forts that surround the city.

I surely do not have to tell you that the white population has an authentic Spanish look. The Creoles have their own appearance, which is less appealing than their Spanish counterparts. There are many blacks and they are almost all slaves. One of the first things I saw here is a cigar factory, and it happened to be the best one in Havana. They are naturally managed by whites, but it is blacks who handle the fabrication and are quite skilled at it. Besides the good quality of the leaves, it is impossible to imagine better made cigars. The best ones I saw were first-quality Regalias, valued at sixty-eight dollars per thousand, or three hundred and forty francs. It is rare to manufacture anything more beautiful, or to smoke anything better, as far as cigars are concerned.

Instead of leaving Havana soon and arriving (as I was contemplating) in Mexico City at the beginning of next year, I am going to spend more time here. The reasons why are twofold: first, I stayed in the southern United States longer due to the distances, as well as the late start of the Black Warrior; and second, the summer in Cuba is too interesting and offers too many pretty views to sketch, too many beautiful plants to collect, and too much originality to study for me to stay here just ten days. The steamships to Veracruz leave from here only on the 23rd of the month, given the *pronunciamento*,[29] from Tampico to Veracruz which complicates Mexican affairs. I am not really tempted to leave, only to find the road to Mexico City completely obstructed and to have to retrace my steps. Following advice from some people in Havana, I therefore want to wait quietly for more news, and while waiting go somewhere in the countryside where I can collect and do some drawings at my leisure and at less expense than here, where the cost of living is awfully high. What bothers me on the other hand is to remain deprived of news from my parents, as it is extremely difficult for me to be so far away for so long, without receiving any.

I also have to change my travel plans, since I will probably have to cancel my trip to Brazil, due to the total lack of good communications between here or Veracruz and Brazil. I would need too much time to travel through Acapulco and Chile to be able to return (as I would like to) next year in the autumn. In order to go from here to Brazil, the only sound way would be to go back to England to board a steamship that provides service from Southampton to Rio de Janeiro, but I know that it would be impossible for me to arrive in Europe without going back to Switzerland and to Vaumarcus.[30] Although I deeply regret not being able to visit Brazil, I may renounce it more easily, realizing how less enjoyable it is traveling alone. Therefore, if I cannot manage to unexpectedly find an easy way to travel from here to Brazil, I will simply return home, God willing, sometime next summer, in June or early July, even if I have to go back to Brazil some other year.

---

[29] *In a pronunciamiento, a group of military officers publicly declare their opposition to the current government. A form of military rebellion or coup d'état particular to Spain, Portugal and Latin America in the 19th century.*

[30] *A reference to Vaumarcus Castle in Switzerland, home of the de Büren family.*

I wish, dear Uncle, that I would have written you a more interesting letter and one more worthy of you, but I am a little bit demoralized, even dazed, by the enormous heat we are encountering now. It is an even stronger heat than the one we had in the United States, so you see it is not with consequence. During my trip through Mobile, I met a young Frenchman from Martinique and a Brazilian, who are both very nice and polite and with whom I have pleasure to find myself right now. In addition, I am still enjoying Mr. Schnitzler's company, with whom I even share a room. You always share a room here, which is not always convenient.

Farewell, Dear Uncle

MEXICO CITY

January, 1853

Last time I wrote you, it was at my aunt's address, and my letter was dated from Paso de Cuevas. Did you (ever) receive it? I do not know if it was ever sent, especially since before I left, I had a small argument with the innkeeper, who had provided me with terrible horses for our trip to Jalapa, which made a difference since it was roughly an eighteen-league ride. I would be sorry if that letter had not reached you, since I do not want you to worry about me. It was also a long letter, full of details expressing my delight with the island of Cuba that might have interested you.

To continue the story of my journey from Paso de Cuevas, I will tell you that after making me wait until ten in the morning, instead of eight as promised, I was brought the horses I was speaking of. The one I was supposed to ride was a tall horse, Isabelle, very unattractive and old, but what was even worse was that she was stubborn and continuously disobedient. I still do not speak a lot of Spanish, it was late, and the innkeeper was impassive. Therefore, after showing him my discontent, I knew that the best thing to do was to get on the quadruped and to turn my back to the biped. However, once in the saddle, I almost repented, because for a rider coming from our country, it is not in my opinion a very enjoyable thing to find yourself riding on a Spanish saddle for the first time, with your legs behind you and your body leaning forward, especially when the specimen is as bad as this one.

After riding a hundred paces on the animal, walking on one leg, trotting on the second one, cantering on the third one, and I do not know which gait it was doing on the fourth one, I decided that my guide's (or *arriero*'s) animal was much better than mine. I kindly requested him to dismount his little dapple-gray horse and ride my Isabelle, which he did without too much fuss, since I have to say that at the outset, I can attest a certain respect paid me and my six-shooter pistol. We rode, sometimes trotting, sometimes galloping, but most of the time walking on a path which unquestionably and without exaggeration was worse than the one leading to Mount Aubert, and nevertheless still the royal road from Veracruz to Mexico City. It was bordered on both sides by low forests, similar to a thicket, mainly composed of mimosas, acacias, and trees with large white flowers which I think are from the begonia family. We encountered large convoys of carriages from time to time, either in groups or isolated; Indian houses; thatch-covered cages which were picturesque, but often dirty and squalid. But we rarely encountered any passersby.

Following this road, I arrived apace at eight o'clock at night in Plan, a sorry village with an even sorrier inn. After our horses were watered and we dined, we continued on our way around eleven o'clock at night and arrived the next morning on New Year's Day in Jalapa, after encountering a road quite similar to the one we were on the day before. I had not slept for two nights. The saddle and the road were both really poor; therefore I arrived (I have to admit) quite exhausted, but not enough to not think about all of you on such a sweet day to spend with the family.

Since you are six hours and a few minutes ahead of Mexico, I was still on my horse when I imagined you arriving at nine o'clock (three o'clock for me) seated around the table, covered with presents and pretty things. I then would have loved to exchange night for day. It was also party time in Jalapa, since New Year's Day is also celebrated in Mexico. The men were wearing their most beautiful serapes, a sort of colored blanket in which they wrap themselves up to their noses, while the women cover their heads and part of their face with shawls that they all know how to use with much grace.

Nature in Jalapa is indeed beautiful, still rich with flowers, despite the season. Therefore I went on a walk around the city in order to pick a few of them for you. The temperature was like the one we enjoy during our best spring mornings. I could see, on one side, the Orizaba peak, with its snow, and on the other side, Perote's coffer, and between them, a chain of mountains that reminded me also of my country. Despite the fact that I could not be among you, I was still happy and grateful for such a nice New Year's Day.

I had a recommendation for Jalapa from Mr. Lesanna, who was, during the whole duration of my trip, very kind to me. Furthermore, I made the acquaintance of a few gentlemen who were staying, like me, at the foreigners' hotel, among them a young Belgian, Mr. Magherns, who was a miner for four or five years in this country and who is a great storyteller. Unfortunately, he speaks just a little too much to inspire any confidence. He draws very well and together we drew a view of Jalapa that I thought turned out well. However, its details took me so long that I could not draw as much as I wished I could have. I have to say that I have rarely seen any other country that inspires me to draw more. Anything can be represented, every sight is worth a good painter's brush, rarely therefore have I regretted so much not to have enough time and talent during the ten or eleven days I spent in Jalapa.

I rode nine times in the area, once to Guatapa, the other time to Nolingo, equally remarkable because of their picturesque locations. I made four original drawings and copied two of Mr. Magherns's (the crater of the Orizaba and the crater of the Popocatépetl) and collected between two and three hundred plants that I asked Mr. Lesanna to send to Veracruz for me.

You can see that I have not exactly wasted my time and I am not counting the day trips that I made into the neighborhoods of Jalapa. Here, more than anywhere else, you cannot be scared of wasting your time, since life is expensive in this country. You do not have any idea at home, and when I will tell you that a pair of boots, for example, costs fifty francs here, you will still not be able to figure out the rest.

I met with good people in order to travel from Jalapa to Mexico City; the Marquis de Radepont,[31] among others, is a very agreeable man. We were two Swiss, three Frenchmen, two Germans, and a Mexican, and finally a native of Yucatán, Mexico, who was very happy to travel in such good company, since (you may understand) we all were in a good disposition and well equipped to go on this trip which, although somewhat unsafe, is by far less dangerous than one can generally imagine in Europe.

The road from Veracruz to Mexico City is indeed interesting. In three days, you go through all areas and climates in the world. From Veracruz, we traveled through tropical regions to get to Jalapa, similar to Italy in terms of climate, but even more beautiful. From there, we climbed up to Perote, through forests and mountains resembling ours, without forgetting the wind and the cold that you can find at the top and that chills you like our month of February does at home. We traveled across lands of sugar cane, oranges, and pine (the last always present in these cold areas) to find again, heading down to Mexico City, the same variation in nature, although it is less important in its contrasts since in the valley, one can see wheat and potato grow next to sugar cane which would not survive in caliente soil—that is, the warm areas closer to the Gulf.

---

[31] ***Aimé Louis-Victor du Bosc, Marquis de Radepont.*** *The policy of installing a satellite monarchy in Mexico and thus expanding France's power in the region is generally attributed to him. In 1861, following Mexican President Benito Juárez's suspension of interest payments to foreign countries (which angered Mexico's major creditors), France invaded.*

Altogether, nature has been kind to Mexico. Its soil is good, and from sugar, coffee, cocoa, olives, cotton, to barley and oats, all of the products the earth offers are gathered here. Nevertheless, what is more necessary to the happiness and the prosperity of a country, the active hard-working and industrious man, is not to be seen, represented (in a country which is five times as large as Spain) by five to six thousand foreigners, defying the little guarantees that these parts offer. I must add that half of these foreigners live in Mexico City and that just a few among these thousands are farmers, or busy exploiting a soil, so rich in all its respects, be it vegetable or mineral.

We spent the first night in Perote, and on the second day, we rode until Puebla, which we left the next day at three o'clock in the morning to arrive at five in the evening in Mexico City. Leaving Perote, we first went through immense plains that resembled an ocean, since they are so vast, flat, and sterile. But since they are at the same time surrounded by very pretty mountains with soft forms, however varied and picturesque, still overlooked by the magnificent Orizaba peak, the picture is not without poetry. I enjoyed it—despite the enormous heat that immediately followed the icy cold that we encountered throughout the morning until the sun rose. As I said earlier, this plain is sterile, as far as vegetation is concerned. From time to time, you can make out cacti that are spread out and that from a distance resemble sheep. Sometimes you encounter swamps filled with water birds, as well as small isolated mountains, which look like little islands in a lake, lost in the middle of this vast land.

We arrived that day in Huamantla at noon. A little further away, we could see to our right the craters of the Malinche, a mountain with very jagged and picturesque forms. Traveling towards Puebla, the land became more cultivated with barley, oats, corn, wheat, and scattered with aloe hedges. Villages began appearing more frequently. Surrounding the gardens, we could see fences made of cacti, which are called saguaros here because of their resemblance to organ pipes. The sight of churches, built in a Lombard Venetian style, grew in number, with somewhat of an Arabesque touch and all with a very artful appearance. It is curious that their numbers grow at the same rate as the scoundrels who live in the surrounding towns or villages. Puebla is the one that has the most of both, which does not prevent you from admiring it. Its numerous glaciers[32] help it stand out. All around Popocatépetl and Iztaccíhuatl, that are the background of this painting, are pretty, snow-capped mountains topped with churches and convents.

Not far from Puebla, we started to climb a hill, the summit of which was the highest point of the whole trip, roughly nine to ten thousand feet high above sea level. Then we descended again through large pine forests that extend all the way to the valley of Mexico City, which presented a stunning view. On your left and very close by, you have the two glaciers and at their feet, a large part of the valley, surrounded by mountains. In all directions you can make out many villages (thanks to their smoke) then isolated mounds, like the ones on the plains between Perote and Puebla, which here are called cerros.

Upon my arrival in Mexico City, I was settled in a most commendable hotel, the Bazar, where the first thing I did was to get rid of an immeasurable quantity of dust; then I rested until the next day from the bumpy ride we had just finished. The day following my arrival, I brought the letters of recommendation (that I owe to my Uncle Wilhelm's[33] kindness); one addressed to Mr. Bénéché, the other to Mr. Ansoatigi, in addition to Ms. Falconnet, whom I

---

[32] *Henri refers to Popocatépetl and Iztaccíhuatl throughout as glaciers. It appears that in 1853 that terminology was accurate. Until recently both still contained glaciers, but due to warmer temperatures and increased volcanic activity they have decreased considerably.*

[33] *Wilhelm Sillem was Henri's uncle. Henri was by all accounts betrothed to Madeleine Sillem, his first cousin and Wilhelm's daughter before he left on his trip for the Americas. Wilhelm Sillem had been a speculator for European business interests in Mexico during the 1830s, and Henri's voyage through Mexico was certainly made more agreeable thanks to his uncle, who was still well connected.*

am able to meet thanks to the kindness of her sister, Mrs. Freuden-reich. Mr. Bénéché and Mr. Wild greeted me well, Mr. Falconnet[34] and Mr. Ansoatigi even more so. I had dinner last night with the former. This morning, I had breakfast at Mr. Falconnet's country house in Tacubaya and I dined tonight in town at Mr. Ansoatigi's. So far, Mr. Falconnet has shown me the greatest kindness and if you could in any way thank his sister on my behalf, I would appreciate it. I also would like you to thank my Uncle Wilhelm for his letters of recommendation from which–given the initial hospitality—I dare to hope for more amiability and congeniality. Mr. Bénéché and Mr. Wild still live in the same house that Uncle Wilhelm used to live in.

I even found there a few Swiss views left over from Uncle Wilhelm's time. At the sight of this house and of the memories they left here, I, at the same time, regretted not being able to visit such good family again, and had the pleasure to see something that reminded me more accurately of them and of their life in this town.

Mr. Ansoatigi, his wife, and their son, were so kind and considerate to me which I owe to the good memories that they had from Wilhelm's family and from the friendship that bound those two ladies (which I conceive easily) since they must have been a perfect match. They asked me a lot of details about the extended Sillem family, so we spent most of our time discussing Geneva.

Farewell, Dear Father

---

[34] *While in Mexico, Henri stayed at the home of **François de Palezieux-Falconnet** in Tacubaya (now part of Mexico City), the agent for the Committee of Mexican Bond holders. He was in the midst of securing payment for the Mexican debt to the British bond holders.*

Letter Eleven

MEXICO CITY

February 2nd, 1853

Although this letter is the fourth to your last one, I am following the impulse of friendship that does not count such things, and I cannot let a steamship go each month without giving you some news about my doings. This is especially true as I would not want to make you worry about me, something which could accidentally happen if I did not enjoy every opportunity, since the letters get lost so easily in this country—one of confusion without equal.

From the date of this letter, you can see that I am still in the capital, which means that I have been busy for the last fifteen days roughly finding my bearings and visiting this city, so interesting in its originality, and so rich in monuments, combining fine architecture and color with the powerful and picturesque weathering of time.

I continue to make further acquaintances with people to whom I am recommended, and among whom I most prominently place Mr. Falconnet, who still shows me great kindness. I spent two days with him in his country house in Tacubaya, where the lodging was excellent, and where I took advantage of my time to draw two sketches.

An Englishman, Mr. Brennan, Mr. Falconnet's secretary and his housemate, was there, and since my arrival here, I have gotten to know him well. I also happen to enjoy the company of Mr. Bénéché and Mr. Wild, with whom I frequently dine. In addition, I met with all sorts of people, either through these gentlemen, or as traveling companions, the latest one being the Marquis de Radepont, about whom I spoke in my previous letter. As far as fellow countrymen go, I met, through Mr. Falconnet, a Mr. Jeker of Porrentruy and his nephew.

I rode a few times in the close vicinity of the city. I went to Tamba twice, in order to admire the magnificent cedar tree under which Cortés rested after the battle of Noche. It is a venerable old timer, with a circumference of about forty feet, but whose crown has been beaten and bruised by the centuries. Then in Guadalupe, you can see the pretty Saint Marie church, where people come on pilgrimage from all across this vast republic, especially as you also find inside the nicest little chapel a sulfur water spring that possesses all manner of virtues.

Afterwards, I went for a walk to draw along the canal in the Las Vigas neighborhood with a young French painter, Mr. de Laval. It is as picturesque as it is interesting, not only for the nice shadows and the pretty houses on its banks, but most of all because of all these small canoes which endlessly pass by. The canoes are steered by Indians or sometimes by just one Indian woman, each with a countenance and dress more original than the next, the boats laden with all sorts of produce; vegetables, fruits, and more. Besides the artful nature of their countenance and dress, the people are also extremely different one from another. The largest race, the purest and the most characteristic, is the Indian race, with coppery skin, black flat hair, long bodies, and slim but vigorous limbs. Their expression is usually cold and indifferent, sometimes dazed and wild. Their nature is very distrustful, but rarely mean. Their outfits vary, depending on the region they come from.

However, what is generally worn by men are pointy straw hats, a sort of sleeveless blouse, going almost to mid-back, made of a brown, striped fabric, and finally, a pair of large shorts, going down to their knees. Women commonly wear a large skirt whose upper part is white and the lower generally blue. To carry their children, they use a sort of shawl tied around their neck in which the child is placed behind their back.

The black race, despite their emancipation and due to the hatred that exists between them and Indians, are sparsely represented here. The same is true for the mulattoes: this mean and cruel race is replaced here by mestizos, mixed-race descendants of Indians and whites with a less coppery skin and wild features. They don't like any work and they only go out to eat and drink, their arms underneath their serapes, a sort of a long rainbow-colored blanket that they wrap around them like the Carbonaris[35] do, mostly on their left shoulder, in order to hide their features up to their nose. Since they also wear a hat with wide brims, you can only see their eyes. They are almost always wearing two pairs of trousers—underneath, one made with white fabric and over that, another pair, often open on each side, and which hangs around their legs. They do not work much, since they only need very little to survive, and are usually bigger drinkers than eaters; therefore you can often see them spend long hours warming in the sun, leaning against a wall.

The *mestizo* women usually wear a very full skirt and a kind of shawl or scarf that they throw around their figure, in order to stylishly surround their face. Sometimes the mestizos are rich *rancheros* (ranchers) and then their outfits become as shiny as their horses' harnesses. The Spanish race, composed of Mexicans descended from former Spaniards, have nothing remarkable about them, nor their dress; a mix of Mexican and European clothing, a style that the foreigners living in this country also choose to wear.

Upon my arrival in this country, or rather in its capital, I was hoping to make up for the non-sociability of the United States

---

[35] *Secret revolutionary societies founded in early 19th-century Italy.*

by embracing again the charms and the pleasures of good society. However, since our dear Wilhelm left Mexico City, this city has changed a great deal in this respect. The first time I paid Mr. Falconnet a visit, he told me that I could not count on the pleasures and resources of good society, because they were non-existent. This is a truth that I was perfectly able to verify.

Life in Mexico City is actually sad for those who are not established in business, especially for young people and particularly for young girls who are locked up at home as if it were a convent, from which their parents only allow them to leave to go to vespers, or to shut them up in a carriage that leads them to the Paseo. Walks do not exist here. It is very rare to meet a man of good upbringing on the street. *Tertulias* (evening parties) are not any more than a balm, and I prefer to spend my evenings reading, or at the Lonja, where I take my Spanish lessons (in which I don't make huge progress) instead speaking most of the time to fellow countrymen.

Bullfights regularly take place on Sundays and sometimes during the week, which I attended once. They actually are quite marvelous for their drama and skill, but even more revolting for their cruelty. The bull is barely in the arena before three or four *picadors* arrive on horses who strike it with their lances. When they think that they have done enough, that there have been enough horses gored, and that the bull has received enough hits, trumpets sound to leave an open field to the *banderilleros.* Until then, they were just busy avoiding the bull, using flags, but now they make the bull's blood run by very skillfully planting in him a series of sticks, at the end of which are hooks, and once inside the flesh, cannot come out. When at last the animal's back and shoulders are so covered with sticks that you cannot place anymore and drenched with blood, it shivers and stamps its feet with pain, a third trumpet sounds, and the *toreador* arrives and kills the bull with a sword. Once dead, a carriage pulled by four mules arrives that drags the bull outside the arena, in which a new bull is thrown. Thus, I saw them kill five of them, three horses gored and a rider almost crushed.

I was so disgusted at times, not so much to see the picadors, banderilleros, and toreador killed, since I would have liked the bull to take care of all of them, but to see the poor animal suffer—I had to turn my eyes away from that spectacle. I saw many people of good society in attendance, even young ladies, who were following with great pleasure, not showing any emotions whatsoever at any point of the fight.

As I was telling you earlier, I have not left Mexico City, but it is not because I do not want to travel through the country. I have a lot of ideas in this respect. One is to accompany Mr. Falconnet on a brief excursion up to a very famous cave which is located by Cuernavaca, then to visit the Guanajuato mines, the largest in the world. I would also like to travel in the vicinity of Valladolid to see Pátzcuaro Lake which Humboldt calls one of the most interesting sites on both continents, and lastly, a short excursion with the Marquis de Radepont to Puebla.

Before going on the road for my excursions, I am also waiting for two young Germans whom I met in Havana and who told me of their intention to go to Mexico. Their ship has finally arrived. Since I last wrote you, I again have been told so much about Brazil's beauties, that I am for the moment torn between the desire to see you again sooner and spare you worry, and the will to visit one of the most beautiful countries in the world. To go on this very interesting trip, I have now found a way to do so while ensuring my return before October or November. I will go from here to Acapulco, then to Panama. There I will catch one of the steamships that leave for Valparaíso every twenty days, stopping in twenty different locations in Peru and Chile. I will continue by land to Buenos Aires by crossing the Andes, which is supposed to be extremely interesting, and then from there to Rio and Bahia.

As I told you, I have not yet decided on this new route, but if I could find a travel companion, and you are at ease about my situation, please let me know through the letter that I am expecting one of these days, and I think I would go for it. Be kind enough, in the meantime, to write me at Mr. Zangroni's address in Havana and also at Schroeder and Company in Rio de Janeiro (Southampton Way).

The young French painter, Mr. de Laval, would love to come along with me, but at my expense. As agreeable as it would be to have a companion on a long trip, I am however not rich enough to grant myself this kind of luxury; therefore I had to refuse, despite his insistence, even offering me many paintings in exchange.

I wait with an impatience that I cannot express for your letters, on which I count very soon. I do not know why, but this long silence worries me. It has been two months since I have not had news from you; may God make them agreeable to my wishes. I am heading tomorrow with Mr. Falconnet to Tacubaya in order to attend the Candlemas festivities, and I expect the letters to arrive by ship upon my return.

You have probably learned by now some things about the Mexican revolution which, I can tell you, has been the most innocent in the world. Not a shot was fired. Ceballos,[36] the current president who orchestrated the coup, shows a lot of knowledge and energy. At the same time, he is a rich and honest man. As for me, I hope he will remain in power. That is, I assure you, a great task in such a disorganized country, both morally and politically; although so beautiful, so rich, and so full of resources. I can only hope and wish to see it rise again by itself, thanks to a citizenry capable of giving a new and better impulse to the political system, as well as to ideas in general, without needing (like many Mexicans admit

---

[36] *Juan Bautista Ceballos (1811—1859) was interim president of Mexico from January 6th to February 8th, 1853.*

shamelessly) an American from the United States to do so to reach a good and solid state.

For this moment and given the situation, the future of this country is a maze from which it is very difficult for a human imagination to escape. I feel fine and this mountain climate and rarefied air suit me better than the hot temperatures of the coasts.

Letter Twelve

MEXICO CITY

February 23rd, 1853

Since I left you at the foot of Cortés' cedar tree, I made two trips which interested me a great deal: the first one to Miraflores, home of the Ansoatigi family, the second to the famous Cacahuamilpa caves. Kept in Mexico City by two invitations, I was not able to leave here on the same day as Mr. Ansoatigi. However, I accepted his invitation to meet with him the next day, which is easy to do: if you leave at six o'clock in the morning with the stagecoach, you arrive in Miraflores by ten o'clock. After a beautiful spring morning ride, I arrived at the country home of Mr. Ansoatigi, whom I found at lunch with Mr. Robertson, the manager of the cotton factory he owns in Miraflores. As I was finishing lunch with them, Mr. Ansoatigi offered to accompany me on a ride to Amecamer where that very day, Indian religious festivities were taking place.

Let us speak first a little bit about Miraflores, which due to its location is worth talking about. It is a village roughly as big as Vaumarcus, whose greatest part consists of a factory and its outbuildings built as an amphitheater which slightly dominates the whole. Immediately behind the village, you can see the majestic Iztaccíhuatl glacier, and further away to the right, the Popocatépetl. In the foreground, you can catch a glimpse of Mexico City's beautiful valley, which was unimpeded by even the few volcanoes that rose from the plain. All around the village, or rather on both sides of it, you find the same terrain, somewhat uneven and a little dry, especially at this time of year where nature in these parts resembles ours at the peak of autumn. Therefore, the name of Miraflores, which I have been assured is well deserved during the warmer months, appears to me at first a little pompous.

At the bottom, finally, the road to Mexico City winds around, and you can see a few *haciendas* (farms) in the distance, and towards Popocatépetl, a big village with a large church, as well as the very picturesque remains of a monastery built by Cortés. It was probably conceived by a Spanish artist, but executed by Indians, which gives it a very original style.

Mr. Ansoatigi's one-story house has, on its front facing the valley, one of those large galleries like the ones you often encounter in this country's houses. The house faces a courtyard where one dries cotton threads. A part of the house is inhabited by Mr. Ansoatigi and his family, and the other part by his manager; which seems to me rather well planned.

I gladly accepted the invitation to go to Amecamer (or Ameca-meca, as some people say), especially since I was told a great deal about their unique festivities. We therefore nimbly mounted our horses and formed a rather sensible caravan. Besides Mr. Ansoatigi and me, it was comprised of a young English woman and her brother who were visiting the Robertsons, and by an American senator and his two servants, also on horseback. After having crossed a small valley which hid the glaciers from our view, we arrived on a mountaintop, from where we were able to see the glaciers even more closely, with the town of Amecamer at our feet. Amecamer is the site of a pilgrimage that is very respected by the Indians, who come from far away at this period of the year in order to venerate the Virgin Mary and ask her for the forgiveness of their sins.

After dismounting, we passed through a large crowd of people, spreading across the side of the village where the market stood. The marketplace was laden with many kinds of produce, primarily fruits and vegetables, from all over the country. After we traversed the length of the village, we arrived at the foot of a small mountain. A considerable crowd was climbing on a well-paved and quick path shaded by magnificent trees, most of them oaks covered with orchids and long, hanging mosses that give them a sad yet artful appearance. Some pilgrims were walking up the road, some were coming down, and others still were kneeling in front of holy niches by the side of the road. The crippled were on their knees in the middle of the road, begging charity of the passersby.

From time to time, you could see the sun break through the clouds, which cast upon the scenic crowd of people in their traditional dress a light that contrasted with the dark shadows coming from the trees. About two-thirds of the way up the road, there was a penitence house with two chapels: In the first one, all were kneeling, some saying their rosary in a low voice, the others screaming in a strident and contrite voice. In the other chapel, young male and female Indians danced, surrounded by flowers, to the sound of violin and guitar music.

On the second floor of this penitence house are the cells that house those who come to repent. They are small and poorly furnished: a few images, some rules of prayers, and for those who want to punish themselves, a whip; these are the only ornaments. You are however well rewarded for this ascetic spectacle by the charming picture you can see from every little window destined to give light to the cells. It is either the view of the road you've just climbed, or of the valley beneath the village, overlooking the magnificent glaciers. Then to the right, the valley becomes dark and severe. The rest of the path turns, and turns again, climbing to reach the chapel that sits on top of the mountain. There ends the pilgrimage, either for the Indian, the Catholic fanatic, or for the man who also puts some fanaticism in the admiration of the beauties of nature.

Where do these people go, after they descend the mountain? If you follow them, you will see them go from religious dancing to profane dancing; you will walk with them inside those gambling houses where you will see them play monte, and then bet on cock fights. In their pleasures, as well as in their religious exercises, their faces stay fierce, their look malevolent to the stranger, and as fanatic as they can be deep inside, they still stay apathetic, in their rare virtues, as well as in their numerous vices.

The reason is that their fanaticism comes from a deep ignorance, a great sluggishness, and also from the absolutions they are granted with great ease for all these bad tendencies they bring to the bottom of the mountain, which they easily obtain pardon for. They will be here again at the bottom of the mountain next year, with an equally brief repentance.

Amecamer, this holy place, might also be home to the most thieves. For a long time, they used to rob travelers on the road from Mexico City to Puebla. For a few years now, however, some good people, seeing that the government was not doing enough to punish the thieves, combined forces to finance a sort of a private militia that now shoots the bandits without warning and which has made the roads much more secure.

I next made the excursion to the grotto with three young Englishmen: one of them, Mr. Mildmay, was highly recommended to Mr. Falconnet. On the first day, we went up to Cuernavaca, a city located eighteen leagues from Mexico City. This is where Cortés rested after his conquests and his disgrace. You can still see the ruins of his palace, magnificently located in a large and beautiful valley, facing the famous Popocatépetl and Iztaccíhuatl. I call them ruins because as they have now been turned into Mexican barracks, it is difficult to call them by another name.

After spending the night in Cuernavaca, we left the following day to go visit the old hacienda of Cortés that still belongs to his family and in Tamixco, the hacienda of Mr. Del Barrisa's, who greeted us very warmly. These two haciendas almost exclusively cultivate sugar cane on a very large scale. The one in Tamixco by itself produces thirty-five thousand arrobes of sugar and seventy thousand of molasses that are used to make brandy. This necessitated the construction of a very large plant, together with the buildings and machinery needed for the production of sugar and for the distillation of alcohol, which take place night and day. There might be at least two hundred workers, some busy producing the sugar, and the others busy irrigating and cultivating the sugar cane fields, which are in this region less humid and less fertile than the ones in Havana, Jalapa, and Veracruz, and therefore have to be irrigated all year long. For transportation, they have no oxen, no horses, nor any carriages, but at least two hundred mules that after taking the cane from the field to the plant then transport the sugar, either to Acapulco or to Mexico City.

On the next day, after visiting a former *teocalli*, otherwise known as an Aztec pyramid, then the Miacatlán hacienda, where we dined, we spent the night in Cocoyotla's hacienda, which was only three leagues away from the final destination of our trip, the Cacahuamilpa cave. The next day, after making our acquaintance with the administrator, a fine man indeed, we rode our horses, since the road from Cuernavaca up to the road is not passable in any other way. After crossing a very rocky path and duck hunting for a little while in a lagoon, we arrived in Cacahuamilpa. After a discussion with the judge of the village (inhabited only by Indians) and paying him about fifteen piasters for the toll, we headed towards the cave accompanied by twenty Indians, whose duty was to guide us and to give us light in this immense and gloomy maze.

Once inside, we were flabbergasted, awestruck by one of those grandiose spectacles that nature sometimes offers and that render us incapable of finding words that could describe how we felt. You can only bow your head to the Creator of all things, marvel at His almighty powers, and give thanks to His magnificence. The vault of the cave is so immense that its dome is lost in the darkness. Stalagmites rise like towers, next to which a man looks no taller than a fly.

After leaving the entryway, where the light of day and the light of our torches were fighting one another, we moved forward so we were only lit by the latter, the glimmer of which had the crystals that form almost all stalagmites sparkling like stars. From time to time we launched rockets high overhead into the darkened void, which ended up bursting into stars, but only after treating us to a magical and grandiose spectacle illuminating the cavernous space. After spending three hours there, as our torches were closer to dying down than our admiration would allow, we had to bid farewell to the most magnificent cave in the world and return to the surface of the earth, which in these parts is rather sorry and monotonous–mainly large treeless arid plains.

We spent the following night in Cuautla where a celebration was taking place, half religious and half profane. We saw people gamble with the equivalent of eighty-franc coins until the end of the evening, since all here, rich or poor have a passion for gambling. The market square was almost entirely filled with gambling tables where we could see people sell their shirts to satisfy their passion, which is one of the biggest ills in this country. We were back in Mexico City on Monday where I was able to meet with my acquaintances, including Mr. Falconnet, who is still the best and most agreeable of them all.

I am writing you from Puebla now, as the Marquis de Radepont, the Count de Béarn, and I are traveling together in the vicinity. We intend to visit the area, as well as Izúcar de Matamoros, Atlixco, and San Rafael, from where we will head back to Mexico City through Paluca. It will be a very nice trip that will reward us with many pleasures, drawings, and plants.

MEXICO CITY

March 19th, 1853

Returning from my little trip, I was very happy to find your good and excellent letter which like all the others gave me so much joy that I cannot thank you enough for it. As soon as I arrived, I hurried to Mr. Wild and Mr. Bénéché, sure that I would find some letters there, but I did not. These gentlemen greeted me with empty hands, telling me that since nothing had come to their address, nothing therefore had arrived for me, and warned me that it was useless to go check at the post office. Having however the intimate conviction that some words had arrived for me, and knowing in what a mess the postal department is, I did not give up, but on the contrary went directly to the post office.

Unfortunately, it was six o'clock at night and totally dark. I tried as hard as I could but was unable to find my name on the letters list that was posted in the post office courtyard. I then had the idea to ask one of the department servants to bring me a light, but he refused to oblige me, with the poor, lethargic attitude that most of the natives of this country share. Since I desperately wanted to see, I started to walk up and down the street, until I was able to find a shop where I bought a box of phosphoric matches. Using this luminous system, I managed to my great satisfaction to light the number *1273 de Buren, Enriquez.* I then hopped to the office where I was given two letters, one from you and the other from Pillichody. Since they were both wearing the necessary mention care of Mr.

Bénéché, I took the liberty to lecture the employees, who told me that although Mr. Bénéché had been living in this city for the last twenty years, his name was only recognized when followed by the title Consul of Prussia.

Back home, I took great delight in reading your excellent letter over and over which, despite its eight pages, still seemed far too short. I praise God with all my heart for keeping you all in good health and for allowing you to enter this New Year all together. May all the letters I receive during the next six months of traveling that I still have ahead of me continue to bring me the same good news of you. I need it both for my happiness and for my peace of mind. They bring me courage during my long and solitary voyage, and while I encounter ever more selfishness and ever less true and real friendship, I learn to love you, my parents, my friends, and my country even more. I thank you all dearly for the good health you wished me for the year ahead. May it, coming from hearts like yours, bring me luck, so much luck that one day my turn will come again to clink my glass against yours.

I left you in my previous letter in Puebla, at the start of an excursion that I was embarking upon with the Marquis de Radepont and the Count de Béarn[37]. The former, whom I met some time ago, is a man of an amicable and obliging character—a true Normand. A former officer in Africa, he deals here with agriculture. Mr. de Béarn is part of the French embassy in Washington and is traveling across the country for his pleasure and his education. Although very nice, he is not of a cultivated spirit, but I enjoyed having a serious and amicable conversation with him.

In the charming vicinity of Puebla we visited the old pyramid of Cholula and a chapel perched on a summit from which one enjoys an admirable view of the town on one side and the Popocatépetl

---

[37] **Louis-Hector Galard-Brassac, Comte de Béarn,** *was a diplomat and Member of the French Embassy in Washington D.C.*

and Iztaccíhuatl glaciers on the other. We saw some of Murillo's remarkable paintings inside the Carmelite convent as well as a great collection of paintings that belonged to a lawyer. After seeing all this and after being very well treated by Mr. Garalli and Mr. Ross, friends of Mr. de Radepont, we finally put on monstrous spurs and climbed on our horses. We were equipped like real Mexican travelers with goatskin pants and serapes, followed by a servant, also on horseback, and by another one carrying our effects. We formed a very respectable caravan and therefore went without incident across these rather ill-famed lands, although we had been told that we would be at risk.

The first day, we reached Atlixco. From a distance, we could already make out a gathering of steep rocks, on top of which stood a chapel, with a nice convent on its left side. At the foot of the mound, the town spreads gently through a plain, or rather a valley. At the bottom, we could see a tree, famous in Mexico for its age and its huge dimensions. The ahuehuete is a cedar tree whose trunk has been ravaged by time and can easily contain seven riders as well as a whole quadrille of dancers.

After a ride around the town and two drawings (rather two sketches) we had dinner, slept, and climbed back on our rides the next day at four in the morning, before dawn and the start of the sun's heat. We rode for nine consecutive hours through a large valley flanked by volcanic-looking mountains covered with Nogales and Organus cacti often as tall as trees. We reached Izúcar de Matamoros, a miserable town, due to both its houses and the morality of its residents; however, it was still picturesque, surrounded by greenery that spread out in all directions.

There are no inns there, only what they call *mazons*, which are houses where you and your horse can rest during the day but where you cannot stay for the night. Next door was an Indian house, where the female residents managed to make us a dinner that we all enjoyed despite its frugality. We then went for a walk, and after doing a small sketch and smoking the usual cigars, decided to deliver ourselves into the arms of Morpheus[38]. Unfortunately, this friend of humanity has organized, regimented enemies, so after fighting them hopelessly, I decided to get dressed and to wrap myself in my serape. After taking a saddle to use as a pillow, I quietly went to sleep under the arcades of the courtyard where this time, sleep finally won a complete victory.

The next morning, we went to visit St. Nicolas' hacienda, belonging to a Mr. de Zamora, a very rich man and a skilled administrator of his vast estates. His lands bring him between sixty to seventy thousand arrobes of sugar, and incur an annual expense of fifty to sixty thousand dollars, due to the four hundred workers employed during the eight-month harvest. I have seen so many of these haciendas that I can depend enough on my memory to be able to, upon my return, tell you everything about the whole process, whose description would be too long and too dry to be made in a letter. Mr. de Zamora is very polite, amicable, and well informed; and it was a distinct pleasure for me to go with him through his huge property. At two o'clock, we were back in Izúcar de Matamoros. We then immediately left to go spend the night in another hacienda belonging to a Mr. Turnbull from Puebla, whom we also left to go to the Bosquet, a charming little farm located near the town, and which is owned by a Flemish farmer, a Mr. Leisen, who greeted us in the best of ways.

I will explain why we turned around by telling you that we first had decided to go back to Amecamer using the famous road through the glaciers (famous for first allowing Cortés to enter the valley of Mexico City). Being so close to the Popocatépetl, we were brave enough to decide to climb it. So there we were, headed towards San Nicolás de Los Ranchos, the last village at the base of

---

[38] *A reference to the God of dreams/sleep.*

the volcano, where we were planning to spend the night before the ascent. However, instead of one night, we had to spend two—since upon our arrival in the village, we learned that we had to have an authorization from the owner of the volcano sulfur mine in order to allow us to climb it. We were then obliged to send our servant to Puebla to get the authorization, which we finally received, but not until the following evening, which forced us to spend an extra night in Nicolás.

A brief description of our inn and innkeeper: he was the first grocer in the area, and did the utmost to settle us as well as possible in his hotel, which had two doors, no windows, and—as far as rooms went—a shop, a warehouse, and a kitchen. As for the feast, we made do with some local chicken, and as for beds, Mr. de Radepont and I lay down on the shop's tiles after wrapping ourselves in our serapes and setting our sleeping bags under our heads. Mr. de Béarn had the place of honor atop the counter of the shop, just large enough to accommodate a quiet sleeper. We dined on chicken accompanied by a good red wine that we brought from Atlixco.

The Indians from these parts were as picturesque as the area itself, and we were in a good mood. I drew a landscape and sketched four little Indians, an Indian woman, and her child. We had a much more agreeable time than I expected, with so much pleasure and ease that even if the local priest had taken me for a pagan, I would have still been able to defend myself!

We left the next day at four o'clock in the morning, accompanied by three Indian guides carrying the necessary supplies. Before arriving in San Nicolás de Los Ranchos, we rode for a while next to a pedregal, which is a volcanic bed of basalt that flanks the volcano. This dry and tormented basalt, topped by a pine tree forest, is somewhat wild and unique. Both Mr. de Béarn and I, amateurs of geology, found it especially interesting. Further away from San Nicolás de Los Ranchos, we crossed through forests composed at first of a mix of alders and pines, eventually by the latter only. The trip, although quite long, went easily and without trouble, while Mr. de Radepont was telling us about his Algerian campaigns. Our horses started to have some difficulty breathing due to the high elevation that we had reached and that was not much different than up on our Jungfrau.

Finally, at ten o'clock, we reached the last rancho, Flamargan, where the furnaces that use the sulfur coming from the crater are located. After getting rid of some of our effects and having a light lunch, we returned to the horses that would be taking us up to where the snows are. This means of transportation was quite important, since from there, the terrain quickly became sandy, and covering it on horseback allowed us to conserve energy that we would need for the rest of the trip. We were thus at the bottom of the Popocatépetl, this giant (seventeen thousand, nine hundred feet high, according to some; seventeen thousand, five hundred, according to others) that stood upright in front of us, so upright in fact, that instead of using a path that wound around the slope, you went straight up a forty-degree angle slope.

Before starting to ascend from the cross where we dismounted, our poor animals seemed to really suffer from the lack of air. They began stopping regularly, bending their heads as if they were hoping to find something more, looking around trying to find out where we were taking them, and shivering pathetically. They looked at us for pity, a pity we would have had gladly given, had we not wanted to conserve our forces for the last part of the trip. It was definitely the most difficult part of the climb, first because of the sharp slope and then because of the ever rarefied air. We first climbed on top of a mixture of snow, ice, and sand that made our ascent uneasy and tiring. Further away we found a more compact and thicker snow that would have allowed us to continue at a faster pace if the air had not started to rarefy so much that every ten paces, we had to stop in order to catch our breath.

Finally, after a walk of four hours (others do it in half a day), we reached the top, if you can call the top the sharp ridge that surrounded the crater. In front of us was the most grandiose and at the same time bizarre spectacle that I ever laid eyes on, an immense crater that took two hours to walk around and that is seven hundred and fifty feet deep. It is formed by rocks, sometimes in regular layers that cross each other, sometimes torn apart and shredded, in all possible colors — red, black, gray, yellow, green — mingled with snow and with huge ice blocks that seemed to lay on their sides hanging from the prominences. Swirls of gas and smoke came from the bottom of the crater which rumbled like the thunder, throwing whirlwinds of smoke into a sky ten times darker than Havana's.

All of this is so beautiful, so original, that we forgot about the strain we had gone through. After the first moment of surprise and admiration, we all took out our sketchbooks (since the three of us are artists) but just as our pencils were starting to draw this masterpiece of nature and tame its lines, we began to feel odd. We felt the cold at first, then headaches and nausea which forced us, whether we liked it or not, to put an end to the artistic ardor that this subject had inspired and to find refuge at the Popocatépetl hotel. This hotel must have some similarities with the hotel of the Neuchâtelois by the Aar glaciers. It sits about a hundred feet away on the crater's slope on a rock prominence which was enclosed by a few planks and made into a hotel. Our hotel (or our hut more specifically) must have been only fifty square feet.

This is where six out of the twelve to fifteen Indians who are responsible for the exploitation of the sulfur actually live. Their companions reside at the bottom of the crater, which we reached later on. One of the Indians knew how to make coffee which was complemented by some cordial I had. That, along with a little rest that we enjoyed stretched out on our serapes, allowed me at least to have the pleasure and energy to return to the top of the crater to admire the sunset. The view, as it was sunrise, was somewhat spoiled by a few clouds that were wandering below and around us, but not enough to prevent us from admiring Mexico City's gorgeous valley and the whole plateau of Puebla that lay at our feet. The latter was so far away that we could not grasp the horizon. Between these two impressive spectacles rose the other glacier, the Iztaccíhuatl (the Woman of Snow) that our eyes could see over, since it was at a lower elevation.

After satisfying my admiration, although tempered by nausea and headache, I walked down to our hotel, where we had decided to spend the night. That little space managed to accommodate three travelers; the administrator who was accompanying us; and the six Indians of the plant—with enough room to allow them to cook for us as well as for themselves, without a fireplace. In addition, the cold was intensifying, and the volcanic gases and smoke were coming through the walls in big blasts that were even more obnoxious than the cooking odors, since they carried a strong smell of sulfur which caused the three of us to become more or less sick. After all of this you will surely have no difficulty believing that this night will not leave any good memories as far as comfort goes. Thus, we woke up the next morning at dawn with great ease.

We had decided to visit the bottom of the crater, which we did immediately following breakfast. It is the most difficult part of the expedition since in order to complete it, you first have to let yourself go two hundred feet down with the help of a *malacate*. A malacate is a rope tied to a wheel, activated by human force, at the end of which you are attached. You go down and back up hanging in the air. Beware of the rocks, though! Every bump can be avoided, either by kicking appropriately with your foot or pushing yourself away with your hand so you go back into the air and you do not graze or hurt yourself against the rock. The descent is somewhat easier than the ascent, which makes the rope tighter against your chest, enough to take your breath away, especially at that height, but this is something you must endure.

Once on the ground, we still had to walk another four hundred and fifty feet down, on crumbled rocks, in order to get to the bottom. There we found some interesting minerals, as well as the second abode, and finally the thickest and most active fumes. The largest of all must have an orifice of twenty feet in diameter from which came a noise similar to two furnaces that you would unload, then an immense column of smoke carrying a large quantity of sulfur in suspension and finally, next to the orifice, some very hot water, acidic enough to burn your feet. If you place a stone as big as your fist near the orifice, it is thrown up in the air as though it were nothing, but a larger one will on the other hand be covered in less than three minutes with sulfur deposits. After an hour or two spent in this sulfurous environment, we reattached ourselves to our malacate to finally go back up to our hosts, whom we left some time later, they as happy as we with the day's events.

It was ten o'clock in the morning—the descent went quite easily and became easier as it progressed. At two o'clock, we were at the Flamargan ranch, where we found our horses and a dinner made mostly of tortillas and chili, which was definitely appreciated as at the top of the volcano our appetite had totally disappeared. Altogether, though the expedition does not present any danger, it was rather tough and tiring.

As soon as we returned to Mexico City, Mr. de Béarn and I departed again to go visit the mines in Real del Monte. After going up almost eighteen thousand feet above sea level, eight days later we went down two thousand feet into the bowels of the earth (I will send you the story soon.) I will only tell you that upon our return to Mexico City, Mr. de Béarn and I will leave for Acapulco tomorrow, where we will arrive after a ten-day ride, and from where we will embark for Panama City. Mr. de Béarn is wishing to go and visit Guatemala, and I am wishing to reach Valparaíso, from where I will continue my voyage to Rio and Bahia, and eventually returning home (God willing) next November.

PANAMA CITY

April 19th, 1853

I was actually expecting to leave Mexico City around March 26th. As soon as I returned from Real Del Monte, I thought about saving a few days in order to go visit my best acquaintances in Mexico City, finish a few drawings, and finally attend the Holy Week celebrations. But Mr. de Béarn, my travel companion, also goes to Panama and Acapulco and has set his departure from Mexico on the 18th, hoping to find an extra steamship leaving Acapulco on May 1st or May 2nd. Therefore I had to make a tough decision between staying in Mexico City for another week, and immediately preparing to depart for a ten-day trip with an agreeable companion. I decided on the latter, settled some business, bid farewell to my acquaintances, and then left Mexico City for a seventeen-hour horse ride to Cuernavaca.

We had some difficulties with the person who rented us our horses, an unscrupulous Yankee whom we had graciously paid in advance. He then tried to cheat us by giving us a mule less, and by adjoining to our party two former Garibaldi supporters, whom we really could not have cared less about. Although our guide was witty and hardheaded like they all were, we managed to get rid of our two Italians and to keep an extra mule by the time we arrived in Cuernavaca, which was more agreeable. Leaving Mexico City at four o'clock in the afternoon, we reached San Agustín de las Cuevas that day, a village where our Sillem family members had their country house, which I visited and tried to sketch, as well as one can do in the moonlight.

Before daybreak, we left and headed towards Cuernavaca through a rather notorious forest and road where only two days before, Mr. Del Barrio, a minister in Guatemala, together with his brother and with all the occupants of his stagecoach, had been robbed. This had been done in such a way that the thieves who attacked them forced them to head back home in their birthday suits. As for us, it is true that we did not have such good rides, but on the other hand, we were armed to the teeth. Not only were we not attacked, but even in places preceding dangerous locations, we found many natives who, seeing our respectable look, started to follow us, as if they wished to be under our protection.

Leaving Cuernavaca, we made a detour to visit the famous Cacahuamilpa cave a second time, which I was really happy to see again in the company of Mr. de Béarn. We had been poorly equipped the first time (as far as lights were concerned) and this time we took our torches, flares, and Bengal lights; the lights allowed us to appreciate the beauty of this magnificent cave all the more. The detour lasted three nice and uneventful days and our expedition would have been very successful if not for the heat, the hunger, and the thirst, and without the disagreement caused by the local Indian rascals, who more or less own the cave. From there we reached the road to Acapulco, which leads to Puentes de Isla.

We rested after the fatigue of the trip and I do not need to tell you that as soon as I lay back in my hammock, I fell deeply asleep. We only had nine days of travel to Acapulco and rode for eleven hours per day, which is not much. But in warm countries like this where you sit constantly on the same horse's back (and ours are not the most vigorous), it is rather difficult to do more. It took us four days to travel to the small town of Zumpango, and an additional day to Chilpancingo, the only two towns you find along the way. To arrive there, we crossed an arid country without any scenic interest, especially during the first part of the journey

In the second part, however, we entered some *cañadas* that looked rather new to us. These are very narrow and deep valleys at the bottom of which usually runs a torrent—dry during winter, but furious and intense during the rainy season. The sides of these cañadas are covered with cacti, mainly of the Organus species, which sometimes look like gigantic tree-like candelabras, and sometimes like long and isolated porches that you could confuse at times with a hop field. Coming out of one of those cañadas and entering another one, we crossed the Messala River where we paused and even spent the night after enjoying a bath and hunting the alligators which, despite their impressive size, are not considered very dangerous. This river is also remarkable in the way you cross it, in boats made of gourds, but its banks are arid and bare, which disappointed us since we were hoping to find a river of a more or less tropical nature hiding in the shade and the greenery.

Chilpancingo, although at the same latitude as Jalapa, which is the latitude of perpetual spring, is nothing at all like that town. While Jalapa is charming with its magnificent location and its beautiful vegetation, Chilpancingo is the opposite, thanks to the dry and monotonous mountains surrounding it. After bidding farewell to these two little towns, which to put it bluntly are highly forgettable, we soon left the Sierra Templada to enter warmer lands, where we found beautiful trees and vegetation, orchids, and bromeliaceae covering the trees that fed them, as well as convolvulaceae and lianas galore that were beautiful. To my disappointment, very few were blooming at the time; therefore I could only collect around a hundred plants for you.

We also discovered new birds—budgerigars, many parrots, charming doves and pigeons, pheasants, a lovely black egret, and also a local jay which, as noisy and curious as ours, has much shinier plumage. From time to time, we saw iguanas run on the rocks; they are huge lizards, and quite delicious to eat. As for the trees, besides those you can see at home, such as the oak, the acacia, and some others, I have not seen any others that could be linked to our own.

We arrived in Acapulco on April 4th and learned we would have to wait until the 8th for the steamship. Since such stops are quite frequent in this country, where communication is still so difficult, we came to terms with it very easily and spent a few very quiet days—not as active as we would have liked. This was due to the enormous heat that prevented us from going on long walks. You can hike only in the morning or in the evening and both times of day are very short in this country. Acapulco's harbor is one of the most beautiful the eye can behold, but that is its only merit and that city has not even taken advantage of it. Indeed it is rather a sorry village, made up of huts and a few shacks, even more dilapidated since the December 4th earthquake.[39] For a painter, however, these ruins, next to this pretty harbor, completely surrounded with palm trees and overlooked by beautiful mountains, are worth admiring.

We also took advantage of this stop to go for a serious hunt, seven leagues away, in Tres Palos, which is a little Indian (or rather mulatto) village. In two mornings and one evening, Mr. de Béarn, his servant, and the pair of us shot enough pheasants and ducks to completely load a horse. We enjoyed a triumphant arrival in Acapulco, as well as a good dinner at the French consulate something—that we had forgotten during our voyage, where we lived frugally (roughly speaking). We spent our nights in (or rather in front of) the Indian huts we had chosen, sometimes in a hammock, but more often on racks made of rush, linked together so you feel each one of them without forgetting the knots. You sleep in your

---

[39] *"On December 4, 1852 at 22:10 [local time] there was an 'indescribable' earthquake, which struck and totally destroyed Acapulco. At Acapulco, the sea retreated about 6 m from shore, and the residents were very much afraid that it would return with greater force and flood them all; however, the regular sea level was gradually restored." – National Geophysical Data Center (NGDC)*

clothes, and despite this, when you awaken they are not terribly creased. For the next couple of days we either ate the game we had hunted, or we pilfered eggs from the local chickens.

For nearly the entire duration of the trip, the water was bad and unsafe and therefore we were glad we had taken a few bottles of wine with us. Bread is something as rare as good water, since Indians prefer tortillas, which are a sort of corn and water pancake made by the Indian women, who turn them and hit them again and again until they reach the desired shape, which is flat, round, and thin. The Indians, who are fond of them, season them with chili (pepper from Spain).

Imagine our two beasts of burden, our Negro guide with two hats on top of each other, worn-out shoes, one spur only and us three with our rifles on our backs, our pistols at our sides, our albums and herbariums hanging down, with our lassos hanging from the front of our saddles, and our serapes and travel bags hanging down, traveling sometimes next to each other, sometimes in a line when the path became too narrow and poor, and you will then have an accurate picture of our caravan. The population, as we came closer to the coast, was of a blacker and blacker blood and became increasingly coarse. Although they seemed better on the outside, the Mexican people are really a very bad one; their faults are so numerous and so disagreeable to list and describe that I give up doing it.

After embarking on the 9th aboard the Cortés, we reached Panama City on the 15th after an agreeable crossing. The company on board was made up of three hundred and fifty passengers, mostly from California. The largest contingent was Yankee, with a rather dirty and forbidding look; it was hard to believe that most of them had pockets full of gold. We did come across two Frenchmen, however, whom we were happy to meet. Both of them knew

California quite well and were able to provide us with some interesting and new details.

We also had on board a company of fifty Chinese comedians and jugglers, whom some Yankee entrepreneurs had booked to perform during the New York industrial exhibition. Unfortunately, these entrepreneurs had consigned them to the bottom of the ship in a dirty and unhealthy place, so I was not able to study them as I had wished. One of the two Frenchmen I spoke of earlier is a ship owner and knows Chile, Peru, Lima, and Valparaíso very well. He told me that it was too late for me to cross the Cordilleras like I expected and therefore advised me to only go to Lima and Arequipa and from there to take the route to Bolivia, which he told me was good for its locals and interesting for its nature. Some people also assured me that the road from Valparaíso to Buenos Aires was closed and I decided to continue for now on the road to Bolivia, until further information that I expect to find in Lima.

It is truly unbelievable that in this America, it is so hard to obtain information from country to country. The locals are very ignorant as far as traveling and geography are concerned, and it is almost only through Europeans who live in this country that you manage to learn something true and useful. I expect to embark on the 23rd towards Lima; my first travel companions will be the French ship owner, then a young Swiss from St. Gallen, whom I met with here, and who seems to be a nice fellow. On the other hand, I am parting with Mr. de Béarn, which I seriously regret, since I really started to like him after getting to know him so well. He is a young man of depth, good principles, and natural wit. He is going back home, traveling through New York, and will leave one day before I do. I wish in all respects that he would have made the same trip I will be making, but he left his family more than two years ago and wants to see them again. I can anticipate all the happiness that I will enjoy upon my return; therefore I cannot, nor do I want to encourage him to join me since I would not want (precisely because of my friendship towards him) to bear the responsibility of the trip.

Panama City nowadays is a perfectly healthy place, despite the crowds of foreigners who make a stop there or pass through twice a month when the steamships arrive. To give you an idea, I will tell you that in this city of less than three thousand inhabitants, we found upon our arrival at least nine hundred travelers who had arrived on steamships from across the Atlantic. Three hundred and fifty of us disembarked and six hours later, the California, a steamship coming from San Francisco, dropped off another five hundred; finally, the next day, around six hundred came from Chagres. Total: twenty-three hundred voyagers lodged here for three days, until the steamships departed anew.

The fact that a lot of them die is not surprising, given that these people, especially the Yankees, are not inclined to cleanliness and are piled up in steamships' second-, even third-class cabins, which are dirty and badly ventilated. They are then dropped off in Chagres, and part of the trip is by railroad, but the last twenty-six miles is on foot and they have to carry their luggage in the worst heat, while crossing swamps and humid places. They drink alcohol to feel better and nonetheless reach here suffering from exhaustion, heatstroke, and thirst. Then, they are again piled up and badly fed in their hotel.

As for me, I am in good form, thank God, despite the immense heat that we avoid as much as we can by relaxing at home from ten o'clock in the morning until seven at night. It is said that Bolivia and Peru are healthy places; therefore you do not have to worry about me in that respect.

During my stay in Mexico City, I sketched more than forty drawings, landscapes, and views, all of them more or less passable. These two little drawings that I am sending, one to Mother, the other to Wilhelmine, show islands in the ocean, one day before arriving in Acapulco, then a small church with its leaning tower, in Mexico, between Chilpancingo and Acapulco. I will almost certainly write to you from Lima but beyond that, you will probably go two months without hearing from me. Do not worry; it is out of my hands.

Farewell

Letter Fifteen

LIMA

May 29th, 1853

It has been a long, long time since we last wrote to each other and consequently we are both ignorant of our goings-on. This is the sad aspect of traveling which, together with time and oceans, is more powerful than friendship in the sense that they, at least, have some power over relationships and communications. Yet thoughts go only more eagerly towards those who are distant from us, and one then looks for a recourse through confidence in God and in hope, this precious gift that He put in the hearts of men.

As I was telling you in my letter dated from Panama, I have for the last three months been without any news from you, and I will probably have to wait at least as long before I receive any. I had decided to spend two weeks in Lima, first to visit the city and then mainly to gather all possible information on the long voyage I was going to undertake. I have the choice between three different routes: the one through Arequipa that would take me to the bottom of the tallest mountains in America, the Nevadas of Sorata; Illimani, where I would travel through La Paz, La Plata, and Potosí, which are the largest and most important cities; or through Bolivia, the most interesting but also the longest of the three routes. The second route, the Arica route, although less remarkable, did not take me through deserts as vast as the ones on the Cobija route, which is the shortest. Upon my arrival here, I received some disagreeable news.

War was about to break out between Peru and Bolivia. However, since the first people I met told me that the difficulties between the two countries would probably be settled amicably, I had decided to choose the first route when, for a matter of letters of credit and later recommendations, I found myself joined up with the two of the strongest and most commendable English establishments in Lima, which also have the largest commercial relationship with Bolivia. While willing to be helpful, these gentlemen annoyed me a great deal by urging me to forego my voyage, telling me that Bolivia was in a state of anarchy, that foreigners were not welcome at all, and that the roads were not safe anymore, thanks to the armed and ill-disciplined gangs that were following them. All this vexed me incredibly, since I really preferred this journey plan which I elaborated on so much.

I think that had I no family ties, I would have taken a chance, but being a son, a brother, and a nephew, I renounced the trip. Furthermore, since I am actually traveling only for my pleasure, I think that very few people would appreciate my courage, while many would blame me, should I needlessly encounter misfortune. Another reason that weighed on my decision was that I had been offered the chance to join an expedition which was going to settle on the banks of the Amazon. At first, I had refused, holding onto my first project. I preferred the idea of traveling on my own rather than with a large contingent, and had also heard that communication on the river seemed somewhat uncertain — two things that would definitely slow down a voyage. However, leading the expedition are two agreeable and knowledgeable gentlemen, the first one from

Peru, Mr. Ijurra,[40] who has already made the trip twice, the other one a German, Mr. de Schütz,[41] still young and a very nice fellow.

You will therefore understand that when I realized that my trip through Bolivia was a hazardous enterprise which could fail in all or part, I finally decided to join the new project that offers more security as well as beauty, although I would have expected more from the other one with respect to nature and the variety of aspects to be discovered. So we will leave at the end of this month, with one hundred and twenty people: men, women and, children. We will travel for two months with this contingent until we reach Loreto, where the colony will be founded, then from there to Pará, at the mouth of the river. For two-thirds of the voyage, I will probably be able to travel by steamboat, either by myself or with Mr. de Schütz, who is also planning to go back to Europe. According to his calculation, we would reach Pará quite late, in the middle of autumn. In that case, from Pernambuco, through which we have to pass, I will return directly to Europe. If on the other hand we should arrive there earlier, then I would still go and spend a month in Rio de Janeiro.

You will therefore understand that one of the things that trouble me most in this new plan is the impossibility of my receiving any news from you for such a long time, or to send you any. This is one of the reasons why I have to renounce, with the greatest sadness, my trip to Buenos Aires. After two to three months, I would have at last learned something about you; whereas now, I am going to go deeply into the solitudes of this great river which will feel even more silent, since nature's silence will add even more to

---

[40] **Don Manuel Ijurra** *was the Peruvian government appointed head of expedition to found the town of Caballococha in the Amazon River basin. He wrote "Travels in Maynas" and was also the interpreter and guide for the 1851 U.S. expedition of the Peruvian Amazon by Lieutenant William Lewis Herndon.*

[41] **Baron Damian de Schütz** *was a German author, traveler, colonizer, and humanist. He was the expedition second in command and leader of the first wave of German emigrants to Peru.*

the one already created by not hearing from you. I have heard that this tropical nature—as we will always be traveling under the ninth degree on the southern latitude–is the most beautiful one can see, as far as vegetation and grandiose spectacles are concerned. As we will travel up to the colony at a slower pace, I expect to enrich my album, if only also to give you some idea of this magnificent country.

You should not worry about the dangers of the trip, since there are few. We travel across rather inhabited areas, but orders have been given by the government to have everything that is necessary for us prepared in advance. We should therefore not die from hunger or thirst. As far as the climate is concerned, we will travel at the best time of the year, since we are entering the winter of this hemisphere. I understand the climate in Pará is very healthy, despite its equatorial location. The natives that we will likely meet are peaceful people; however, we are all carrying arms, so if some bellicose tribes from the Amazons were resurrected we would use them, just like we would for the fierce animals that we may encounter along the way.

But let us allow the future to become history and let us review for a while what I have seen since I left you in Panama City. I told you about the immense crowds of Californians that congest that city, which has played such a big part in Spanish-American history. Its sorry state, the degradation of its churches and convents, and its immense ramparts, bereft of canons, are all too noticeable. I told you about that large bay which, scattered with islands and sometimes as still as our lakes, constitutes by itself the true beauty of that site. I told you of the view of the mountain that overlooks Panama City, and on top of which one can see, on one side, the peninsula on which the city is built and its immense bay, and on the other side, a wooded land, composed of a quantity of little round mountains between which winds the Rio Grande, a river that looks black in the shadow of the mountain, but which follows a smooth and majestic course.

I also told you about that hike we went on with Mr. de Béarn in the surrounding countryside, where we found a land of magnificent fertility, but where you only encounter, in terms of agricultural industries, pastures with their herds, but no fields. The Negroes and mulattoes, that lazy race which in Panama City forms the base of the population, find it more convenient to earn a living by transporting effects and people from this myriad of voyagers who cross the isthmus. Some become mule keepers, some boatmen, some cargadors, and all demand a financial ransom from voyagers.

It is expensive to cross the isthmus, half of which is already occupied by a railroad, but for the rest of the trip, the price of the mules is excessive. You usually pay fifteen dollars per day for a mule and ten cents per pound of effects. This is the reason why Mr. Sand of St. Gallen, who is a thrifty man, had to pay sixty dollars for the trip from Chagres to Panama City, although he only had two trunks.

I also told you about the hotels' barrack-like system and how the streets were literally covered with old hats and old clothes, since everyone wants to buy a Panama hat. Many hats are left beside the clothing; therefore there is a quantity of Blum's colleagues[42] who do a superb business. Last of all, that Californian influence, being made up of the most ordinary Yankees, naturally also have the worst manners.

I was very sad to see Mr. de Béarn leave Panama City two days before me. Wishing to remain on the Pacific Ocean, I embarked on the Bogota, a good-looking English steamship that operates between Panama and Valparaíso. I found on board a Mr. Berger, a French ship owner, Mr. Sand from St. Gallen, and a Mr. Anschlitz, who is on his way to work in the Copiaco mines in Chile. Our crossing lasted only a week.

---

[42] *A reference perhaps to Germans.*

From time to time, we could glimpse Ecuador and Peru, which always had a dry and desolated appearance. We only stopped once in a harbor in order to take coal on board. It took place in Payta, whose claim to fame is selling straw hats, a fame that must have developed quite naturally since there is absolutely no shade in the whole vicinity, although being near the Equator, it is quite necessary to protect your head from the sun. What will astonish you is that we were extremely cold during a big portion of the trip, especially as we were crossing the equator. I was therefore very glad to have two sets of clothing to wear on top of each other. If I am not confused, we arrived on Sunday morning, May 2nd in Lima's Callao Harbor. The arrival in the harbor was astounding, due to the stunning island of San Lorenzo that faces it perfectly but more so for the large quantity of French war vessels and lastly, because of the first chain of the Cordilleras on the horizon with Lima's numerous towers at its feet.

Callao in itself does not add anything to the beauty of the view. This place is only remarkable for its picturesque forts. After a short walk in the neighborhood, we climbed on wagons that took us to Lima within a half hour, moving through a plain that would have been insignificant if it had not been next to the capital city and decorated with large gardens and fields of bananas and manioc — the local potato.

Just like Mexico City and every other American city born under the Spanish domination, Lima bears the weight of the conquering country. All streets are right angled and form large squares of houses, vast enough in order for each to contain a yard as well as a courtyard of good dimensions.

Around the latter, you usually see one or two galleries supported by discreet columns that give the courtyard a more gracious look than was the case in Mexico City, where the architecture is heavy. There, the galleries are usually festooned with flowers, which make the courtyards extremely cheerful. In Lima people find refuge inside courtyards in case of an earthquake, which are very frequent in this country. For the same reason, the houses are rarely built with more than a first floor, often just with one story. They are built with lightweight materials, since light construction copes better with the jolts from earthquakes. In the galleries, you find numerous French doors, each one leading to a private bedroom. Therefore, during the day but especially at night when you are walking by, you can have a look inside at a Peruvian family scene and know (should you be curious to step into their dwellings) just whom you might meet.

Furthermore, the houses here have balconies facing the side street which resemble large sculpted wooden sideboards and whose shutters can be raised when the local ladies, who love to stay there (which happens often), treat themselves by leaning over to observe the activity on the street. I also assume they do it in order to be seen, since what is said about their beauty is not an exaggeration to me. In this respect, they deserve their reputation which, for most of them, could only come from the generosity of Providence. I would be inclined to believe that although gifted with a happy and festive character, one rarely seeks to develop and improve it through good education—they are taught to ornate their beauty more than their mind.

Like all women in Havana and Mexico City, they almost never read, work even less, and could not care less about their home, which must not count for much, since I have been assured that people live here very cheaply. They never have a foreigner over for dinner; therefore there is no particular reason why I should be invited. There are however two places where I can go and have a cup of tea whenever I feel like it and that is already something.

While I have only been in Lima for two weeks, it still seems that it is rare to find here a really educated man with a deep spirit, and as a result it is also rare to have a truly interesting and significant conversation. For recreation, there are bear and bullfights, ferocious spectacles that usually crowd the arenas, as people are very passionate about this here. The bulls and bears are chained by one foot, which barely gives them twenty five feet of freedom, therefore a fifty-foot diameter circle. The fight loses a lot of its interest without losing the cruelty, but at least there is some kind of equality which does not exist in the regular bullfights. At the beginning, the bear and the bull were of equal strengths, the bull was greatly bitten and lacerated and the bear received a few valiant assaults from the bull which, being very brave, was the main attacker. It was different the second time. The bull was not as strong and caught itself in the chain, so the bear immediately took over, threw it down to the ground, and sitting on it, started to tear it apart and bite it in order to satisfy its hunger. I was told that it managed to eventually kill it after I left. I was filled with disgust, not for the spectacle itself, but for the people who seemed to enjoy it so much.

To go back to the society in Lima, I have to admit that despite the terrible level of education you can encounter, the foreigner is welcome and I can only be grateful for that. I even believe that should I stay longer in Lima, I would end up discovering some families that I would have the pleasure and use for spending time with.

On the other hand, I was fortunate enough to be introduced by Mr. Wahl, the captain of the Bogota, to the family of Doctor Smith. Mrs. Smith, a British national like her husband, is a very charming woman and immediately appeared kind and benevolent towards me. Like me, she enjoys drawing as well as natural history, and although in charge of her three children's upbringing and taking care of her house, she nonetheless finds the time for drawings and plants. She has talent, knowledge, and a level of education that makes her completely amicable without being at all blue stocking.[43]

---

[43] ***Bluestocking*** *refers to an educated, intellectual woman. Due to the fact that he is using it disdainfully here, I would say it would be synonymous with feminist.*

She shows a lot of interest in my voyage, but her interest is not only expressed with good wishes—she also shows an attention which made her gain my friendship. She spent a great deal of time telling me about various useful things for the collections that I wish to make, and she taught me the way to take care of butterflies, also providing me with the paper that is used for plants, that I could not find in Lima, although I had visited more than forty stores.

As far as paintings go, this lady paints the many fruits of this country in their actual size with their leaves, their flowers, and their seeds. She has recently switched to flowers, which she really paints perfectly. I am sure that she would have been as good friends with my father as she has been with me, his son, since she passionately loves flowers and has a delightful collection of orchids, some of which are very rare.

The vicinity of Lima is rather dry, but from the mountains that overlook the city, the view is truly magnificent. You can embrace the whole of this great city, with its hundreds of steeples. The Rimac River crosses the city and flows into the ocean further away. The plain that I mentioned to you is rather cultivated between Lima and Callao, and further away to Callao itself, you can see forts, vessels, and islands. Then onto the great horizon of the ocean, finally to your right as well as to your left, you can gaze upon the dry and rocky foothills of the colorful Cordilleras, at the bottom of which lie some lonely, large, and beautiful convents, like the ones that the Spaniards built with the gold of their conquests, which they acquired through great crimes that they thought they could absolve through great charity.

Lima does not offer many curiosities. Its museum is really poor even with this country's antiquities, although the ancient Inca Empire was so immensely rich. The only and truly magnificent monuments are the churches and convents, particularly San Francisco. The convents have beautiful cloisters due to their architecture, which bears, like the whole city, a Moorish influence which distinguishes Lima from the other cities built by the Spaniards in America. The main plaza that my window overlooks resembles Mexico City's, offering on one side a view of the archbishop's palace and the cathedral; and on the adjacent side, the government palace; and finally, on the two last sides, long and tall arcades, under which are large stores, most of which sell ladies' fashions. At the center of the plaza stands a pretty fountain around which a crowd of aguadors always gathers. Sitting on their donkeys with their little barrels in front of them, they come there for supplies. The main street, where the majority of people and stories can be found, is Mercadores Street. It is also there that two of my fellow countrymen, a Perret from La Sague and a Müller from Thun, have their beautiful jewelry. They are both nice fellows with whom I like to chat. Comparatively speaking, there are a lot of silversmiths' shops in Lima; the reason being that women here love to adorn themselves with jewelry and naturally spend a lot of money. Therefore it is at the jeweler's that they like to bring their taste as well as their money.

As far as interesting souvenirs worth bringing back, there are almost none, therefore I will abstain. These countries are hopeless for their lack of industries: everything you buy here comes almost entirely from Europe, Paris in particular. The greatest wealth and the biggest revenues of the Peruvian state come from the guano mines, some thirteen million piasters, that Peruvians themselves cannot claim credit for discovering, since all the profit goes to the Frenchman who first had a feeling for the importance of the business, and to the British who came to exploit it. Most of Peru's commerce is within the hands of foreigners: Germans, British, but mainly Frenchmen who, once their fortune is made, take it back to their countries. It is in the same in Mexico City and all cities and states of Spanish America, a reason for the states to fight against financial disasters, which they could easily avoid with more energy, industry and activity. In this respect, it is much better here than in Mexico, since the Peruvians are beginning to enter the business world, while in Mexico, everything is falling apart, cities, finances as well as people's character.

To my great sorrow and despite three trips to Callao, I was not able to get your letters, the captain of the Santiago having answered me in the most polite way. He was very upset about it but there was nothing he could do, since the bags all bore seals that he had to strictly respect. I therefore have to find consolation and to reason with myself, which I am at great pains to do since I cannot picture myself without any news of you until my return.

Since I told you that it would be unlikely, although possible, that I would still leave Pernambuco for Rio de Janeiro, please be kind enough to send your letters from now on to the general delivery in Pernambuco, so I can at last after such a long silence receive news from you. We will leave from here shortly, probably in five to six days. I am so impatient to get to the Cordilleras and then to the banks of the Amazon. I will only be able to let you know of my return once I am in Paris, where I will ask you to write me to the address of Zelaeger and Co. Be therefore patient, dear parents, and instead of worrying, keep your trust in God, who will not allow anything to happen except for my own good. Imagine that until Loreto, a third of the trip, we are one hundred and twenty people and that from there, it is easy to navigate the river. I will do so with the company of Mr. de Schütz, who is even more accustomed to traveling than I am, and who is a very good and brave young fellow, and whom I shall return to Europe with. In the meantime, I long to be on the most magnificent river in the world, while praising God to bless my journey, to keep me from harm's way and to grant me with a happy return to my family for whom I always ask Him for His blessings.

Farewell

Letter Sixteen

MOYOBAMBA

August 6th, 1853

I hope you have received the letter that I sent you from Lima in which I warned you that it would be probably impossible for me to give you any news before my return. But here I find in these uncivilized countries, after a two-and-a-half month's voyage, a place that communicates every month or every other week with Lima. I have to admit that since I have been without news from you for so long, I do not travel with the same pleasure, and as far as I am from Pernambuco, I am longing to get there as I hope to find some news from you. I am currently so far into in this immense continent and so close to the goal of my trip, the Amazon, that I cannot turn back now and I must be happy to think that each step brings me closer to the East and therefore to my family and my country.

We just ended our horseback riding trip and are more than two hundred leagues (Spanish leagues, which are very long) from Lima. It is, if you will, a small distance covered in two-and-a-half months, but in order to move forward faster, we would have had to put two powerful obstacles aside, the first one being the nature of the trail, which is so dreadful that I had never seen anything like it, even in Mexico, and which is impossible for the sedentary European to have the slightest idea of. The second obstacle is mostly the lack of organization and know-how of our leader, Mr. Ijurra, who caused us to lose precious time and caused the government to lose a great deal of money by stopping for far too long at the main stages of

Chachapoyas and Moyobamba. This is unforgivable of him since he knows the country very well. The fact that he delayed the expedition by a whole month (under the pretext of organizing it so we could march faster), together with the slow pace and his negligence, is so deplorable that it harms the morale and trust that are so necessary in such expeditions.

I will not give you any descriptions of these gigantic mountains of the Cordilleras that we have not ceased to cross until now because since I cannot write you these long letters in which I summed up all my travels month after month, I write as steadily as I can, in my journal called *"Voyage on the Amazon,"*[44] which I sincerely hope you can read some day, if its volume, its thin handwriting, and its poorly constructed sentences do not scare you away!

Since I cannot leave you in total ignorance in this respect, I shall tell you in a few words of our trip from Lima to Moyobamba, which is the capital of the Maynas province. We embarked on May 10th from Callao aboard the schooner Clorinda. We were all happy to leave, especially those of us who had to wait for a month on a pontoon, and who formed the greatest part of the expedition. Due to this delay, many of them had become sick and renounced the trip. So instead of the hundred or so people that were supposed to leave, there were only eighty. After five or six days of a rather favorable crossing, we disembarked in the little port of Huanchaco, near Trujillo, where we found four hundred mules and horses waiting for us. Those who had not done what I had done, which was to take a saddle, and who had trusted what the governor and our leaders had promised, were proven wrong, since almost all rides only had their aparejos (a packsaddle, since carriages and carts are not well known in these countries, and are only used in the cities, but never for traveling). Most of the travelers had to sit as best as they could on the *aparejos*, which was difficult, especially for the women carry-

---

[44] *The journal that constitutes the second portion of this adaptation.*

ing children in their arms. This is how we proceeded towards Cajamarca, which we reached after a seven-day march, the first three days of which we traveled along and across the plain that separates the coast from the Cordilleras, and the last four days to cross mountains and valleys. Then in one of the valleys, we found our stage, the famous Cajamarca, well-known for being the residence of Atahualpa, the last of the Incas, and for being Francisco Pizarro's first and most important victory.

This fame is the only merit of the city, since it really is as ugly and sorry a town as it is uncivilized, contrasting with the beautiful mountains and the rich valley that surround it. We spent four days there, which were enough to convince me of the lack of education, activity, ambition, and ideas of its inhabitants. It only applied, however, to the pure-blood Cajamarcans, since I found one Italian there who gave me more information about the city and its province than any native could have.

The Cajamarca province is, together with Chile, Peru's wheat loft. However, agriculture carried out by underpaid Indians is still old fashioned, because fallowing is still in use, very imperfectly. As land is cheap, and you can get a good size property for nothing, you look here and there for pieces of land that are the most appropriate for culture, since all of the areas we traveled through have very poor vegetation and are consequently deprived of trees and forests. The almost complete lack of vegetation, and almost perpetually gray rocky terrain, give the country a drab look, which the beautiful, large, and imposing mountains can only somewhat compensate for. We left there to head towards Chachapoyas, which is the capital of the province that bears the same name. We traveled through more large mountains and deep valleys. It was after three days that at the bottom of a valley and from the top of one of these huge mountains, making the panorama even larger, we had for the first time a glimpse at the Marañón, winding like a silver snake through the morning haze that was coming from the valleys facing us. After nine days, we safely arrived in Chachapoyas, located, like Cajamarca, in a nice valley, but in itself as unattractive as the latter. The locals are even less civilized.

I was, however, happy to make the acquaintance there of the young Señor Besséril, who, having already traveled a great deal, and having been raised and educated in Europe, is now here, outside the Chachapoyas line. Since he made the same voyage as the one we are going to undertake, commanding our chief (although our chief is a lot older than he is) he was able to give me much information of real value. He also shared a few interesting details regarding the province and it was with him that, taking advantage of our long stop in Chachapoyas, I went to visit the large and beautiful ruins of Malea, a former Peruvian city. The sub-prefect, with whom I was staying and dining, and who considered himself my friend, insisted on lending me his horse for our three-day trip.

The resources of company and conversation naturally disappear as you penetrate more of this great continent. Thus, in Chachapoyas, even more than in Cajamarca, the men are generally totally ignorant, as are the women, who are also fabulously shy and possess a completely insignificant talent at playing the guitar. The arts, strictly speaking, are nonexistent in this country, the arts and crafts not much better. The men spend their existence as grocers, and women, who are more active than the ones in Lima and Cajamarca (who do nothing), spend their time spinning, weaving, and embroidering. These are activities they excel at, helped by the quality of this country's cotton, which is remarkable for its beauty and finesse. All they use to spin is the old distaff that Queen Bertha[45] used; they hold it in their left hand and spin with their right hand, while walking.

---

[45] *A reference to **Perchta**, a goddess who oversaw spinning and weaving in Germanic mythology.*

In the Chachapoyas province, all white people are exempt from paying taxes, while the Indians, on the other hand, have to pay them, which they do—not with money, but with tobacco, at the rate of twenty five pounds per year per person. The agriculture in this province is almost nonexistent and is limited to sugar cane and banana trees plantations that you find, together with their sugar mills, on the ever narrow valley floor, along with wheat and corn in locations that are sheltered by the mountains.

The racial type of the locals is definitely Indian, and since the white blood of the old Spaniards has been mixed with the Indian blood, the facial appearances are all more or less the features and the color of this latter race. The character of the Indian is gentle, shy, helpful, generally deceitful and lazy; the ambition and the desire of a better intellectual and material state are unknown to them. This is and will long be one of the major obstacles to civilization in these countries which, if inhabited by industrious people, could be the richest in the world despite the locals' laziness. The voyager that travels through the various provinces of Peru cannot ignore the wealth and diversity of the gifts that Providence granted it.

When the Chachapoyas aristocracy wants to be entertained, they ask their servants to play instrumental music, which is a prelude and invitation to dancing—restricted to fandango—the only child that Terpsichore[46] has in this country. Then gentlemen and ladies make a sustained effort of swapping *copitas*, which are small glasses of pisco (the local brandy) made with sugar cane and corn, drunk to each other's health. The people entertain themselves and the music only becomes noisier with the amount of the copitas. One or two persons know the polka, but it is only a very new dance here. Books and newspaper are exceedingly rare and little sought after, even in the best homes. Every person of any importance or wealth owns his chacara (country house) with a more or less large surface of

---

[46] *A reference to the muse of music and dance.*

fields, cultivated with sugar cane, corn, or bananas. All spend most of the year there, but without enjoying any of the pleasures of the countryside as we do at home. They only live a lazier life, with the men not taking care of their agriculture that they charge a sort of steward to deal with, and the ladies having no interest in flowers or walks. I am not exaggerating by saying that people vegetate rather than live in this country, regardless of their social class.

At last we left Chachapoyas, after giving the prefect more than two weeks to have the necessary horses brought over, which he did in a remarkably slow and messy manner. We managed therefore to leave Chachapoyas after three days of total disorder, heading towards the village of Taulilia, where we were supposed to again change horses and where we found the same negative attitude coming from the authorities, which was only exacerbated by the reputation of our incompetent leader. After three days we were still missing many horses, so we finally used an incentive of offering three piasters to those who would continue on foot, which was accepted by forty-two members of our expedition to their detriment, among them two women. I say to their detriment since it was the worst part of our trip, thanks to the rain which accompanied us the whole time. At the end of the day, all pedestrians had lost their shoes and were cursing the three-piasters agreement.

After six days on an abominable road and two much more reasonable days, we arrived in Moyobamba, where we rested, waiting to continue our trip, which took us after five or six days to the river and at last allowed us to embark. Then after another fifteen days of navigation, the colony will reach Loreto, the end of its journey. I have, coming from Mr. Besséril, a letter of recommendation for Don Ignace Alvares Bonfin, a Brazilian businessman recently established here and who greeted me in a very amicable way, inviting me to share both meal and lodging. Although I already had a place, since I stayed in the barracks intended for immigrants, I only accepted the meal.

Cajamarca's population might be ten thousand, and Chachapoyas' eight thousand. Moyobamba's in my opinion is also eight thousand, but as the Moyobambins want to glorify and enhance the importance of their native city they pretend it is more like twelve thousand. Cajamarca has the appearance of a shabby little town, as does Chachapoyas. Moyobamba, despite all the space it occupies, is still a large village since not only are all its houses covered with thatch, but they are also separated one from each another by their courtyards and gardens, the latter only planted with banana trees. The natives here are even lazier and without any resources. Since there is no market, they each provide very basic food composed of bananas and yuccas for their own nourishment and for their families. Yuccas are roots, as floury as they are tasty, and in my opinion, as good as potatoes.

People in these parts rarely eat meat because even though the land would be appropriate, very little cattle is raised here, out of sheer laziness. Pigs are the exception and all the streets in Moyobamba are overrun with them. They are bred more for fat than anything else. Moyobamba's richest people and aristocrats—who are excessively respected—own a total wealth of five thousand piasters (twenty-five thousand francs) and support themselves by making straw hats. This business is so widespread that all homes without exception engage in it—Moyobamba trades more than thirty thousand hats per year. Havana, Brazil, Chile, and the rest of Peru buy them. A hat that is here worth one piaster sells in Lima for four piasters and in Havana for six or seven. They are not made with real straw, but instead with the leaf of a palm tree.

In the vicinity of Moyobamba, nature transforms. Two days before arriving here, we traveled through forests with real tropical vegetation, full of mangroves, tree-like ferns, parasite plants, and immense lianas. The forests are also inhabited by monkeys, hummingbirds, tigers, and clouds of butterflies, admirable for the variety and the beauty of the colors they display. In short, the forest is a brilliant precursor of all the wonders that will be revealed to us on the banks of the Amazon.

Upon embarking on the Clorinda, I hired a young German emigrant to serve me during the voyage. I am very happy with him since he has not ceased to provide me with zeal and friendship. I am telling you, so you know that I have with me a man I can count on, which will help reassure you about my safety. I generally feel good with my expedition fellows, who show goodwill and trust towards me.

Finally, my health is resisting well to the strains of the journey, the greatest of which are, I believe, overcome. May God continue to protect me and to advance the happy day when I will be back with you. Since the expedition is moving forward very slowly, I do not believe I will be back before the end of the year or the beginning of the new one, therefore do not worry about my arrival being delayed. Please tell dear Papa that I very often think of him when I see the admirable vegetation of this country.

Farewell

<u>*The end of the letters*</u>

A Voyage Across the Americas – The Journey of Henri de Büren

Portrait of Henri de Büren (1825-1909), painted by Rodolphe Léon-Berthoud, 1859

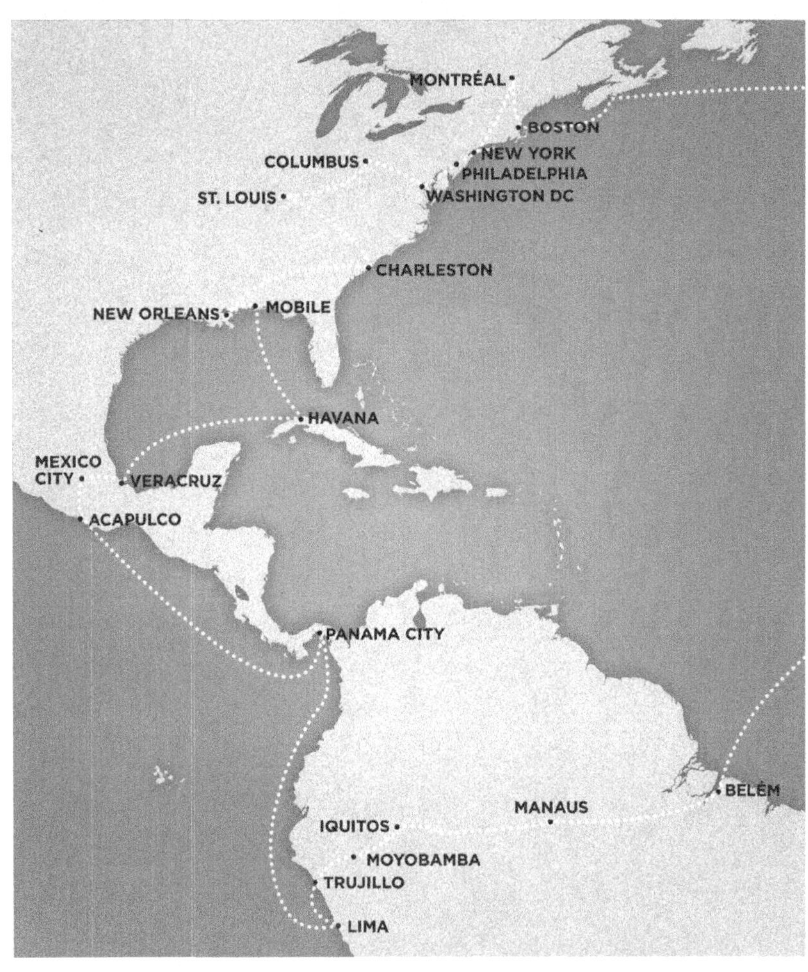

Overview map of Henri's two-year journey

*Photograph of the Letter book. The surviving letters from Henri's journey
were copied and compiled by his sister Wilhelmine.*

Photo of "Voyage on the Amazon" journal

Havana Harbor, watercolor, 1852

Count Fernandina's gardens, Havana, pencil, 1852

Cuernavaca, Mexico, pencil, 1853

Miacatlán, Mexico, pencil, 1853

View of Mexico City, sepia watercolor, 1853

View of Tacubaya, Mexico, sepia watercolor, 1853

View of Puebla, Mexico, sepia watercolor, 1853

View of San Augustín de la Cuevas, Mexico, sepia watercolor, 1853

"American Landscape", Southern United States, pencil, 1852

Church near Jalapa, Mexico, pencil, 1853

Peru (location unknown), pencil, 1853

Xochicalco, Mexico, pencil, 1853

American warship, ink, 1852

Amazon river, ink, 1853

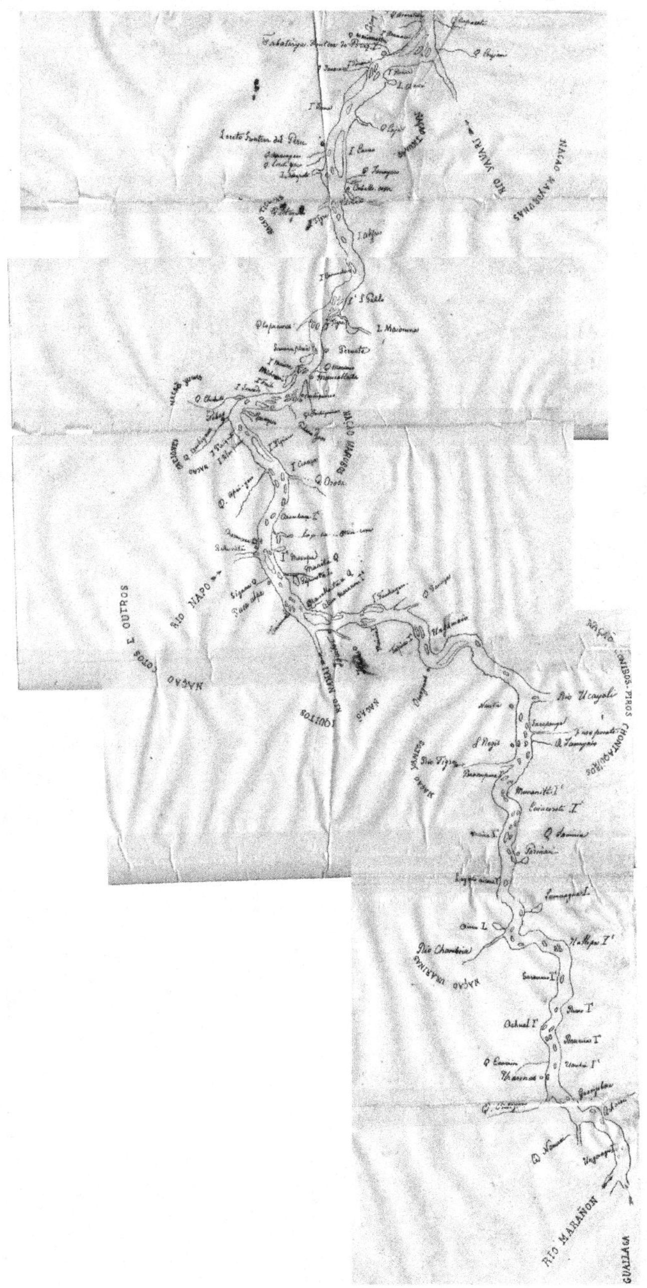

Portion of map, drawn by Henri of Peruvian Amazon, 1853

Mundurucú headdress that Henri brought back from Brazil in 1853.
Photograph courtesy of the Musée d'Ethnographie de Neuchâtel, Switzerland.

Late 19th-century photos of Vaumarcus castle, home of the de Büren family.

Henri's father, Baron Albert de Büren (1791-1873), painted by David Sulzer, 1820

Henri's mother, Baroness Catherine de Büren-Senarclens (1796-1857), painted by David Sulzer, 1820

Henri as an older man at Vaumarcus

Journal – Voyage on the Amazon

HAVANA

December 9th, 1852

We made the crossing in fifty-three hours, fortunately avoiding a storm which threatened us last night. By law, no vessel may enter Havana Harbor after sunset, or risk of being fired upon. In that event, escape would be difficult, due to the extremely narrow harbor entrance and its protection on both sides by imposing forts. So while we were in sight of the city of Havana, we would have to wait.

Our captain, however, had decided to force his way through if the storm broke out, rather than let us be driven towards the coast. I even believe that he would have done it willingly; although much more polite and better behaved than the Yankee race in general, he seemed to share their anti-Spanish sentiments.

On board were two young men with whom I made good acquaintances. One was a Mr. *(left blank)* from Martinique, the other a Mr. *(left blank)* from Bahia, both of them gentlemen in every respect. We conversed a great deal, both on the limited rewards of a trip to the United States, and on subjects such as slavery, education, politics, sophistication, history, travels, and many other items. It was a very agreeable medley of topics, since opinions were shared with enthusiasm and were based upon information, education, and knowledge of the subjects.

My traveling companion, Mr. Schnitzler, was still with me. From time to time, he joined in the conversation, all the while humming Spanish songs.

What a gorgeous entrance Havana has! Is there anything more beautiful? It is a view that presents the elements of a great painting all at the same time, as if by magic; beautiful nature, picturesque architecture, and a magnificent harbor, all dominated by hills topped by majestic forts of various shapes and colors.

Everyone was so delighted with this magnificent spectacle that suddenly appeared that they were immediately transported with admiration. We dropped anchor at the end of the bay, far from the city. A mass of small boats made their way towards us, crowding against our ship—whoever shouted the loudest would have the honor of being chosen first!

We would need to wait to disembark. The police, who came on board, took our passports in exchange for a residency permit costing two piasters, reserving the right to give us back our passports when we left with the payment of six dollars or piasters. Total profit: Eight dollars or forty francs, which could be spent, in my opinion, much more agreeably.

After dealing with our police business, we left in one of those small boats for the custom house, where they were, I have to admit, very polite and easygoing with us. From there we headed on foot to our hotel, the Colon, managed by Mrs. Almy who welcomed us graciously.

While walking across the city, we briefly studied its features. We passed through long and very narrow, unpaved streets, lined with houses which all have more or less a Spanish look, and consequently are a tad Moorish. The low-slung houses have large windows with bars, whose lower ones are at the street level, so once in a while you find yourself directly facing the occupants. Sometimes this is not unpleasant, since in Cuba, the ladies love to sit at their windows or nearby them, which only enhances their charming appearance.

We met many Negroes who have lighter-colored clothing than what's worn in the United States. They were occupied with various tasks, either on the street or in houses, some coming from the countryside. The Negroes push horses so loaded up with feed (mostly young Turkish wheat stems) that one can barely see the horse and would almost mistake it for a small moving mountain. Afterwards, we encountered the *volantes*, also known as putrines, by far the best Cuban mode of transportation. A volante is a sort of open carriage with two extremely high wheels, harnessed far forward and drawn by one or two small, rather plain local horses. A crisply attired Negro sits on top wearing tall riding boots, carrying a postal driver's whip.

It was in one of these carriages that Mr. Schnitzler and I rode in this morning to visit the beautiful gardens of Count Fernandina, one of the island's richest land owners. One would find it difficult to see anything more charming, rich, or gracious, as far as vegetation and shade trees are concerned. The count's garden is designed in the English style, with paths crossing in all directions, separating different groups of trees and flowers—but what trees and what flowers! The lush vegetation and rich colors are almost as impossible to comprehend as they are to depict.

I did not tire easily of admiring this vegetation, especially the palm trees which are new to me and which displayed themselves in various forms. However, our volante had been waiting for us for some time already and Mr. Schnitzler is always a bit in a hurry; therefore unwillingly, I had to cut short my visit, although I had decided to return if possible to explore the garden at greatest length and bring back lasting memories.

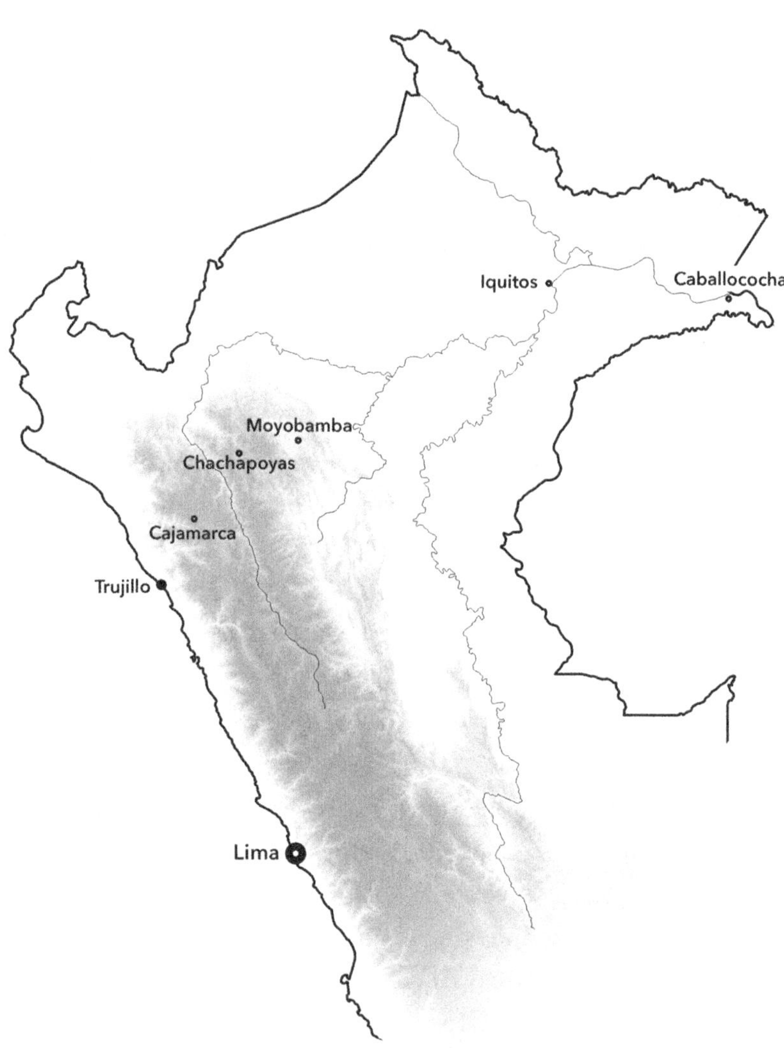

Map of Northern Peru with Highlighted Locations

SANTIAGO

June 14th, 1853

Farewell, Lima! Farewell to bulls, elegant women, Alameda, and uncultured locals! Here we are, heading to Callao, aboard the brigantine schooner Clorinda, which is the inaugural vessel for our upcoming expedition. Thanks to the lengthy emigration process, many of our hopeful companions abandoned us, which reduced the expedition from one hundred and thirty people to ninety. This turn of events appeals to us since except for the prettiest member of the expedition who was kidnapped two days before our departure, the ones abandoning us are not exactly the cream of the crop and have nothing of what is needed for such an enterprise.

Out of the ninety people, more than half are Germans. The rest are French, Irish, Americans, Italians, Scots, Spaniards, Peruvians, and Chinese. There is only one umbrella, which is carried by a Jew from Berlin. The expedition is a real tower of Babel, but one where everyone gets along rather well, since, after four days of a rough and ill-sustained crossing, we arrived inland at the end of the first day without any breach of harmony. On the contrary, it seems that these first tribulations strengthened our relationships. Let us hope this will continue and grow.

We disembarked at the poor and dirty little harbor of Huanchaco. There, we found two hundred and fifty beasts of burden, most of them mules, and only a few horses. The Prefect of Trujillo welcomed us, wearing an authentic prefect uniform, with a three-level crinoline petticoat, a blue tailcoat with gold buttons under which you get the hint of a white vest, followed by black trousers with boot straps. It is all topped off with a slightly worn hat properly sitting on a sphere of nothing noteworthy, if not for a nose that had a tendency to stay in the air, his arms crossed with elegant disregard.

The mules are less well equipped, all of them bearing no more than their packsaddles. Therefore, except for those of us who were prudent enough to bring our own saddles, all the men and women will have to sit on these packsaddles instead of proper saddles. For all of those not sitting in this awkward position, the look of the caravan must be somewhat entertaining, the riders perched as they are with a tendency to assume an excessively horizontal position.

We followed the shoreline for three hours, along which the beautiful blue ocean cast its foaming waves up to the hooves of our horses. The mule, on which an authentic German school teacher (i.e., old hat, long coat and long pipe) was riding, got scared and threw off the German in the middle of a big wave, and they both almost went for an unintended swim. As for me, I had my heart set on a small white horse seemingly built for the journey; I had removed his packsaddle, replacing it with my saddle, and in doing so moved a forty year-old Indian to tears.[47]

With all these details, I expect that I have completed the description of our party. I will therefore tell you that there are on paper two groups of emigrants. The second one is composed of craftsmen and farmers; in other words, future settlers. I will now skim over this category without giving details about their personalities; it would be too long and too premature. I will only say that for the most part, they seem like very good people, benevolent and obliging, especially the Germans.

---

[47] *I can only assume that the Indian wanted the horse for himself.*

The first group is composed of Mr. Ijurra, the governor of the future settlement and the actual head of the expedition. He is accompanied by his wife, Señora Carmen, an excellent lady endowed with a happy and generous nature, which is so precious on a voyage such as this. Next, there is Mr. de Schütz, a young German appointed by the government, who is to be the first aide to the governor and who will manage the future German settlement.

After these are a Spaniard and an Italian, both former sailors. The Spaniard is forty-five years of age, the Italian roughly fifty-five years old. As little as I know these gentlemen, it seems to me that the Spaniard is a first-rate fellow and well educated.

Fifth, there is Don Pedro! He is also from Spain and a former merchant marine captain. He abandoned the salt water of the ocean for the fresh water of the Amazon, upon whose shores he dreams of settling down with his "better half." But Don Pedro is not young any more, nor is he handsome or even rich, and yet he wants a wife who is young, beautiful, and wealthy. Since women usually have more ambition than men, this leads me to believe that if Don Pedro were more realistic, he may well be dreaming all by himself on the shores of the Amazon.

The next-to-last member of this group is the Doctor, a man who although of small and stunted stature seems to be a scientific giant. He continuously lugs around two huge cases full of medicine that are gifts from the government. At his core, he seems to have a good and sweet nature, and is especially very interested in all things Portuguese, which is rather natural since it is in Rio that most of his acquaintances reside and where he practiced medicine.

Finally, turning to an individual that I found insignificant until now, there is me! I am well known to you, so I will tell you nothing about me, except that after planting my tent, I find myself at nine o'clock at night busy writing the present entry in my journal.

June 15th, 1853

I woke where I left you, that is to say in my tent, which inspires admiration and envy from my fellow travel companions. It is true that the tent is quite pleasant, and roomy enough for my bed, my servant's bed, my personal effects, and even my tackle table. Yet it weighs no more than twenty pounds.

Naturally, I planted it at headquarters, which is a sort of large yard or field, where in one corner sits a decrepit shack, with only half a roof. We spent the entire day in Santiago, which is one of the saddest places that I have ever encountered, including Mexico.

My legs and head still ache from the passage on the Clorinda. This however has not prevented me from lightening my strong box considerably, which seemed too heavy to me. I have kept my rifle and pistol, and acquired a bird preparer, a butterfly net, and a seed collector from my German companions; all three items are perfect for my needs. The countryside around is very fertile, but wholly uncultivated due to the laziness and carelessness of the native Indians, who have very few needs, and certainly feel no need to work.

CONTUMAZÁ

June 19th, 1853

Here we are in Contumazá, four days after leaving Santiago. I have written nothing since then because I was not feeling terribly well and because a journal needs physical well-being to support a writer's moral character. Nevertheless, recapitulating what occurred over these four days is simple: on the first day we continued to move away from the ocean and towards the Cordilleras. Like the following day, however, we only found large plains that were rarely cultivated, so rarely that I must certify that on that day, I actually saw two Peruvians who gave the impression of work—I think they were harvesting rice.

As is the rule with this expedition, the caravan started to move forward in disorder, the carriages generally together, and their owners in groups. As for me, I sometimes rode with them, sometimes not, but I was always followed by my servant Auguste with whom I continue to be pleased. We risked getting lost once or twice, since the *camino real* (royal road) is no more than a beaten path.

We spent the night in Chapate, a pitiful village, similar to the one before and the one following. It has only poor huts made of adobe or reed, whose interiors look equally meager with no fields surrounding them, although the soil is excellent. At most, some gardens will have banana and orange trees that grow of their own accord rather than through the care of their owners.

We stayed in the most beautiful building in town—a school dedicated to Lancaster by the good will of the local priests. In order to make the advantages of schooling more understandable, the priests have painted two illustrations on either side of the door.

The first illustration depicts a shepherd playing the flute while guarding sheep. Underneath, the words read: *"completamente un rustico,"* which means, a total peasant. On the left side of the door, there is another illustration displaying the same individual holding a book and sitting very graciously. The words here read, *"Entrando à la ilustración,"* or, enter and learn to write.

I rather liked the idea. But the models of writing that I observed proved to me that the youth of the place will never walk towards the illustration of calligraphy, not even toward that of freedom. Freedom is the big word of these poor countries, in which they are thrown complicated examples of writing that are so unclear and so untrue, that after digesting them, they become either Jesuits or bad students. Rarely or by chance do they become good citizens, as one encounters in countries where liberty is well understood.

On the following day, we spent the night in Escope. We still found ourselves on a dusty plain that led to houses plagued by laziness and misery. These two days, we only rode six leagues (the Spanish leagues are arduous.) Tomorrow we anticipate a difficult and long day: we will travel more than fourteen leagues, which will take us over the summit of the first Cordillera mountain range.

The mountains themselves are devoid of most vegetation; only small tufts of green—especially from the dianthus genus—appear here and there. The summits of the mountains are steep and have many points. The flanks, which are not covered by any vegetation, show bare rock which often is porphyritic and unstable. Therefore, falling rock and avalanches are frequent, and the crushed rock amasses in small piles at the foot on the small hills.

The sun's heat that is reflected off the rock faces becomes intolerable as the valley begins to narrow. In the valleys that we travelled through on that day, there was little or no vegetation; however, in some places, willows grow next to the river beds that are more often dry than running wildly.

After leaving Escope at seven in the morning, we arrived in Cascas at eight o'clock at night, without having crossed even the smallest village, only shabby huts here and there. Those who had to travel through the mountains and valleys on an uncomfortable packsaddle, especially the women who had children to hold, arrived very tired—needless to say, the animals were just as weary. We had to wait for a long time before we could eat and even longer to sleep, as most of the luggage including the beds, had yet to arrive.

All, however, were refreshed and rested this morning. So after a light breakfast, we climbed back onto our animals that were less rested than we were and still had a tough journey ahead of them. This was due to the fact that for more than four leagues, we climbed a steep, rocky path that was reminiscent of the roads I encountered in Mexico. As bad as the road was, the climb began next to a beautiful creek and the route was bordered by beautiful shade trees. Then the flowers which lined the road began to change as rapidly as our ascent, and among these flowers were fluttering butterflies, one shinier than the next.

Our path zigzagged up the steep slope of a high mount standing between two other mountains and we could only guess at our location, or the valley from whence we came. At the summit, the view became quite expansive, allowing us to take in nearly the whole road that we had just covered up from Huanchaco, where we originally put ashore. So it was from this point that we viewed the Pacific Ocean for the first time. We also looked out over the plain that separates the ocean from the Cordilleras, as well as all the other mountaintops and valleys we had crossed over the past day.

It was only for a brief moment that I was able to admire that magnificent panorama, for shortly afterward, we began our descent. After a league and a half, we reached Contumazá, a veritable one-horse town at the center of a very narrow valley, lined with ugly shacks. When we arrived, nothing had been prepared for our arrival. Thus someone had to go and butcher a young bull a few leagues from the village, which they served us piping hot. The heads of the expedition arrived long after we did and it was only later, at nightfall that we managed to dine. *Caramba!* You really have to plan ahead and cross your t's and dot your i's with the natives in these countries. If order is necessary in most places around the world, it is even more critical in disorderly countries like this one.

June 20th, 1853

Our animals were very tired; therefore we took a day of repose. Almost everyone was happy about it, since not only did we feel the need to do so, but some were also in desperate need of rest. Our day went by in a manner that was almost as inspired as the countryside surrounding us. The only industry to speak of in the area is in the hands of the women, who, armed with a small distaff, spin cotton like we used to spin hemp before the invention of the spinning wheel.

The women do not spin cotton to make stockings—they do not wear stockings here—but rather to make *ponchos* (a sort of man's coat) that the women weave by hand for very modest prices, although it often takes them six months to weave one. Life seems to me to be very cheap here. For example, you can purchase six small loaves of bread or a dozen eggs for a total of six cents.

It seems that hens here have a passion for laying eggs, since one of them came up to lay its egg in a little hole above my bed. Once the egg was laid, the Spanish sailor grabbed it and ate it, still warm, to satisfy his hunger. As for me, I went to visit with the second-class settlers whom I found rather poorly housed in what appeared to be an ancient convent.

My butterfly net showed its first exploits, and my bird kit is not without courage or hope. After dinner, I sketched the courtyard of our hotel, more to stay busy than for any interest in the site. Tomorrow, we will leave at seven in the morning for *Tambo*,[48] an inn of some sort that is six leagues from here; there, I will tell you what it is all about. In the meantime, I bid you good night for today and good day for tomorrow.

---

[48] *His first mention of "Tambo" would appear to be a town, but rather is simply the name of an inn beside the road. He mentions many other Tambos throughout his journal.*

TAMBO

June 21st, 1853

We spent an entire day traveling over mountains and through valleys. From Contumazá to here, we have made three dramatic descents as well as two huge climbs and perhaps not even twenty paces on flat land, since as soon as we arrived in one of those deep valleys we immediately had to start climbing again, only after fording a small creek whose water was as cold as ice.

Once we had finished one of those climbs and arrived on a ridge, the horse would have to begin the descent almost immediately, as there was no space for both horse and rider on the ridge. The slopes are excessively steep; therefore, seen from the bottom, they look like a wall you would have to climb, and indeed you do climb it on a narrow, zigzagging path, with each zig and zag no greater than ten paces. It goes very quickly, however, so the ascent that appears to you interminable at first sight is achieved surprisingly fast.

A tambo is nothing more than a dirty cabin where most sleep in the open air; as for me, I installed my tent and invited the Spanish sailor to share it with me, which he accepted. Our comrades are still in good spirits and were well fed, thanks to the herd of sheep that we found here.

CAJAMARCA

June 23rd, 1853

I am told that I had my dates wrong up until today, the proof being that St. John's Day, which is to be celebrated tomorrow, always falls on the 24th of June. I surrender to such a strong argument and beg your pardon for the previous errors, which I attribute mainly to continuing to suffer the after-effects of the pitching and tossing that I experienced aboard the Clorinda.

From Tambo, we went to Llama the following day, which is located approximately six or seven leagues away. To reach Llama we had to make a huge descent of five leagues before getting to the narrow and pernicious Magdalena Valley. When one has such a descent in front of him, the view is unquestionably expansive. Indeed, at our feet we could barely make out the valley floor and the river we had to cross. Before us rose the beautiful Cordilleras range—massive and more powerful-looking than ever—with multifaceted terraces, ravines casting dark shadows and reflecting bright sunlight. These are mountains that we would need to cross for another hundred leagues.

Our path down was fast and difficult; more than one mule was surely lost here. Thus, for the first time, our caravan was surveyed by the flight of the majestic condor that was waiting for a prey, but this time in vain, as we did not leave him any. More than one of us (especially me) would have liked to salute this beautiful animal with a pistol shot and not simply a piercing gaze.

But the condor is so voracious that once gorged, it will let itself be beaten to death. He is so prudent when his stomach is empty that we could barely recognize the beautiful white collar that is his main feature. Next to him, another bird flew with a wingspan almost as grand, but instead of a white collar, he had a brown one. Were they young condors or another bird species? My eyes were not able to determine this.

The path down from the summit was strewn with stones, and the mountain slopes had no greenery other than a few cacti and some aloe vera plants with long and flexible leaves. At the bottom of the valley, we later saw a few sugarcane fields, as narrow as the far end of the valley. These fields constitute the industry and agriculture of San Magdalena, a little village known mostly for its fevers and the insalubrity of its water.

I will not make the same critique of its food, since one particular lunch was a highlight of the day, and one of the happier ones of our voyage. The *chicha* (a local drink made of fermented corn) that we washed down placed our diminutive doctor and our rotund priest (the Spanish sailor Don Luis) in such good moods that they instantly started a local dance that was as fast as it was original. The wife of the governor of San Magdalena even joined in, her husband deeply appreciative of our cheerfulness.

The music was excellent for we were making it with our hands and our walking sticks. We eventually hoisted our tired little doctor and his large riding boots up onto his huge white horse and then departed, after a gracious *buenas tardes caballeros*, to find our beds as well as a frugal meal in Llama, which we reached after a two-hour ride uphill.

Llama's location is very picturesque. It abuts the deepest part of a semicircle of mountains, with two large peaks on either side, the same mountains that we hike down in the morning. Before us appeared stunning view of the Magdalena Valley. We had a cup of coffee and some eggs, sitting cross-legged around a large fire, which was a source of light rather than cheer, since we were already in a very good mood.

During a rather deep philosophical conversation with the priest after the meal had finished and the fire was only embers, we saw the glow of the moon with a silhouette of the large peak which stood to the east (to our left). A moment later, we saw the moon emerge from behind the summit—like fire coming out of a volcano—to illuminate our camp and the amphitheater of mountains that surrounded us. Our camp was near the few huts that distinguish Llama but had been abandoned by its pure-blood Indian inhabitants. They had completely fled in advance of our arrival, so we were forced to sleep in the open air.

The night was mild and at daybreak, everyone—including emigrants and *arrieros* (muleteers)—departed, in order to reach one of the principal stations of our voyage, the city and provincial capital of Cajamarca. We arrived there after a climb to a long plateau on which a bitterly cold wind was blowing, and then descended steeply into Cajamarca. The city was in turmoil and in revolt upon our arrival. Strangers are a rare occurrence here; you can only imagine for a moment what it must be like when close to a hundred of them show up with weapons and luggage! The balconies, sidewalks, and the road leading all the way up to a large cross in the middle of an intersection were lined with curious, admiring locals, shouting, laughing, and welcoming us.

If such places, unknown to the rest of the world and even to their own country, and inhabited by ignorant, lazy, and superstitious people, could have a history, I would say that our arrival and our stay would be one of its main chapters. Here, nobody can really judge what a significant event is, even one of the smallest importance.

As far as any attributes of Cajamarca are concerned, I will tell you that they are vastly enhanced by the picturesque valley in which Providence has placed it. As for the city itself, should you choose some of the worst neighborhoods of our poorest villages, make them large enough to house ten thousand inhabitants, and then place a large square with five to ten half-built churches at the center, you would have something similar to the *"famous"* city of Cajamarca.

I say famous because Cajamarca was once the seat of power for the Incas, where Francisco Pizarro won his first and most important battle. It was on this very square that he personally fought hand-to-hand with the last of the Incas. He decapitated[49] the Inca leader who had not, as he had promised, been able to fill up a chamber with gold and riches,[50] additionally mocking Pizarro's illiteracy.

Despite the role that Cajamarca played in the times of the Incas, you can barely find traces of its antiquity. Should you be interested in such matters, it is first of all pointless to inquire of the locals, because they will remain mum, which in these Spanish-American countries is due as much to ignorance as to superstition and distrust.

Let us suppose you want to find ruins (a reasonable desire, I think) that could tell you something about the ancient Indian civilizations, nowadays so sodden, something that could speak of the wise politics and history of the Sun people, or about the descen-

---

[49] *Historical sources say that he was strangled by garotte.*

[50] *Historical sources say that he did in fact fill up three rooms with riches.*

dants of Manco Cápac[51] and Mama Ocllo.[52] Let us further suggest that you wish to find ruins that would enhance your single-minded investigation, one that looks, examines, rummages, and explores; north and south, east and west, from downtown to the outskirts. If this is what you seek, do not ask for help. In exchange, all you will encounter is renewed evidence of the ignorance and unconcern in which the natives of these countries are completely immersed; whether rich or poor, businessmen or craftsmen.

This is why, trusting my own judgment and some texts that I previously consulted, I went searching for the Inca throne by myself. All the locals will tell you, however, that it is a myth. Yet it indeed exists—on one of the slopes of a small hill overlooking the town and from which you really have a very beautiful view of the valley. Then I understood very clearly why the Inca chose this location.

The semi-circular throne is carved into a small rocky hill and can be accessed by one or two very narrow terraces. Sculptures nearby are too weathered by time for an amateur archaeologist like me to be able to make any real sense of them.

The customs, habits, and social relationships of the locals fit, or are rather framed very well by the geography of the area. Both rich and poor live miserably here: the poor, because they are lacking in both resources as well as activities; the rich, because they are very self-conscious and must resort to ingenious ways to spend their piasters sensibly in this city, which has a dearth of communication, commerce, and reasonable luxury. Therefore, whatever the number of piasters the rich may have, theirs could only constitute an imaginary wealth. Once wagered, the small amount of money necessary to satisfy most people offers poor odds for the charms and comfort that Cajamarca can offer in return.

---

[51] *The legendary first Sapa Inca of the Kingdom of Cusco and a figure of Inca mythology.*

[52] *The sister and wife of Manco Cápac who discovered Cusco with him. She taught the Inca women the art of spinning thread and was deified as a fertility goddess.*

The rich here, admittedly, do encourage one luxury: silver—a luxury that they indulge in to great extremes. I only realized it this morning while walking down the street where people have their silver cleaned. The sheer quantity made me realize that the wealthy do not really know what to do with their money. As far as social amenities are concerned, we were only able to find La Tonda, where we went at night for either a cup of coffee or chocolate, during which the priest and the rector danced a light minuet for us to the tune of two discordant guitars.

June 26th, 1853

I just came back from a walk with a Mr. Degola, a Genovese who has been established in this country for about ten years, where he took a wife, bought some land, and built a grocery store. I cannot tell you anything about his wife because I do not know her, not much more about the store because all the grocery stores in the world resemble each other and are not terribly interesting. Nevertheless, I will tell you more about the land and its agriculture since they do present something natural and original which may be of interest.

Three leagues from Cajamarca, Mr. Degola owns a piece of land whose size he does not know; he guesses it might be around three leagues in circumference. He is essentially devoted to the grocery store; as a result, the land is in the hands of a manager who receives a yearly pension of a hundred piasters, or five hundred francs, plus some land for his own needs and lodging.

On the property, he grows wheat, barley, potatoes, corn, and clover, and follows the practice of fallowing, whereby the same land is cultivated for four or five years, usually starting with potatoes, then the land is left fallow for ten years. The land is cheap, the agriculture out-of-date; fertilizers and their advantages unrecognized. Yet after the first harvest, which takes place in the month of February or March (the end of the rainy season), sheep are left to graze the field for a period of two weeks. Then the second and third harvests occur in November, after which plants are sown.

Here the growing season, which is also the rainy season, runs from November to February or March. Winter, on the other hand, is from March to October, a season which is dry, and where there is a frost almost every night, which renders agriculture quite impossible. The Indians are armed only with very poor farming tools, such as a plough without curved handles, and a short, thin ploughshare. For their work, they are only paid in kind. It is the alms which they receive at the end of the week, or at a time determined in advance, and consists of barley, wool and potatoes.

The Indians receive very little money, just enough for their needs. In order to give you evidence of the meagerness of their salary, I will tell you that Mr. Degola usually hires one of these Indians each week to take care of his house in town. At the end of the week, the Indian (the *semanero*) receives one real (around 60 cents) and is then replaced by another Indian the following week.

On Mr. Degola's land, there are around a hundred and twenty oxen, twelve cows, sixteen hundred sheep, and about forty donkeys. The price of cattle is very low here: a good five-year-old well-fattened ox is worth ten piasters (fifty francs): a sheep, one piaster: a pig, six to seven piasters; or when a pig is young and healthy like the kind we sell at home, six reals, which comes to around four francs. Wheat, which is the main yield of these lands, is sold in three-hundred-pound loads for five to ten piasters, depending on its quality, and then ground. Mr. Degola owns a mill on his property that can grind sixty loads per day, and he charges two reals per load for milling.

Mr. Degola's land is one of the most fertile in the area. Some lands are far more suitable for farming, with a circumference of forty leagues or more, and on which over three thousand oxen may graze. He assures me that one cannot expect more than the five or six per cent yield. Therefore, a piece of land which costs from five to six thousand piasters yields two to three hundred loads, that is between six hundred and nine hundred net tons of wheat. This wheat, mainly produced in the neighborhood of Cajamarca, provides for the whole province and part of the coast to Lambayeque, but cannot compete in Lima with Chile's wheat. This is not because of the transport, but because of the quality, since bread made with this wheat cannot rise, which always gives it the appearance and the taste of poorly baked bread.

Yesterday, in order to sketch the square, I ingratiated myself into a house with a balcony from which I had estimated the view to be quite favorable. I was warmly greeted by the *señores* and the *señoritas* who asked me countless questions about our expedition and about Europe, after they had accepted and smoked some very fine cigars that I had offered them. In my opinion, the ladies prevailed over many other Peruvian women, as I admired their work ethic, as well their talent for silk embroidery, as sophisticated as that of China.

The ladies gave me a sheet of paper to write my name upon. When I gave it back to them, they first admired my calligraphic talent, then having read it, made fun of the heretical turn of my name. Since they did not ask for it—in countries as Catholic as Peru, it is more or less futile—I did not share my own religious testament, so that we left each other last night on very friendly terms. Today when I returned to finish my sketch, I was greeted graciously and was asked to dine with them.

I am not saying that I was invited to sit down at their table, since that would be a totally inaccurate description. I do not know whether one can call a wooden plank elevated one foot from the floor a table, around which one has to squat down, almost like a Turk.

As I was presented with a very decent rug next to the prettiest señorita, I crouched without the slightest greeting. This was the easiest of my duties as tablemate, for when the meal began, it happened that the dishes were so peppery that I found myself in a position, if not less patriotic, at least similar to the Roman who let his hand burn. Yet, politely, I managed quite calmly to finish my meal, while sharing with my hosts a *"muy fuerte"* (very spicy), almost as an excuse for my expressions. I was also not given a knife, and was truly very thankful for the young guest on my left who periodically came to my aid and cut my meat with his pocket knife.

As for the ladies, they ate everything with their fingers, even a kind of soup—that is what you call living well in Cajamarca. For me, I do not explain to them what living well is in Europe because these good people would only feel insulted. I believe that you have to leave everyone happy with their own position in life, especially when it pertains to the material aspect.

Later, my dinner friend of pocket-knife fame and I went to visit the ancient palace of Atahualpa, the last Incan Emperor of Cajamarca. When I arrived, I found an old shack where an older lady and her daughter lived, but apart from a wall covered with slightly ugly paintings, I did not find the smallest vestige of antiquity. The lady assured me, however, with all the power of her eloquence, that the bedroom in which she lives was the main and favorite room of the unfortunate Inca.

The stone on which the emperor was beheaded, she explained, was part of the house, but was later donated to the prison. Due to security regulations, we would not be able to visit it. This was especially true since yesterday we incarcerated one of our emigrants, a Peruvian named Domingo, who is going to be sent back to Callo, his point of origin, for trying to disrupt our expedition. This is a good move for everyone concerned, including Domingo, because I know a few Germans who were disturbed by his behavior and were already trying to figure out how to lynch him.

THE POIANKA HACIENDA

June 27th, 1853

We finally left Cajamarca, and Don Pedro had still not achieved the goal he had set himself at the start of our expedition. Despite his coming and going on the worst footing possible; despite his relationships, which I think were not very agreeable towards the local priests; despite his attractive uniform; and lastly, despite all the advances and all the gallantry he is capable of, Don Pedro did not succeed in finding his mate, this better half for whom he took an entire case of the best wine that he was able to find in Lima to tempt a human being to join him in holy matrimony. Don Pedro does not appear to have the gift of devotion, an essential component of a successful marriage.

This hacienda where we find ourselves at day's end does not offer anything remarkable. There are only a few miserable shacks and a rather quaint church, located at the bottom of one of those dry, bare valleys you commonly find in Peru.

It seems to me that the products made of sheep's wool play a rather big role here. There are at least two large buildings, the first one, a mill; the other, filled by looms. Both are used by Indians who get one gold *real* for a day's work, while the weavers get it for a pound of wool, which they manage to weave rather roughly in a day. Their machines are all very primitive; they are the perfect counterpart of the simple distaff that every Indian woman holds in her arms and from whom she habitually pulls a rather nice thread, which goes around a small spool that she turns with her left hand.

We waited for quite some time for the heads of the expedition who habitually arrive last. For example, today, we got here at three in the afternoon, while they arrived at eight at night. Thus, our little doctor, who had been resting on the table wrapped in my cardigan (since his effects had not shown up yet), had to squat down in a corner of the table, while the latecomers were busy preparing a rather late dinner. They were all cursing the bad ride they had, as well as the people, like my servant and me, who had made sure to choose pack animals that were strong and well suited for the poor roads that you encounter in these countries.

As for me, I would have had a good laugh, had I not been vexed by the eternal slowness which destroys much of the harmony that should always exist between chiefs and subordinates in such an expedition.

CELENDÍN

June 29th, 1853

Since we had more than ten leagues to cover, we left first. Our quality saddles and pack animals allowed us to collect plant samples along the way and still arrive before anyone else. We rode across mountains and high valleys where a cold wind was blowing, which would have been an inconvenience if it were not tempered by the heat of the sun.

The landscape is still dry and treeless and is interesting only for several panoramic views and a few rather pretty flowers. Among these, I recognize two species of anemones, two species of calceolaria, a lobelia, a geranium, and a cornus, all bearing a rather alpine character, due to the elevation where we find ourselves.

Once again, I arrived first; *"the first member of headquarters,"* as the second class of the emigrants nicknamed me. I went back and forth two-and-a-half times, from one end of the village to the other, before I could find the shack that had been prepared for us and inside of which I got settled in advance of the others. After having spent a good night and been spared by the *garapates*, a rather dangerous indigenous insect that has attacked some of our expedition members, I may, just like the others, spend the rest of the day in this poor village. Why? I have no idea.

Today, I changed quarters and am going to stay with three of our companions, Don Ruiz, and Señores Lama and Ortiz, with whom I partnered so I would not have to face the slowness and the indecision that our chief seem to be willing to impose on our endeavor. It is through this friendship that I also became the priest's housemate, who greeted us all very cordially and seems to me to be a very enlightened man in the otherwise ignorant realms of this country's clergy.

Thanks to the priest and his recommendations, we are finding our way (at least until Chachapoyas) into good quarters in which we are able to settle as soon as we arrived. The priest complains about the idleness and the poor habits of his parishioners, as well as about the small stipend he receives. That will not stop him from having only silver, porcelain tableware, dishes, and the like at his home. He tells me that while the population of this country is small and scattered, the people are still believers.

Tomorrow, we will leave very early. We have a journey, twelve leagues long, that will take us across the Marañón for the first time, then to a valley renowned for its fevers and its garapates, which we must pass through to find healthier and more comfortable quarters with one of our priest's colleagues.

TAMBO VIEJO

July 1st, 1853

The priest did not keep his word. We only had old horses, and some of us did not have any at all, at least not at four o'clock this morning, as we were promised. We really would have liked to have left at that time since we had been told that we would have to cross a very hot region.

Indeed, after having left at seven thirty instead of four, we descended a very steep slope, sometimes even on the ridge of the foothills that are so distinctive of the Cordilleras. In the distance, we were already able to distinguish a silver ribbon in the midst of heat vapors coming up from the Marañón valley, which will be our companion, guide, and host for a long time to come. Once arriving at the bottom of the valley, we had to cross the river on a raft led by two Indians who stood behind us and who knelt down in order to use their short oars more effectively.

As for the horses and mules, we were merciless; we whipped them until they were out of the current and could be led safely to the other bank. Once on that side, we had a light meal, after which we marched on.

When I say "we," I do not mean the entire column, but only the Presbyterian Society of Celendín which consisted of Don Ruiz José; Señores Ortiz and Lama (former worker, and secretary of the general government of the Amazon, respectively, who joined us halfway from Huanchaco to Cajamarca); an ex-military Peruvian businessman, and myself.

All this led to a rather dramatic episode. When leaving Celendín, Mr. Lama had warned Mr. Ijurra that we would not sleep at the bottom of the valley in Baltsa because of its fevers, but that instead, we would have to find our lodging four leagues farther on and higher up on the other side of the valley.

Had Mr. Ijurra not understood or did not want to understand, I am not sure. What seems clear is that a dispute began between Mr. Lama and Mr. de Schütz, who had stayed behind in order to load our personal effects onto the mules that had arrived late. Following this dispute, Mr. de Schütz had my effects unloaded just as the mules were about to depart. This was an act that seemed truly spiteful, which I will hardly pardon him for, especially when I think about the rather friendly relationship that existed between us before we left Lima. I must say that since then the relationship has changed for the worse. Perhaps Mr. de Schütz wanted to transfer me to the general category of the emigrants, which I cannot accept in any way, and which has placed a chill in our relationship that shows no signs of thawing.

Upon our return, I will tell you that after four hours of ascent, we arrived in the Caraset, a poor hut filled with garapates, which forced us to sleep out in the open. I was deprived of my bed, thanks to Mr. de Schütz's unkind actions earlier in the day.

Comfort aside, I was so exhausted that I easily fell asleep on a bed that I had made for myself from pine needles (which are quite thick here). The following morning, we again climbed to the Tambo-Viejo where we arrived at ten thirty in the morning, and where Mr. Lama and I, while the three other gentlemen went ahead.

The road is singularly beautiful. We followed a mountain ridge for some time with magnificent views on both sides. There are aspects of nature so intense, so beautiful, and so important that even my memory could not recreate them with fidelity. However, this beauty remains: this perfection, this development of our best faculties, which is the fruit of worthy achievement, should come from God, or that it is born from the pen, the brush, or comes from the genius of a great man.

On all sides there is such an intermingling of immense mountainside and deep valleys—hiding, crossing, and mingling in such a way that the eye only succeeds in taking it all in only after a long moment, especially when thick mist rises in the morning from those deep gorges, and slowly dissipates before reaching the summits.

It is true that neither the trees nor their forests cover the sides of these mountains. They do not leave the valley floors, where they then appear in all their tropical luxury, ornate with birds bearing shiny feathers and peppered by richly colored butterflies, and where they are traversed by a small refreshing creek which, after a thousand twists and turns, merges with the power of one of the greatest rivers in the world.

When the sides of the mountains are bare, or only covered with a grassy vegetation peppered with cacti, the color of their rocks on the other hand is so beautiful, their shapes so rough, so picturesque, and so varied, the paths which wind around them so bold, the majestic flight of the condor stands out so well, that you have to admit that even sterility can have its beauty.

If at first the roads seem to be impracticable or very dangerous, this impression vanishes once you arrive at the location. The reason is that in the Cordilleras, real precipices as abrupt as the Alps are very rare, and the path that seemed suspended in the air from a distance does indeed overlook a very steep slope close up, but one that is not steep enough to prevent a man to find a way to hold on, should he fall.

According to the sketches I had seen in Europe, I imagined the Cordilleras to be very slender and pointed, but reality has trumped this notion. In my journey so far, the Cordilleras more than once have displayed powerful massifs and immense boulders. It is a beautiful display as much for its raw power as for its soaring, bare forms that I have only rarely encountered.

Composed mostly of limestone, the Cordilleras reminded me more than once of parts of our Alps and our Jura. I think that this resemblance could be even stronger if, like those mountains, the Cordilleras possessed vegetation that would prevent the disintegration of that limestone, already visible, and responsible for those long and fast slopes I spoke of earlier. I must also add that together with the limestone you also encounter shale and shale deposits.

From Balza (that is, from the Marañón) we climbed for more than seven leagues. After leaving Tambo-Viejo, we continued our climb uphill for yet another league or more. We arrived at the sharp ridge of the Sierra Calla-Calla, which therefore forced us to immediately to start our descent, but a surprise was waiting for us! We had ended our ascent with a soft and gentle breeze; however, as soon as we started our descent, we were assailed by the coldest and most furious winds that I ever felt in my life. You barely remain on your horse and you can barely breathe (the name of Calla-Calla comes from the Spanish verb *callar*, which means "to silence.") Your fingers grow so numb that you throw the bridle around your horse's neck and you hide your hands under your poncho.

As for me, at first I did not feel anything, and I heroically took my thermometer out of my bag which I held for the time necessary for it to stabilize at a fixed temperature of five degrees above zero, thus a temperature five times colder the one in Balsapuerto, which we had just left.

Such a sudden and unexpected arrival of cold air comes from the fact that the wind follows the top of the mountain sideways. Once at the top, it proceeds impetuously into the air, especially since the latter would only offer the wind a powerful enough obstacle, to push it down to the other side of the mountain with difficulty.

Arriving on the ridge, I heard a piercing scream coming from the other side of the mountain, so I sped up my horse. It was from the little daughter of one of our emigrants, who had nearly fallen off her horse. I arrived just as her parents were trying to secure her position. As we were descending an almost five-league-long slope, the wind slowly diminished over time. In the middle of our trip, it had almost stopped and had been replaced by rain. The precipitation drenched those paths, already so impracticable, and worsened them so greatly that I did not understand how our caravan with its three-hundred pack animals could have arrived at the end of our journey, safe and sound at Leymebamba, where nothing memorable had occurred.

I immediately left the next morning for Suta, located only four to five leagues away. The road was excellent and I therefore traveled it rapidly on a good dark chestnut horse who after a series of fruitless kicks finally decided to start trotting in long, elegant strides.

The road followed the banks of the Tambo, a tributary of the Marañón, remarkable for its lovely clear water and green, shaded banks, and dominated on the left by a high mountain whose rocky face, inhabited by flocks of parrots, rises almost perpendicular to the river.

Suta is a small, very picturesque village that overlooks the Tambo and is surrounded by high mountains. The village is not only picturesque because of its location and its small church, which stands out against the black mountain background. It is also attractive because of its Indian inhabitants, who come from a race that especially among the men seems more pure, distinct, and beautiful than the races of the other Indians whom I have met until now in the Peruvian Republic. They have long faces, defined features, aquiline noses, beautiful eyes, and magnificent teeth. Their faces are framed by long jet-black hair that hangs down around their shoulders, tied simply and elegantly by a light-colored handkerchief.

Their attire, which consists of a black collared jacket, a vest, and wide pants that extend to mid-leg, reminds me somewhat of the attire I have seen in the drawings of Freudenberger, as well as among peasants in Brittany, especially when combined with their distinct facial features and the long hair. But the character of these Peruvian inhabitants is thoroughly Indian; that is to say, they are thieves, with little honesty and supreme ignorance and bigotry. At the same time they possess a curiosity which, although mostly unspoken, is somewhat phenomenal.

My tent greatly intrigued them above all, and when I made coffee with my Lebrun coffeepot, they were even more fascinated. We left the next day, my casings full of lead pellets, which they had found a way to swindle from me while I was busy drawing, despite my servant's vigilant eye.

In order to get from Suta to Magdalena, you take a path that is in good condition but very slow going. We followed the Tambo for some time, and crossed it on a small covered bridge which reminded me of those in Bern. The village of Magdalena has nothing welcoming per se, and nothing of note took place, except for when the local priest, a sworn enemy of Mr. Ijurra's, forbade his flock to sell us anything.

While in Magdalena, some of us had a fervent desire to drink chicha, and as luck would have it, the local mayor offered us some of his own. We all crowded into his small residence, drinking late into the night. The following morning, after sleeping late in my tent, which I still enjoy as it protects me from the garapates and from a society which does not always amuse me, I decided to take my leave. But then my horse that had spent the night in rich local pastures ran off, despite my good treatment.

Many of us did not have horses and cursed the arrieros. As for me, I had my eyes on a horse which Mr. Ijurra had reserved for himself in case his got tired along the way. I took him, in the knowledge that he was not used to the bridle and would have been too difficult for Ijurra to handle.

Since I am now so used to chomping at the bit and know that it is not fatal, I think that my horse, which is far more of an animal than I am, will get us safely to Chachapoyas. Having only been on the road for fifteen minutes, I had an encounter that shocked and moved me painfully.

I came upon the wife of a German worker who was part of our expedition. She was in very grave condition—lying by the side of the road on a blanket, her dog by her side, and her husband standing next to their horses and unsure of what to do to assist her. I gave her some sherry that I had in my flask, but she was not able to swallow it and coughed it up through her nose.

After begging the husband to stop at the first house and to meet us later when his wife was strong enough, I moved on. Some travelers, walking by five minutes later, reported that they had found her dead, and I, further away, caught up with her twelve-year-old daughter bounding ahead joyously. I could not help lecturing her about having abandoned her mother who had been sick since the very beginning of our voyage.

The dead woman and her husband had been warned by the physician that this sad end might come to pass, but she was stubborn. I will say that because of the courage and self-sacrifice of women like this, who would have rather faced severe pain than gone back to Lima—a pain so terrible that I can hardly imagine it. It seems to me that once we arrived in Cajamarca, the heads of the expedition should not have allowed them to continue and given them the money to go back to Lima. At the very least, they should have provided the sick woman with a new bed, which she had been deprived of for the last four nights.

I finished my trip quietly, alone as usual, that is to say, with my Auguste, with whom I am still pleased since he serves me with zeal and friendship. This time, my reflections were less joyous, but I usually prefer my reflections, my observations, and everything that nature in all its bounty reveals to me, rather than anything I can find conversing with my fellow travelers.

The trip from Magdalena to Chachapoyas was six leagues long, which we made for the most part through rather wooded country. On the way, I caught up with the physician and invited him to share my small luncheon on the grass, which he accepted without the smallest word of thanks.

CHACHAPOYAS

July 7th, 1853

Yes! How deeply I miss a friend; a comrade, a companion who shares some of the same tastes and ideas as me, and with whom I could converse—a bond, one that enlivens both the heart and the mind. This someone, this friend with whom I could forget the weariness and hardships of the trip, while sharing our time and our thoughts, this someone I have yet to find and will not find. Here I sit, with self-reflection as my only recourse, which is neither good nor agreeable, nor instructive.

Mr. de Béarn, with whom I did most of my travel in Mexico, spoiled me in this respect, since we shared a similarity of ideas and tastes, as well as a desire to learn new things. Such an easy and agreeable exchange of impressions is difficult to find when you are looking for it. This is especially so when you depend on the odds that such an expedition offers, in a country where it is rare to find men who value education and knowledge as one finds so easily in Europe.

Yet I had prided myself on the idea that in an expedition with close to a hundred people, within a first class consisting of eleven persons, I would find such a person, but I had to forego this hope early on. The more I progress in my voyage, the more the absence of such a man is hard to bear. Nobody from first class fills that need, which torments me. To study, to observe, and to understand the masterpieces of creation that we encounter so often, and for which

I would like so much to have an interpreter at my side. Someone more knowledgeable, more handy, and more gifted with observational talents than I. A man who would know something of that sweet science, and possess a kind and spiritual nature as the prominent scientists of our time possess. Like the man who welcomed me at his home so hospitably as soon as I arrived in the New World.

Out of all my companions from the first class, none of them possesses the inclination, to admire, study, or observe the spectacular masterpieces of nature that we encounter so often now and which will increasingly come our way in, even more brilliant, beautiful and rich than we have yet witnessed.

July 8th, 1853

My companions seem more motivated by the need for locomotion that now attracts so many people—young, new or unknown—who are hoping to find a great fortune with ease and speed in these countries. Like California for some, the Amazon region attracts more than one of us with that promise, and with the probability of finding gold mines such as those lavaderos who gave a part of this country the pompous name of *"El Dorado."* People say that they will clear the land, and then scatter seeds of coffee, cotton, corn, cocoa, and more, in those open spaces, I say that the four-fifths of the column already has their lavadero in mind and is dreaming of pockets full of gold.

One thing that surprised me was that I found more taste and more knowledge of natural history among individuals from second class. I met a gardener who knows botany extremely well, much better than I, which in a sense pleases me since I have now someone I can learn something from. Then comes my butterfly collector, who catches ever more unique butterflies; followed by my skinner and bird taxidermist who become unnerved in a town like Chachapoyas where there is nothing to shoot at, let alone to skin.

Finally, I will say that very often when we march or arrive at the end of our journey, one of the travelers from second class presents me with a beautiful flower, a brilliant bird, or shares an impression of such depth that none of the caballeros in first class could have ever made nor have probably ever felt. I turn away from Man in order to return to this nature that I feel at times to be beyond my insight, and well beyond my descriptive capabilities.

The view from a nearby hill in Chachapoyas — its valley and the surrounding areas — is one of the most beautiful spectacles that I ever encountered in the Cordilleras until now. The town itself is pitiful. On the other hand, its location is fortuitous, because both ends of the town rise gently towards the hill and on the side of the mountain that overlooks it. What is really beautiful in the larger panorama is the great mountain with its half-hidden precipices that one can see in the hills that overlook the town. Then to the left, there is a narrow valley formed by mountains; their flanks are perpendicular, and their summits form gracious plateaus with slightly rounded surfaces. Above them, through the haze, you can make out even more gigantic mountains with white, tortuous, serpentine paths. The ground continues to be uncultivated, so that from time to time in the distance, you can barely distinguish fields that seem to have been misplaced.

On the outskirts of the city, however, I noticed a small estate. It belonged to the sub-prefect, someone I will discuss later. Its polished look, its well-irrigated fields, and its tree groves surprised me. A few horses were smashing grain on a small knoll that looked like an old tower. They were trotting in a circle on the grain beneath their hooves, as is customary in these countries.

Once in town, we headed to the house that had been reserved for us. There I found three of our companions who had preceded us, Don Ruiz, and the Señores Montoya and Ortiz, along with Señor Don José, the local sub-prefect, and the owner of the house and hence our host. He immediately declared that his table was ours for the entire duration of our stay. I accepted without hesitation, because first, the sub-prefect is an excellent man, with frankness and a warm manner that I appreciate, and second, because his offer is a blessing, not simply considering our location but as a comfort from the fatigue of the meager, irregular meals that are every voyager's lot in these countries.

The sub-prefect is essentially a practical man. On top of that, he is more educated, and has a more open and active mind than you would expect of a Peruvian, especially in this area. A man wealthy in years and experience, he easily mocks the theories of closed-minded people. Along with some of his ignorant compatriots, he employs humor as a foil, and will answer a difficult question or one that goes beyond their understanding with a poorly constructed joke, because you cannot gain access to a house if there is no door.

Since I insisted on benefiting one way or the other from the knowledge that his position as the Chachapoyan sub-prefect had brought him, I asked him the following questions, the answers to which, given his mocking and his sense of humor, I cannot guarantee are true.

Q. Do we know anything about the foundation of Chachapoyas?

A. We know that it was founded since the day it was built.

(We laughed a lot to please the sub-prefect.)

Q. Are we really sure of that?

A. I would think so, yet people say that the foundation goes back to the depths of time.

I have nothing against that, since nothing in the town is beautiful and striking enough for me to believe that it was built in one night, even in its obscurity.

Q. How many inhabitants?

A. Eight thousand.

The exact figure is probably closer to four thousand. Every Peruvian who loves his country (especially its civil servants) is always looking to enhance the standing of his hometown, from his first day forward.

Q. What is the tax to the Government?

A. For the city, almost nothing, since it is mostly inhabited by whites, and they made sure to preserve the ancient Incan custom that requires only Indians to pay taxes. Furthermore, we do not pay any business or professional license fees.

Q. What is the population of the province of Chachapoyas and its contribution?

A. The population is thirty-two thousand, six hundred and fifty people who pay their contribution to the Government with masos of tobacco, representing a value of thirty-two thousand piasters, which would represent twenty-six masos for each Indian, or six and a half piasters per year, payable every semester. The Cajamarca Province pays its contribution in silver; the Moyobamba Province does not pay anything. The Cajamarca civil servants and other towns are paid regularly; the ones in Chachapoyas are paid very irregularly, probably because it depends on the sale of their tobacco.

Q. Do Indians have large families?

A. Three children, on average.

Although I now know enough Spanish to get by, if need be, I have not mastered this language well enough to be able to lead a conversation and obtain all the information that I would like about these countries. It is partly for this reason that I extracted what follows from the first-hand account of our leader, Don Manuel Ijurra, from a voyage that he undertook a few years ago, in which several persons advised me not to place too much confidence.

Topographic description of the Chachapoyas province:

Dimensions:

Length: a hundred and eight leagues from southeast to north. Width: thirty-seven leagues from south to north.

Location:

Between five and eight degrees latitude south. Between seventy-five and seventy-nine degrees longitude west.

Chachapoyas is a northern province of the Peruvian Republic. It sits on a mountain chain belonging to the Cordilleras. Therefore, its directions are south to north. Through its elevation, it is located more than two hundred leagues north by northeast from Lima, and thus lies in the northeast quarter of Peru — northeast from Trujillo, northeast from Moyobamba and Pataz.

Physical geography:

The land of this province, located in mountainous country, is composed of deep valleys, of barranca[53] and of generally inaccessible steep slopes. Most of these mountains end with considerably large

---

[53] *A deep ravine or gorge.*

and convex, flat summits. Their large surfaces are covered with dirt, pebbles, and different kinds of rocks, and are surrounded by high mesas that at first glance seem to lack the earth needed for proper vegetation. On their surfaces, all those mesas have great rock veins, and ridges of marble, granite, and quartz, which are the products of underground eruptions (*ovitas de cartaepia*) that nature produces in order to create human richness and demonstrate its luxury.

July 9th, 1853

What I just translated here is neither beautiful nor clear. Is it the author's fault or the translator's? My self-esteem aside, I believe the former shares a good portion of the blame. I will provide the rest at a later date hoping that it improves. For now, we are staying in Chachapoyas. I believed we would be busy drying plants without the sub-prefect, enjoying his good spirits and his fine dinners. Sadly, they are the only part of the day we look forward to. Our current location presents little of general interest for the curioso voyager, as the Spaniards say. No game to hunt, very few plants and butterflies to collect, and not enough variation in nature that could sustain artistic inspiration, day after day.

We will not leave until this coming Monday. This is close to eleven days wasted, but the meat of fifteen or more cows are being salted, a necessity for the rest of our voyage. We require the extra supplies so that we will not need to stop in Moyobamba, which I would explain simply by saying that there is no love lost between our leader and the Moyobambins.

In general, I view this situation with some sorrow. Our leader seems to be remembered only unfavorably, and generally encounters little friendship along the route that he has made twice before. I realized that his education was lacking, but what I have heard is worse, and because of it I have reserved my esteem. In general, and despite what Mr. de Schutz, his second-in-command says about him, I find that he leads the expedition with little skill. I believe that a man who claims to know this country as he does could easily bring more care, foresight, and swiftness to the execution of his duties. Since I am not one to accuse too harshly nor judge too lightly, I will let my journal and its detailed summations either condemn or absolve. I believe that in any case, this long stop in Chachapoyas is a bad calculation on his part. In my opinion, the people in second class are not sufficiently fed. Given the climate and their mostly Germanic habits, they have a tendency to become discouraged, just like a troop during a military campaign that stays too long in one location. Those who have a taste for liquor get drunk often and complain even more than those who already complain sufficiently. Everyone is tired of our inactivity. Our current situation focuses only more attention on the moment that everyone yearns for, that of the arrival at our final destination.

In speaking about our next stage and our journey to Moyobamba on foot, I believe it would have been judicious to rest between these two cities, or at least not rush this last great stage which I foresee will be difficult.

As we were finishing our dinner last night, our host suddenly rushed from the room, and returned almost immediately with three señoritas at his side. After introducing them and the customary *buenas noches*, he had them sit in a row on a traditional long sofa and presented them two *viguëlas* (local guitars). We collectively asked if they would grace us with a song or two. We paid them a number of initial compliments—which is customary here—then, when the viguëlas were finally tuned, these ladies gratified us with a few sweet, reserved, and melancholy songs, as all songs in these countries are. Then a deafening silence took over, since these ladies are as shy in their conversation as in their songs. At that point the sub-prefect, who really wanted us to be entertained and be as joyous as he is, called out *Manuel! Manuel!*

Manuel, a mixed-race Indian and Negro man, arrived with three companions of the same complexion. He was given the viguë-la, one of his companions took out of his pocket what appeared to be a clarinet, and the other two, holding long pieces of bamboo or sugar cane, knelt down on the area of the floor that seemed to be the most appropriate to their philharmonic intentions.

The sub-prefect insisted on us dancing the old rooster. Once the orchestra was in position, he gave us the signal and the music started, one that resembled bacchanalian music. Manuel could scarcely use his five fingers fast enough to make three strings of his viguëlas all resonate at the same time, although he played his part well, and sang like a vigorous old rooster. The clarinet screamed harshly. The sub-prefect said that it should have been oiled, and finally the other two band members slapped the floor in time with their bamboo sticks and hands. The rhythm was a simple one, three beats, represented by three notes that went on forever.

To these melodious chords, one of the caballeros held a scarf in his right hand, and engaged one of the ladies. She took the scarf and faced her partner six or eight feet away. They then started a sort of fandango. They turned away from each other, they criss-crossed, one backed away, the other came closer, one turned, and the other pirouetted. They flitted about endlessly, always moving and waving the scarf about which gives the dance an air of grace. It is indeed a very respectful and modest dance. The dancers never touched one another and only took small steps. As it is the only dance I have seen here, it must be somewhat entertaining. For the spectator or the amateur, however, it does not seem varied. The sub-prefect wanted his people—that is to say his servants—to dance as well. So to the sound of another tune which is far more harmonious and not as loud, played by a one-handed Indian who also manages to play the pan flute and a tambourine, two small *cholos* (Indian girls) and the sub-prefect's *chacaros* (women) danced their mountain fandango for us. They danced with a great deal of natural grace and energy and in a far more picturesque, original, and charming way than the caballeros and señoritas from Chachapoyas had just danced, and will certainly dance again.

July 16th, 1853

The sub-prefect is decidedly an excellent, frank, and compassionate man, and we get along well. He says that he feels much friendship towards me. I tell him less often, yet I feel similarly. As far as friendships go with their people, in these countries, I rather like proof of such intentions, and without them I find myself easily becoming quite skeptical. This is the result of experience that has a sad and at the same time very useful side.

The sub-prefect absolutely wanted to lend me his excellent moro (gray) horse for a three-day excursion. This act of kindness, in addition to his hospitality—as generous as it is prolonged—seemed to be adequate proof of his good intentions. It gave me strength and belief in the reciprocity.

This leads me to tell you what this excursion is all about. I had heard about some very interesting and vast ruins that were rumored to be close to here, and since we were lingering in Chachapoyas, I wished to make the most of my time and visit them. In this sparsely populated country, where the occupied towns are always far apart, the nine leagues that we had to travel is still considered a small distance, the steep and poorly constructed roads notwithstanding. The sub-prefect at first tried to dissuade me. After seeing that I had made my mind up, he eventually surrendered and went so far (as I was telling you) to allow me to take his prized horse as well as secure other horses for my companions and my servant.

Of the four companions that were supposed to join me, only two were able to do so. The doctor, who had been the first that wished to come along, had to stay, since his services were needed. A Frenchman from the second class asked if could join our group; he was well educated and had a fervent passion for antiquities. Unfortunately for him, his taste and passions did not include a talent for horseback riding, a necessary skill on this continent.

Of the two horses that he was presented with, the first one appeared useless to him since it insisted on turning around on the spot. The second horse bucked him off, along with his load, a quarter league away from town. It forced him to go back on foot to Chachapoyas—and to boredom. He did it without hesitation because although he usually wears three hats on top of each other, two in straw and one in felt, he knows as well as we do that he only has one head.

Our two other companions were local Peruvians, Messrs. Besséril and Ijurra. I made the acquaintance of the former who, although still very young, has already traveled extensively and spent several years in Europe, most of them in England. He also went down the Amazon to the mouth of the river in the company of Mr. Ijurra, after having first been a part of an earlier failed expedition. The goal there was to exploit the gold of the St. Jago River, as well as harvest some of the local products such as sarsaparilla and cascarilla quinoa to sell in Europe. He knows our leader very well as well as the whole country that we are about to cross, and twice he had the opportunity to showcase his courage and skills.

As soon as he knew that I was going to visit those ruins, he volunteered to accompany me, as did Mr. Ijurra. Mr. Ijurra also owns a chacra close by where he invited us to stay. We had planned to leave very early in the morning and were supposed to be on our way by five o'clock. Therefore I woke up at four and immediately sent my servant through the darkness to retrieve our horses from the corral, which also gave him the occasion to be thrown to the ground anew by the horse he chose. My coffee machine was working and we drank a cup each. Five o'clock came; no one arrived. Six o'clock, still no one. Finally at six-thirty, I feared foul play and went to see Mr. Besséril who, I was told, was fast asleep, as was Mr. Ijurra.

This story is a testimony of what I have come to know and experience here. In these countries, it is indeed very difficult to be ready, and impossible to leave on time, especially in the early hours of the morning. Finally, at ten o'clock, after taking a *caliente* at the sub-prefect's and a formal breakfast at Mr. Besséril's, we five were finally able to climb on our horses, including the Frenchman's fiery steed.

We backtracked to Magdalena five leagues away on the same road we traveled to arrive at Chachapoyas. I will therefore abstain from repeating any descriptions that I have already made. Needless to say, despite spending some time in a rather heavy downpour, we traveled joyously. From Magdalena, we descended to the valley floor, climbed up a hill, and went down the other side, arriving in another valley where we were supposed to find the chacra at the end of our day.

These two valleys are equally deep and so narrow that apart from the little stream that runs there, there is only a very slender piece of land, but one that is extremely lush. Almost everything that is cultivated here is sugar cane, so joined with the babbling sound of the river, there are shrill and cadenced sounds coming from a sugar cane press. It is a simple cylinder moved by oxen that walk in a circle, and can be found in every *chacarita*, the thatch of which you can distinguish throughout the trees bordering the road. The trees, watered by the stream, are generally strong and have lush vegetation. They are laden with orchids and bromeliaceae as well as climbing vines that surround them on all sides.

On the other side of the road, where the water does not flow, the rays of the sun beat down on rocks that are almost always bare, and cacti reign as tall as trees. At their feet sit aloe plants with gigantic slender flowers, so gigantic that their stems are used as firewood, and so slender that the eye cannot discern the hummingbirds flying around them. We crossed rivers, torrents, and creeks again and again, sometimes on thatch-covered bridges, sometimes by wading through the water. The night, which falls quickly here, surprisingly allowed us just enough light to distinguish a wood fire in the far distance at the end of a gorge—even narrower because of the darkness. Our companion told us the fire was coming from the chacra, his property.

Indeed, after half an hour, we arrived at the chacra, where we were warmly welcomed by the Señoritas Encarnación and Isabella, our companion's sisters and for now the only occupants of this lonely place. The ladies prepared a nice small supper for us, which we ate with pleasure, and which made us forget how long we had to wait until breakfast. After a little chat that allowed us to become better acquainted, these ladies occupied themselves with making a place for us to rest, that is to say, a bed with clean sheets, which would have been glorious had they not been accessible to the garapates that inhabit this chacra, as so many others insects do. Garapates are small insects from the species that in German are called *waldböcke*. Like the latter, they penetrate the flesh with their head, then engorge themselves with blood and transform from small and flat to very large and round. More than their European cousins, these insects sting and bite, and leave you with a blue-tinted bruise that, due to the decomposition of the blood, will stay for a few days and worsen with some people, to the point of inducing fevers (which afflicted two of my roommates, Mr. Montoya and his servant).

We did not wake up unscathed (they do not ask you here "Did you sleep well?" but rather, "Did you feel the garapates?") This did not prevent us, from mounting our horses after breakfast and climbing to the top of the hill, a league-and-a-half away, to view the famous ruins of Malca.[54] Greatly wishing to excavate the site and return with several mummies, I had asked my companions to adjoin a few Indians to our party with the appropriate tools, which I was told was going to be done and later was told had been done.

We paused only a few moments in the village of Kuelap at the bottom of the ruin. It is a sad village full of poor Indians, among whom we took with us one who is supposed to know the ruins' twists and turns and secrets the best. From the village, you can already distinguish the walls that surround the ruined city, which we had seen emerge from the horizon shortly after starting our ascent to the summit on which the ruins sit.

Once we arrived at the gigantic walls, we dismounted and headed toward a door that would let us enter the venerable, enigmatic, and fantastic world of the ancient Peruvians. This great rampart, fifteen thousand feet long, and sixty feet high, provokes a silent meditation; the power of the work itself calls to the viewer, almost silencing a vague curiosity, as to what this great achievement has engraved and locked within its heart. I then understood why the Indians gave these ruins the singular name of the Muralla. One feels great respect and religious admiration for works that inspire and that carry the imprint of the power of Man, combined with the weight of time. I felt this admiration when I walked under the large doorway that progressively narrowed as you walked through it—as high as the wall and sixty feet deep. Two towers guard it, flanked by

---

[54] *Whenever he refers to Malca, he is speaking of the fortress of Kuelap site.*

trees overloaded with vines that form a canopy, as well as chandeliers that only let a somber and mysterious light penetrate, barely bright enough to allow you to distinguish the narrow, obstructed passage you need to pass through in order to leave the large doorway and access the remnants of a great city.

Unfortunately, the deeply seeded superstitions associated with this place have provoked such a fear among the Indians that no one ever visits the ruins. The tropical vegetation surrounding the ruins is so lush and strong that it was able to take over the fortress completely—so completely that the rare traveler who comes to admire the ruins can only walk among them preceded by an Indian armed with a machete. Even after a path has been cut, it is still not enough to prevent one from walking with difficulty, having to bend down during most of the pilgrimage.

Therefore, given the maze of the ruins and the overgrown vegetation in an area fifteen thousand feet long by three hundred feet wide, it is very difficult to derive a proper appreciation of the site as a whole. In order to fully comprehend it, one would need to spend far more time than the brief visit I made. I suspect you would need five to six days worth of work and a geometrical survey facilitated by a good compass. The sketch I am providing you represents how I remember the site, corroborated by the memories of my companions, as well as the Indians who accompanied us. The Indians were very quiet and circumspect. They are this way when it concerns the ruins of the "gentle ones," or how they refer to their ancestors.

The city was built on the sharp ridge near the summit. On the side we climbed, the slope is maybe twenty degrees. Its terrain is uneven and laden with rocks. On the other side, a chasm of close to one thousand feet (without exaggeration) stands immediately under the walls. The long sides of the city border these two slopes. The wide sides face the ridge of the mountain; the first ones are impregnable and have no other protection other than the wall. The other two, which are easier to attack, are defended to the south by a tower (half a tower, to be more precise) as well as two abutments, to the north by one abutment only. But in front of them and still on the ridge, some fortifications continue on that end, to the north with a twenty-foot-wide precipice, and to the south with another tower.

The inside of the city is full of round stone houses topped with arched roofs with doors and small openings that resemble loopholes. Beside these houses, generally fifteen feet wide, one can find other circular-shaped ruins, but considerably larger. Some of them still appear like defensive towers, while others seem to have been used for other purposes and could have been the leaders' residences. From the layout of the whole city, you can tell that it was built in conjunction with the natural undulations of the terrain as opposed to following a master plan.

As the mountain ridge is very sharp, the builders had to fill up the space in between the ridge and the outside walls in order to turn them into platforms that could make portions of the city level. They built the circular portion of the wall at the greatest and most abrupt elevation, and it crosses into the city at its width, roughly two-thirds of its length to the north. As for main entrances, besides the one I already spoke of, there is another identical door facing it to the east, which opens onto a small plateau that dominates the chasm. Then there are a third and fourth entrance, on the same side as the first one, but to its north, smaller and seemingly less important. The stones that were used for the construction of the city and its walls are all made of pale yellow limestone. The largest carved blocks you encounter can be four feet long, two-and-a-half feet wide, and a foot-and-a-half high, but they are very different from the blocks that you find at ruins in Mexico. These stones are carved as rubble stones, that is to say, their sides are slightly curved and their ridges almost non-existent. Furthermore, their surface is not perfectly smooth, which gives you the idea that the tools that were used to prepare them were fairly rudimentary and were used more to break the stones than to carve them. A cement that is more reliable than these stones is applied generously, to hold the stones together.

Comparing these ruins, their construction, and their materials with the sketches that I have seen from other ruins in Peru, most of them going back to the glorious Inca times, I could not prevent myself from dating the city of Malca to an even older period, despite my archaeological ignorance. Upon seeing the complete devastation at the northern end of the city and recognizing its strong position, I had a hard time believing that the small army of the Spanish conquerors could have inflicted such damage. If they had attacked, they would have surely lost a great deal of their forces as well as their time. Finally, after only finding Indian skulls among the bones, I told myself that the destruction of this great city had to go farther back to the times when some bellicose Inca was expanding his empire by subjecting his neighboring peoples to his theocratic and civilizing power.

Moreover, hearing that ruins of circular stone houses similar to these cannot be found in the vicinity—only in a village located far away from here— I surmised that this city may have been built for the warrior elite of one of the ancient peoples of this land. It is natural to believe that this city did not live in total isolation; to the contrary, neighboring valleys were cultivated by Indian farmers living in simple thatch-roofed shacks like they still do nowadays. How had this large city found the means to survive on the rocky ridge where it is located?

I would have really liked to rummage through one of these houses, but unfortunately when I looked around to find the workers that Mr. Ijurra had told me he had sent forward, all I saw was one of them, armed with an iron crowbar. Very disappointed, I fumed internally. My thoughts turned to the carelessness of the Peruvians in general, and to this ignorant Indian superstition in particular, which makes them believe that whenever they touch any object having belonged to their ancestors, some sickness or pain will befall them.

I reached such a point of anger that I developed and nurtured some very unscrupulous intentions. I told myself that this mountain and its ruins belonged to the church, and therefore to the priest of the local village. As Mr. Ijurra was the steward of the church and of its priest, if they agreed with each other, they could make it easier for a foreigner to discover any rich antiquity that could be found here. I say rich, because when you search in this country, your intention is to find gold—gold that has remained as dear to the Peruvians as it was to their ancestors, the first Spanish conquerors.

I therefore went down the mountain and bid farewell to those ruins without taking back the smallest *guaco* (antiquities, mummies, and vases, etc.), thanks to bad means or bad faith, *quién sabe?* I also left without taking back the smallest sketch with me, because of the thick vegetation that prevented me from seeing more than ten paces ahead of me, and also because of the rain that assailed us and forced us to leave just as I was going to start drawing the door. When I say that I did not take back any sketches, I am talking about landscapes, since you just saw that little plan of which I cannot unfortunately guarantee perfection.

Upon our return to the chacra, we found the Señoritas Encarnación and Isabella who were waiting for us with a good little dinner that we enjoyed immensely. After dinner, some people started to write, others joked, and I drew a portrait of Señorita Isabella, whom I had missed, since her eyes sparkle with emotion when she laughs. Finally, after Don Ambrosio tormented his two childhood friends, he joked with Encarnación about her admirably true resemblance to a mummy, which made her laugh and enjoy herself in a very endearing way.

The following morning, waking up again to many garapates bites, we enjoyed a good breakfast, and after a very prosaic farewell, mounted our horses around seven o'clock in the morning in order to arrive at our Chachapoyan home by six o'clock at night. We had changed our route and followed a long valley filled with sugar canes and chacras, among which my friend, the sub-prefect's shines, as it is located very close to the river, to the point that it encounters the calmest current and the best shade.

Monday, July 18th

Here we are, still in Chachapoyas. When are we going to leave? I keep asking myself. On Saturday night, there was a revolution among the Germans, which could very well be the reason for the extension of this delay. The first cause I attribute to Mr. Ijurra, who was not able to take measures to end our stay in this town. Our expedition is essentially comprised of people who are used to working; there are also a few who are not used to it and are what you could call troublemakers. Alcohol is very cheap here, and many drink, some out of idleness, others out of habit. The troublemakers keep aiming for new levels of noise and debauchery and are driving others to follow their example.

On Saturday, at eleven thirty at night, as I was finishing my journal, Mr. de Schütz walked in and asked me to lend him my pistol. I gave it to him willingly and since I am in fact and especially in this expedition a partisan of the rule of law, I asked to accompany him. Mr. de Schütz had been told that the prefect beseeched him to come as soon as possible in order to calm people who were threatening to break down his door, were firing shots, and were generally creating a menacing uproar. We reached the square where the sub-prefect resides. It was empty except for a small group of Peruvians, including Mr. Besséril, my companion from Malca.

Asking for information, we were told that some of the Germans had attempted to free one of their companions that the prefect had jailed, because of a quarrel he had with some soldiers who were accused of stealing part of the meat that had been prepared for the expedition. Following this quarrel, the German in question supposedly went to get his gun, and was intending to make good use of it on the soldiers, had one of his companions not been there to prevent him from doing so. The soldiers subsequently threw him in jail, under the prefect's order. At that point, some of his companions, as *borracho* (drunk) as he was, heroically tried to free him. They went first to the sub-prefect's residence, who, hearing shouts and commotion followed by kicks at his door, refused to open it and listen to them anymore.

From there, they went to the prison and exchanged words with the soldiers, which were accompanied by harmless bayonet strokes. Realizing that these first efforts were useless, they regrouped on the square, where some of their more reasonable and sober companions were, who tried to dissuade them and take them to bed. At that point, they dispersed. Some went off singing, some back to their barracks, and some to cafés. We arrived too late to witness this activity, and Mr. de Schütz was then told that he had to go to the Merced barracks if he wanted to prevent his people from further action. We went inside and found a group of Germans who, besides one or two who appeared drunk, seemed to have calm and peaceful intentions.

After talking to them for a while, we calmly went back to bed, thinking that everything had been resolved; but an hour later, a new messenger from the prefect, looking barely alive, arrived saying that the Germans had gone to get their weapons and that the prefect, who saw everything from behind his shutters, was expecting a bloody confrontation. We left again immediately for the square, which was empty, except for an American, a German and a Peruvian. All three were part of the expedition and were quite drunk. They were speaking quietly with the officer and his soldiers at the prison door.

As we were leaving, laughing at the prefect and his false alarms, we met a dozen well-armed Germans at the end of the square walking quietly but with purpose. Mr. de Schütz stopped them and asked what their intentions were.

Their leader was a German from Holstein named Krüger, a former sommelier and ex-army officer, yet hardly an ex-layabout. He responded, with an authoritative, strident tone typical of the commanders of great armies, that as settlers, they could not recognize the authority of the prefect of Chachapoyas, and that therefore he did not have the right to imprison one of their own. Consequently, they were going to free him at any cost, even if the streets should run with blood.

Mr. de Schütz tried his level best, speaking with a cool head, and demonstrating to the Germans the falseness of the argument. However, despite making parallels with our countries and our own habits, despite advising them to wait until tomorrow, and promising them that everything would turn out well, they only truly listened when Mr. de Schütz promised to go to the prefect's with Krüger to see how the situation could be rectified.

Mr. de Schütz, however, was no more successful than the emigrants to end the prefect's deafness, the door remaining closed. Then Mr. de Schütz went to the prison. Finding it not well guarded, he thought that he could avoid a useless and regrettable confrontation by imploring the officer to release the prisoner to him, promising that he would keep him at his house, which the officer did. As for me, seeing how the situation was steadily worsening, I also tried to persuade a Frenchman, who was part of the military band. He acknowledged the correctness and logic of my discourse, and said he could sense that I was right, but that he could not turn back now as his honor was also at stake.

I was suitably tired of making so many peaceful, conciliatory efforts, and was thinking—listening to these men bragging and uttering such absurdities—that it would be much wiser and even more prudent for the rest of the expedition to let them go, even if it meant that they received a few bullets and bayonet strokes. It would have saved the principle of order, and would not have given them this appearance of triumph that, while appeasing them for the moment, would eventually make them even more arrogant and undisciplined.

The next day, Chachapoyans woke up exasperated, local sentiment finally turning against the emigrants in seeing that their authorities' power had been so undermined. It was always the same ten or so troublemakers who had turned the locals against the expedition by trespassing, killing countless chickens and pigs, and engaging in other disappointing activities. To think that the expedition had been so very well received at first by the local residents who upon their arrival had given them a bag of rice, a bag of corn, and other gifts as a welcome.

All this is very regrettable, even more so when you realize that in these lands more than in any other, a good reputation that precedes you must be regarded as something sacred and advantageous for the success of the enterprise, while a bad reputation can be prejudicial. I say especially in these lands because the Indians whom we meet all the time here are subsequently less civilized as we travel inland; these Indians who are our guides, our arrieros, our cargadors, and will later be our river men, are indeed the race that is the easiest to frighten, the most difficult to manage, and the most susceptible to fine or poor treatment that I have ever met.

I will provide you with a recent example to prove my point. No doubt, you know how quickly bad news travels. There can be no doubt then that news of the excesses committed in Chachapoyas during the Saturday night escapade is about to arrive in Moyobamba, after having been announced all along the route we are about to travel. We were supposed to leave today, all the arrieros and their animals should have already arrived yesterday, but half of them are missing. The prefect was told that one of the arrieros had supposedly cut off the head of his mule, that another one had stabbed his to death, and finally that a third one had cut off two of his own toes rather than assist us. The veracity of these tales is unknowable, but what is known is that half the animals are still not here, and I wager that at least a quarter of the Indians here now actively regret their participation or are in hiding. Most of us will therefore have to walk the seven leagues that separate us from Jumbilia, even if the same situation awaits us there.

Mr. de Schütz said with reason that the troublemakers will be the first ones made to walk, and if necessary, he will shoot anyone one of them riding away, in particular the leaders. We shall see if it comes to that. As for me, I praise the good people of the second class—my servant Auguste is one of the best—who are banding together in order to prevent the instigators of disorder from continuing to give our expedition a bad reputation. I believe they met tonight in order to establish a code of conduct, but given the lack of unity, so inherent with the Germans—especially when it concerns something positive–this prevented them from arriving at a favorable conclusion. As for me, I told them that "no rules," which is the genesis for both good and evil actions, can only work if it is enforced by physical consequences.

July 19th, 1853

I just had a long conversation with Mr. Bességil, first about the fateful chaos that reigns in our expedition, and then about the disorganization that appears to threaten it. I am continually frustrated when I feel that it could all be going so smoothly—yet nothing changes. This all makes me very sad, since I wish most of our emigrants well and I would like to see them happy. Despite my hopes for order and harmony, I am often rendered speechless as the emigrants assert the correctness of their recriminations. In spite of his capabilities, I attribute the already tenuous state of affairs specifically to Mr. Ijurra's negligence, who, knowing the country and the people we encounter, should have had greater foresight, and instituted order and speed.

The prefect asked him to provide a list of the number of riding horses and pack animals necessary for the expedition, but Mr. Ijurra forgot to take the beds into account, and therefore we are now short of about thirty horses or more. These gentlemen were planning to place the beds on the pack animals and to have some of the emigrants walk. But the latter knew what they had been promised; they knew about the five thousand piasters that those gentlemen must have received in order to cover the expedition's expenses, and were troubled by the general lack of order. Thus they refused and said that they would not walk. The British and the Americans even told Mr. de Schütz that in case the plans could not be changed, they requested that their effects be brought back. Since our effects left over the past two days with the arrieros and already have a three- to four-day head start on us, walking would not really be the way to catch up with them.

We spoke about this subject for a long time, not because it amused me, but because I was making a case for Mr. Bességil's character, and especially because I wished to hear an experienced man like him talk about other expeditions. Despite his youth, he has found himself leading other expeditions made in this country's mountains, ones he led with great skill. This feeling was confirmed when he shared with me his points of view on Mankind and other subjects. After leaving this topic, I continued our previous conversation on the governmental system of this country. That political description will be on the following page or two and I will do my best to be as clear as possible.

Governing the province is the prefect, appointed in Lima to a term of four years by the government. The prefect is Lima's representative in executing governmental orders. He is also the highest ranking police officer and is in charge of the police within the province. In Chachapoyas, the police are governed on a day-to-day basis by the sub-prefect as well as the *gobernadors* of the villages. The prefect resides in Chachapoyas and his wages are three thousand piasters per year.

The sub-prefect is chosen by the government from the three candidates that the prefect presents. In addition to overseeing the city police, he also collects taxes. Furthermore, he exercises powers over the villages' gobernadors, also charged with overseeing the police and collecting taxes. The sub-prefect also resides in Chachapoyas and his wages are twelve hundred piasters per year. He is appointed for three years.

The provincial judge *(juez de letre o de derecho)* is appointed for life by the superior court in Trujillo and confirmed by the government in Lima. He judges all second-degree misdemeanors, trials, etc., but is also in charge of judging the more serious, first-degree offenses and crimes. He resides in Chachapoyas and his wages are two thousand piasters per year.

There are six judges of the peace or alcades *(juez de paz)*. They are appointed by the college of electors (indirect election) for a year, with a possibility of immediate reelection. They act individually, each having his own degree of popularity or skillfulness. They are the ones who judge the less important infractions, and can levy fines of up to two hundred piasters. They are compensated with two reals per act. The alcades receive two hundred piasters annuity.

If he is not satisfied with the alcade's judgment, the accused can appeal to the judge of the letter first, then to the Trujillo Superior Court, and finally to the Supreme Court in Lima.

The gobernadors are appointed by the sub-prefect for three years. They are the ones who are in charge of collecting the taxes and managing the police department in their villages. The city's gobernador is also appointed by the sub-prefect for three years. He more or less exercises the duties of our administrative secretaries, taking special care to carry out the orders of the sub-prefect. He is compensated on the basis of four percent of the taxes. The two prosecutors (*procuradors*) are appointed by the college of the electors for one year. Their duties consist in part of supporting the people's interests. They are compensated depending on the honor.

Elections are indirect. All individuals aged twenty-one or more enjoy their civil rights and may participate in the election of the second-degree electors. The second-degree electors are charged with electing sixteen first-degree electors who form the Electoral College. They are termed parochial when duties consist of appointing the justices of the peace and the prosecutors, and are considered provincial when the village electors join the former in order to appoint the representative to the Congress, as well as his deputy.

The provincial interests are represented in Congress by representatives. There is only one per province, plus a deputy, who is destined to replace him in case of illness. He is in charge for two years. For his compensation, he receives eight-and-a-half piasters per day for the duration of the session, plus two piasters per league for traveling expenses.

The communal and provincial systems are unknown, and there is no provincial congress in charge of discussing or providing for the interests of the province.

Thursday July 21.

Production of the Chachapoyas province

Raw materials: The cotton from Chachapoyas is of very good quality. Sugar is another high-quality agricultural product, especially in the Guayabamba district, which could alone supply the Pataz, Chota, Cajamarca, and even Trujillo provinces.

Bagua's cocoa is very good and if not for the locals' laziness, its cultivation could be more expansive and worthwhile. At the summit overlooking the Rio Nieve, you find high-quality cascarilla quina, which naturalists used to call negrilla. They say that in the valleys enriched by the Marañón past the Quenico hacienda, you can find three species of negrilla.

The laurel tree or the wax tree can be found in the valley forests and those who farm it can sell a pound of very white wax for three to four reals. There is also a species of shrub called the Chinchango, whose bark and fruit are used to produce a beautiful red ink. The Campeche tree can be found in almost all forests. The indigo plant grows naturally and multiplies in Chachapoyas, without cultivation; natives use the ink to dye fabrics such as wool and cotton in a light blue. The shrub called Chilia can be found everywhere. Its sap has an opaque green color. In some areas of the province, you can find oak trees, chestnut trees (nogales), guayacanos, ash trees, aljobes, cedar trees, and isphingos that can all be used in cabinet-making. Another very useful plant that you may encounter in the province is linen. Lest we forget, tobacco is the major crop and its quality is generally good.

Industry: Industry lies mainly in the hands of the women who provide the country and the neighboring provinces with white and fine bayatas, woolen alforjas, ponchos, bed covers with varied colors and designs, woven mantillas, towels made of fine fabric, laces, very delicate embroideries, alvas, and other embroideries for the church.

In every district, you encounter a number of mines, many abandoned by previous generations. They contain gold, silver, cinnabar, copper, pewter, iron and rock crystals, which proves that their ancestors knew how to work with all these metals. Amethyst, hyacinth, sapphire, and chrysolite can be found in various locations, as well as gypsum (yeto), pizzara, jasper, talc, agate, mica, and other crystallized and impervious stones. Furthermore, salts like alun, salpetre, sodium nitrate, and magnesia (excerpt from Mr. Ijurra's travel narrative) are present.

MOYOBAMBA

August 4th, 1853

I have before me a long, disastrous chapter to place in my journal. Long because it must contain all the details of our voyage since our departure from Chachapoyas until our arrival in Moyobamba, and disastrous because of all the calamities and disorder that accompanied us during this fifty-league trip. I will detail everything methodically by dividing the chapter into seven parts, or the seven stages of the trip.

It was not without difficulty and only after eighteen days did we finally leave Chachapoyas. Much time and money was wasted, in part due to the incompetence and disorganization of our leader, and in part due to the hostile disposition the local authorities had toward him—his bad reputation preceding him. I have the innermost belief that he deserves all or part of this unfriendliness. But what I find undignified and less than honorable from the magistrates of Chachapoyas is that they unquestionably tried to make us bear the pain of his sins by attempting to harm the success of our expedition in order to damage the reputation of its leader. This, like other facts I learned later, confirmed my fear of the Peruvian people's dishonesty and lack of character.

Due to the lack of horses in a country where they are abundant, we were made to wait. After three days of embarrassment and boredom, we were finally able to leave, one at a time, therefore separated one from each other and from most of our effects by one or two days. I have to admit that in the last days of our stay in Chachapoyas, my friendship with the sub-prefect cooled down considerably and became very temperate. The reason is that after promising five or six times to provide me with good horses, he ended up wanting to take away the one that I finally obtained for myself or rather, through Mr. Bésséril's recommendation. His lack of tact displeased me greatly and perhaps I do not need to tell you that my hand did not leave the bridle, to take that of the mule that he wanted to give me in exchange. Nevertheless, I am still grateful for his hospitality.

The goal of our first day was Taulilia, a village toward which I traveled in the company of Don Lucas, the son of the sub-prefect, and Señor Montoya, a former officer who was a retired wholesale businessman. After traveling for a great part in a very narrow valley and lunching near a very picturesque small bridge, we climbed a mountain. At the summit, we found the arrieros loaded with our beds and our luggage, celebrating Bacchus, after first unloading our effects from their beasts of burden that were grazing around them. Since we insisted upon sleeping in our beds and since we really did not want our arrieros to have any more of their *pisco*, I ordered them harshly to reload our beds and to take them to Taulilia, after some attempts at gentle persuasion from my two companions, to the chief arriero. As the arrieros were in the process of reloading, those two gentlemen left, after inviting me unsuccessfully to accompany them. After all the experiences encountered in these countries, I do not trust promises made, and as Doubting Thomas, only believe what I see. After a while, we were off again, my servant and I, walking with two beasts of burden and our arrieros, who were advancing on these bad roads in a very comical way.

As night fell upon us, we found ourselves lost on a bad little path, since the arrieros had missed the one that was supposed to take us down the mountain. They really wanted to start unloading their animals again and to camp where we were, but since I was of a wholly other mind, I admonished them to turn around and go back until we met the missed path that was supposed to take us to the bridge and the river that we had to cross.

Upon going down the path, I had seen, through the forest trees, a number of fires that I had attributed to the village of Taulilia. But upon crossing the bridge, I recognized my mistake. There in front of us were thousands of dancing, hopping will-o'-the-wisps, slightly illuminated against the prevailing darkness. The arrieros, out of fear or ignorance (I do not know which) declared that they could not see the path and expressed a vague desire to unload and camp.

Since I know the Indians rather well, I began with kind words, but seeing that I was not going anywhere, I found myself obliged to pull out my pistol. I placed it so close to the nose of one of them that despite the darkness, he recognized it quickly and suddenly remembered the path. We resumed our walk up to the first house in the village. There we hired a guide to take us to the shoal that we still had to cross. When the guide refused to go any further, our arrieros started to beat him up and asked me to shoot this *maldito cholo*. This is when I delivered him from harm; in return he kissed my hand and conducted himself with greater zeal afterwards.

Upon arrival, I found our emigrants rather agitated. The governor of a neighboring village had been put in jail and was scheduled to be executed because he had not delivered the animals we were promised. Since we all had to change horses in Taulilia, those who did not have their own saddles kept the ones they had brought from Chachapoyas, refusing to give them back until they would be given others. Ijurra was there alone, since de Schütz had to stay in Chachapoyas—for lack of a horse.

The emigrants were right in substance but wrong in their behavior. Ijurra's lack of character and know-how was not making things any easier. He hadn't had the courage to crack down on the reprehensible actions of the emigrants, and I therefore found the latter more favorably disposed towards Ijurra than de Schütz—a result of some ill-considered words that he had hurled at them some time ago during the Chachapoyas insurrection.

Since I know these two men and since I appreciate de Schütz's character, while I do not appreciate Ijurra's, I did my best to appease those who seemed the most irritated against the former, among which was the German Dominico. His experience, actions, and outspokenness carry quite a bit of weight among the emigrants, and he benefits from the leaders' favor and confidence. We expect to see him and his companions move to de Schütz's side. The following day, despite de Schütz's arrival and his energy, we were still missing many pack animals; therefore, when de Schütz offered to pay three piasters to those who would agree to travel by foot, forty-two accepted, ultimately to their detriment. After the column left, Ijurra said that in de Schütz's place, he would have never made that three-piasters offer. He knew the road very well, and knew that it would rain a great deal (we had been told as much in Chachapoyas). If he had concerns, why then didn't he voice them?

After my servant remained loyal to the cavalry and procured the necessary horses and beasts of burden for us, we started our walk, which did not take place until the middle of the day because of the difficulties in finding animals, since the arrieros had hidden or driven them away to the neighboring forests or elsewhere. As far as ours were concerned, my servant found them hidden in a room.

De Schütz stayed, for lack of an animal, until the next morning with Señores Ortiz, Lucas, Montoya, and José. He would have stayed longer, he claimed, if he had not pressed forward with the system of imprisonment as well as threats of shooting people that he had put in place. Most of the effects had been carried on the backs of the arrieros and cargadors, and I have to say that the prefect had only paid half of them. These people are however accustomed to being paid cash, and, defiant by nature, do not care at all (I believe with good reason) about debts that the government owed them. I am telling you this so you are not surprised later on when I tell you later that a large number of them abandoned their loads half-way.

Since we have four nights ahead of us in Tambos, I must first explain what a tambo in this country is, which will be neither long nor difficult. They are made of four beams or more, stacked up and holding up a thatch roof, big enough to cover around fifty people. It is used as a nightly refuge by voyagers who travel these deserted areas, and who have to settle the best way they can. Tambos are certainly more amenable if one is careful enough to bring a bed and necessary supplies. With the neighboring forest and some matches (if the wood is not wet), a good fire can be made to get dry, stay warm, and cook.

In order to emphasize that there is no other shelter, I will just tell you that for five days on the road, we saw no farms, no hamlets, no villages — in short, no houses nor people.

Tambo of Ventilia

We arrived just as night was falling, soaking wet and weary from having traveled on a road that was made even worse by the rain. Since we were preceded by many on foot and on horseback, we found the tambo was already full, with most of its occupants busy making their beds and gathering some branches in front of a small hut where they were starting a fire to keep warm, make coffee, or cook dinner. They had left Taulilia without having breakfast, and although it was already eight o'clock at night and they were famished, dinner was far from ready.

After having eaten a few of the things that the doctor gave me, I crouched down by a fire where I thought I could dry out and sleep. I did not have my tent or my bed. The night was so dark and the road so bad that I had given up the idea of going to get them. I was however proven wrong, since, around ten o'clock, my effects showed up (to my great satisfaction) and I was therefore happy to leave our wet campground for something better.

We woke up the next morning in an even more compact layer of mud, due to the rain that had fallen during the night. Most of the expedition, who had not slept at all, and not who had not had anything to eat last night, resumed their walk without having breakfast, since the cook was late and the wood was too wet to burn. Ijurra and his mistress had arrived in the middle of the night and would not have found anything better than the others, had he not made sure that their luggage (beds, supplies, etc.) accompanied them at all times, an advantage that he had reserved for himself alone.

Tambo of Bagasan

After climbing a long slope pelted by rain and cold winds, the sun greeted us on our descent down the other side of the mountain, which dried our clothes before we reached the next tambo. The expedition was already divided, a part still with de Schütz in Taulilia; another part remaining in the tambo in Ventilia to wait for their beds; and our group of between thirty and forty having gone ahead. Since most of us had not eaten, we decided to have a young bull slaughtered at around five o'clock at night. The bull, brave and mean, started by entertaining us with a spectacle that could have easily ended up dramatically since its rope came undone and it charged directly at one of the Indians in charge of the sacrifice. It knocked him over in the stream and was starting to work on him when his companions came to his rescue. I admired the ease with which the Indian positioned himself between the bull's two horns so he wouldn't be gored.

The next day, after a good night in my tent in the company of the doctor, I decided, despite the rain, to spend the day in the tambo in order to make sure that my chests had been sent, which I had not seen since we left Taulilia. Upon leaving, Ijurra asked me through Mr. Lama to show Mr. de Schütz the bones that were the only remains of last night's bull, completely devoured by our companions. At the same time, he let me know that he had a quantity of sugar and rice transported, that I had to remit to Mr. de Schütz when he arrived with his companions who comprised the rest of the expedition, numbering around fifty. When I walked inside my tent to see the supplies, all I could find was the sugar. My servant told me that he heard Mr. Ijurra order someone to load the bag of rice, so it could travel with him and his companions' company. About ten people had stayed in the tambo with me who were tired of sleeping in the humidity and were expecting their beds, which they had been deprived of since Taulilia. We did not have any lunch, except for the few pieces of meat that we scavenged from the carcass of the bull and that we succeeded in grilling over a fire with difficulty. Because of the rain, there was more smoke than flames.

Realizing that the rice that was intended for us was gone with the rearguard, I abandoned my scruples, and after Ijurra left, grabbed a bag of rice being carried by an Indian who was leaving to join the vanguard. Since he seemed afraid to part with his supplies, I gave him a note saying that I was responsible for the consequences. I then distributed a share of the rice to each of my companions so everyone could cook it the way they liked—without salt, however, as we had been deprived of it since we left Chachapoyas. Ijurra had indeed forgotten to bring this rather necessary ingredient with him, especially when all you have is rice. Rice without salt is not nutritious enough, therefore I decided to give them some of the sugar that I had been given.

It seems that the Indian had not been satisfied with my note. He ran so quickly that he managed to catch up with Ijurra who then told him that I could not keep the bag of rice. Mr. de Schütz was bringing all necessary supplies with him, and that I could only distribute some of it to the people who had traveled with me, which I did. We will see later the sort of supplies that Mr. de Schütz was supposed to have with him.

My trunks eventually arrived and I removed what I needed to be dry again. That was fortuitous, since for the whole day, as with the days before, we suffered an almost never ending rain. Some of our companions arrived at night; those who walked arrived very tired and wet. Among them was Siegnitz, my seed collector who, with his poncho, his long staff, his pants rolled up to his knees, and his bare legs and feet, had a very curious look.

At night time, our division had grown to around ten people, and de Schütz had not managed to find us, or did not know how. Fearing that they would lack supplies—not without reason—I invited my companions to leave early tomorrow so they could catch up with the vanguard that was better supplied and therefore avoid the rear guard whose means we could only lessen.

Since all were in agreement with me, I ordered our arrieros to bring our animals as soon as possible, which they promised to do but did not, as is the custom among Peruvians. We therefore left rather late, which would have been difficult to remedy since the arrieros and the animals had been lodging in distant forests that we weren't aware of. We therefore did not start our walk until nine or ten o'clock, leaving some companions behind, for lack of animals and beds, through the rain that had not ceased to fall.

Tambo of Almirante

I had already seen bad roads in my travels, but never as detestable as the ones we have been traveling on for the last two days (and will have to take for the next three). In dry weather, the roads are already in such a state that someone who has not left Europe cannot grasp what they are like, and would believe them to be impassable if they could somehow see them from afar. Neither in Jura, the Alps, nor in other parts of the ancient world do such terrible roads exist, even for pedestrians. What will it be like, then, when we have to go through them on horseback or on mules, through a never-ending rain that turns dirt into a thick mud, a few feet deep and, wherever there are rocks, makes them slippery as ice, and transforms these swampy passages into ponds?

We suffered through this—and not only this—all along our trip, but what you must not forget is that we had tall mountains to climb. But what descents and what climbs! Sometimes, we found stairs made of bad, rotten logs; other times, we found stone stairs where there were two- to three-foot-high steps that our mule would have to straddle only to find itself with its knees and head buried in the mud or the swamp. Furthermore, these roads, or should I say paths, were sometimes so narrow and so deeply dug into the ground, that one wonders where to put one's legs and one can barely see the sky above one's head.

During the steep descents, you are, thanks to continuous jumps from stone to stone, so shaken up that there is not one of us who has not injured his ribs or had their mule or horse fall over at least once, rider in tow. My mule only did it once, because the saddle was shifting, so I just let myself fall onto my leg and let my mule fall by itself, which wreaked havoc with my saddlebags. As for my servant, I think he knew what he was signing up for, since not a single day has passed by without his falling two or three times—both with and without his mule. His mule is so witless that it is really admirable he made it in such a good shape. I have to say here that, in spite of the road and weather conditions that could have demoralized many, the zeal and the affectionate attention that Auguste always shows have never diminished. Quite the contrary.

The story was different for those who traveled on foot. Due to the fact that most of the luggage had left before there was even a question of walking to the next stage, most only had one pair of shoes and almost all of them were lost them in the mud before the third day. They were forced to continue in bare feet, although none of them were used to it, and walking among those stones, rocks and swamps made their journey especially perilous. Then, as wet as they were, or even wetter since they could not protect themselves against the rain, they arrived at the tambo, finding only a wet tent to sleep in and nothing to eat but salt-free rice. Later when we were among the vanguard, there was at least grilled corn that we bought from our arrieros — not without difficulty.

Because of these paths, our walk was arduous and slow that although we left early, we rarely arrived before nightfall—having covered only about four leagues. Upon our arrival at the tambo of Almirante, we found Ijurra and all of his companions, who had decided to stay there because of the rain, thinking that de Schütz would join.

I found Ijurra and his companions, soaking wet. They were busily dining, in a hut whose roof was leaking copiously. Although I had nothing to eat all day, no one invited me to dine with them, which did not surprise me because of the chill between Ijurra and me. It all stems from the fact that I cannot respect a man who, when called to responsibility, answers so poorly. He is a man who knows his country so well, yet plans a trip across it so ineptly. He is in charge of taking care of his people, yet lets them starve and sleep in the mud, which not only causes such a general discontent, but increases the chance of disease that are the natural consequences of bad expeditions such as this. As for me, after sharing a cup of chocolate with my servant, I retired to my tent and to my bed, the latter as wet as the former. The next day, I woke up early, and decided to get out of this mess and reach Moyobamba as quickly as possible. Others had the same idea; therefore we were twenty to thirty, ready to leave. The arrieros were hiding, together with their horses, and since Ijurra was not at all concerned, some of them, not knowing what to do, took his horse. The same road and the same weather prevailed and we arrived that same evening at the Tambo of Puca.

Tambo of Puca

We did not find anything to eat and had to resort to our arrieros' supplies. Despite this misery, we were still cheerful. We were telling each other about the falls and events of the day, while sharing and cooking the few supplies that some of us had managed to keep. Since my bed had not arrived, I had an excellent and quiet night's sleep on my horse's covers. I am not telling you about the country and the nature we just went through, since in such weather, nothing is attractive, no path can be overlooked, and therefore everything needs most of your attention.

The next day, we had a hard time getting our animals back from the arrieros, who are turning out to be more and more undisciplined. This is because they feel more and more that there is no orderly or strong power in this expedition and that it becomes even more disorganized every single day. Today, de Schütz and some others were still in Taulilia, while the rest of the expedition was spread out in the three other tambos, without any food, except for where Ijurra stayed. Still deprived of arrieros in more hospitable areas, we started our walk, fearing that the road from Lima to Moyobamba, for the chacra or hacienda of Rio Negro, could be the worst road of the entire trip.

Rio Negro

We arrived at four o'clock in the afternoon, after an immense descent that could be considered both as the worst descent of the trip and the worst road in general that we have ever encountered. It is with a true feeling of gratefulness and pleasure that after passing through deserts like those we just crossed, you finally meet a world that is alive again. Therefore, everything appealed to me; the host, the chickens, and especially the fine home that was going to feed us. It finally put an end to that hunger that had been tormenting us since we had left Taulilia. The beautiful Rio Negro where we would wash was a revelation. The host, the owner of the chacra, was a farmer and a sugarcane producer in addition to being a most decent fellow. He gave us everything we asked for—for a fee. He even graciously had a small white hen delivered to me, which I sacrificed to the gods of the Rio Negro.

We totaled twenty souls, including the company of ten and its captain, famous for their planned assault against the Chachapoyas prison. Together with their leaders, they enjoy a bad reputation for being the most impulsive and incorrigible. I do not share this opinion at all. During the few days we spent together, when I was more or less in charge of leading and taking care of this group, I had the best relationship with them and enjoyed all of its aspects—especially their concept of order.

After a night without rain, we all woke up, happy to leave for the great village of Rioja. The village has a charming location in the middle of a large valley filled with magnificent forests. It is inhabited by an extremely white race whose features look really European, I would even say British. I saw charming children who reminded me of the children of our countries and as I was complimenting their grandmother, she proudly responded that they were the descendants of the people who lived on the "other side," and that they had absolutely no Cholo blood in them.

I got along well with the governor of the village who sustained us, as much and as well as he could, with chickens, yuccas, and bananas. I have to admit that among the Germans, fortunately, just a few are very greedy and voracious. Thus, one of them, who is certainly not accustomed to a better table than mine, had something negative to say about our food, which I personally found delicious.

The next day, we had a little trouble in gathering our arrieros, who since the beginning of our voyage did not feel compelled to exhibit any discipline, and who were becoming more independent and insubordinate. However, seconded by the government, I did not let any of them go and only left when all of my companions were all ready to walk. After crossing two rivers, swamps, the pampas, and passing through the charming village of Calzada, located at the base of the Mountain of the Dead, we arrived at Moyobamba, the capital, our present location, at nightfall.

Going through a very swampy forest, we snaked along a road frequently traversed by log bridges. At every moment during this long passage, we were surrounded by magnificent vegetation, including palm trees, whose wide leaves created a vaulted space far above our heads. Then on all sides, in the middle of the surrounding waters, vegetation arose everywhere, amplified in its vigor by the humidity. These immense leaves were a stunning backdrop for cyclamens, dogwoods, cinerarias, and many other plants and trees.

August 8th, 1853

More than a week passed before the expedition, which had spread out, finally reunited in Moyobamba. The last ones made it in yesterday, which was the 7th, while my companions and I, who formed the vanguard, had arrived on Sunday, July 29th. All of them arrived more or less tired due to the bad roads, incessant rain, and many other hardships. The most exhausted without exception were those who made the trip on foot. Many lost their shoes early on, and they had to travel these awful roads in their bare feet through mud and swamps, and over rocks and stones. Almost all of them therefore arrived in Moyobamba with very swollen feet, covered with a host of small wounds. This would be less of a concern if they could stay here long enough to heal and rest, but how can you not worry when you think of the terrible roads they will soon have to travel for the next five to six days to Balsapuerto.

The government surely had promised that the children, the sick, and the elderly would be carried on people's backs, but Mr. Ijurra, whose money had seriously diminished, must have told the local prefect that would be impossible.

Thus, everyone had to make it on foot, even if they had to make it on their knees, as my seed collector Siegnitz did for part of the way on a road that we had just covered. He only arrived today. Generally speaking, the government and Mr. Ijurra behaved like good Peruvians; that is, they promised much more that they could or wanted to deliver. It seems to me that for such expeditions, one should do the opposite, which is to promise less and deliver more. It would not only be wiser but better politically as well.

I do not know whether I already mentioned it, but during the trip and upon their arrival here, the emigrants were furious at Ijurra. Knowing the route as he did, he had allowed and even encouraged people to walk; people who had lost total control of their arrieros and the cargadors. The guides did what they pleased, got drunk, hid, slept wherever they wanted, dropped personal effects wherever it suited them, and most importantly did not take the necessary measures to feed the expedition along the way.

I found myself in the center of these recriminations. I did my best to exonerate de Schütz, who was being blamed, by pointing out that he did not know the road any better than we did. Then I was told there were those who wanted to thrash or kill Ijurra. I knew this was merely bluster and that the emigrants should first try to maintain their composure and not be branded with a reputation for violence. They had to know that if Ijurra was harming the expedition, they could bring their complaints to the local authorities, ask for help, and demand a change. If the safety and the fate of the expedition hung in the balance, they could ask for another man to lead them—possibly a native of the area, who would be well respected locally and would only enhance the group's reputation in light of the voyage they still had to make.

Unfortunately nothing changed. I say unfortunately because I believe that the trip will not be without new troubles, some instigated by the emigrants themselves. No change was made, due to the lack of unity that still reigns among the Germans who are dominated by Dominico's scheming mind. He benefits from letting Ijurra remain the leader, since the latter promised him monies in exchange for those that Dominico invested in a company and partnership that he had in Lima.

If the people arrived slowly and disorderly, the luggage was far worse off, since forty-one loads had been left in the middle of the road and in the various tambos by the arrieros and the cargadors who returned home. Some people are missing beds, some personal effects, while those who arrived last, arrived dirty, shoeless, and covered with mud. Upon their arrival, they received the news that Ijurra had already sent their things forward, and therefore they would have to wait until Balsapuerto to be able to put on fresh clothes or new shoes.

It has been eight days since we arrived in Moyobamba (I will tell you later what Moyobamba looks like) and the group has no desire to leave. The reason now is that the leaders would like to go and the Indians are losing their patience, but the emigrants cannot or do not want to, some because of disease, and others because they want to see their belongings arrive, which seems very understandable to me.

Having left Rioja last, I arrived last in Moyobamba. When I got off my horse at the building reserved for the emigrants, I found my companions rather indisposed because no one wanted to feed them, and on top of that no one wanted to even sell them food, not even bread. I was first told that it was because of the unscrupulous reputation of our leader that has preceded him. The fact is, after being sub-prefect here for six weeks, he was brought in chains to Chachapoyas. Therefore, the natives thought that we would help them take revenge. I personally thought that there were other reasons and that the news of the little troubles that had taken place in Chachapoyas—shooting chickens and storming the jail—had perhaps reached Moyobamba. These incidents had surely been embellished and while they started as a small molehill in Chachapoyas, they could have grown to the size of a mountain upon their arrival in Moyobamba.

Both of these conjectures were somehow true. People from Chachapoyas had written such terrible things about us that many Moyobambins, hearing of our arrival, had fled to the neighboring mountains with their families, their chickens, and their pigs; leaving their houses behind and closed to any hospitality. Learning that the authorities were refusing to feed us, I and four or five of my companions visited Mr. Ortiz, the local sub-prefect. I explained our situation in my best possible Spanish. He responded, saying that he had still not received any order from Ijurra to feed us, but that he would make it his responsibility to supply us with everything that we would need as early as tomorrow morning. The sub-perfect was none other than a former officer who was the brother of Mr. Ortiz, our travel companion. He proved at once that he had good manners and judgment, which warranted my esteem.

From the next day forward, our people were properly fed and found bread that they could purchase, although bread is a difficult thing to find in Moyobamba, where it is often replaced by bananas and yuccas. This leads me to a local and physiological description of Moyobamba.

August 9th, 1853

Like Cajamarca and Chachapoyas, our present residence shines more for its location than for its architecture or appearance. Without even discussing the population and the impressive number of twelve thousand inhabitants that every good Moyobambin throws at you, I have to admit that those thatch-roofed houses separated from one another by courtyards and gardens; the unpaved streets (and every decent Peruvian town is miserably and pathetically paved); the pigs and their barnyard companions that you encounter at all times; the shabby church; and finally the square that looks a lot like a pasture, all give Moyobamba the look of a quaint village.

This mass of thatch-roofed homes sits on a slightly elevated plateau flanked by bare ground everywhere, due to the *aguaceras*, or rain showers, that travel from the capital and flow down the valley.

The valley, where both Moyobamba and its hill sit, offers the visitor the most picturesque aspect. A league wide, it surrounds them with beautiful forests covering the mountain sides and a large plain that extends towards the mists on the horizon towards Rioja. At its center is the powerful and solitary Mountain of the Dead with the gracious village of Calzada at its feet. Hiding in the shadows near the village is the quiet, limpid Rio Mayo that runs and disappears in the distance towards the southeast where the valley narrows. Eventually only mountains can be seen. These mountains are the ones that one has to cross to get to either the Ucayalior or the Huallaga, tributaries of the Marañón River, and finally to the Marañón itself.

When the day is glorious and the banana tree draws its immense leaves, so green against the dark blue of the tropical sky; when the river is ribboned by dramatic shadows and small canoes; when the Mountain of the Dead lets you admire its natural details; when in the distance, located on the side of the mountain and among the palm trees, smoke rises here and there indicating the homes of the Indians; when the horizon, its mountains, and its valley disappear or take on a color thanks to a storm, then you will forget the fatigue of the trip, the inhospitable poverty of the village, and only thank the Creator for so many wonders.

The thatch-covered homes, as I mentioned earlier, have average-sized dimensions. They usually have only a ground floor and never more than one story, and are sometimes adorned by a sad-looking balcony. Adjoining on either side or behind the house stands the yard or courtyard with several little outbuildings. The yard typically contains banana trees and rarely anything else, except upon occasion for large orange trees, as strong and fertile as our best apple trees. The inside of the house contains one, two, or three rooms without any ceiling, and roofs of supporting beams covered only in thatch. There is no real kitchen; you simply build a fire, since there is no floor, and then set the pot above it. Therefore, any room can be used for that purpose. The furniture is as poor as the rest of the house, since it consists of no more than few benches, couches, set against a wall to which they are usually nailed, a hammock, and one or two really massive tables. Armoires, buffets, desks, dressers, and even chairs are unknown in Moyobamba and generally throughout Peru, as they are in all of Mexico and Latin America. I do not believe that you can find a dozen chairs even in the capital of the Maynas province. Some houses, on the other hand, own one or two massive armchairs that are quite unique. You may ask where the clothes, linen, cleaning utensils, and supplies go. All of the above hang on hooks, lie flat, are thrown, or lean, which means that the European style of order is rare to nonexistent here.

Regarding ornamentation, there is none, since glass is not used for windows, nor is it used for paintings. People do not care for flowers here, and I do not know whether the illuminated images of saints that some nail to their walls really qualify as decoration. On the other hand, the rooms are large and well aerated, as the windows have no panes and the two-sided doors, always wide open, are sometimes the only way that light penetrates.

August 11th, 1853

The courtyards of these houses have nothing of the rustic look that embellishes our villages and countryside. It is understandable, since agriculture and even gardening are relatively unknown here. Inside these courtyards, you will not encounter any carriages pick-axes, fountains, or anything like them; more likely, you will find two stones used to crush corn or coffee; a rope from which to dry a few clothes; and a family of pigs. No one owns cows. The local aristocracy owns horses or mules that often graze in the neighboring meadows and forests.

Let me now switch from the houses to the occupants that we shall consider with regard to physical and moral attributes. I do not know whether the cream of the Moyobambin crop fled the town at the sound of our arrival, but if I have to judge—and I have to judge those who stayed behind—this population's physique bears nothing of note, either good or bad. The height of both men and women is average and their forms are slender. They have a very Indian-like appearance: brown skin tone with dark or light nuances, depending on the individual. Their hair is black and smooth. Women wear it in two big braids which hang down their backs. Men in general rarely have beards, but it does not prevent from showcasing whatever facial hair they do have. Aristocratic men wear what was fashionable in Europe three to four years ago. Peasant men wear a short linen shirt over linen pants. Women wear a traditionally blue jumper over their blouses–their only articles of clothing—which are made of wool and finished with a red border. When they go to Mass, they wear a woolen shawl, often brown, sometimes red or blue, which they use to cover their head and most of their face.

As for hair style, all the men and women wear the same straw hat, which is the main industry of the capital and neighboring villages, which I will speak of later. Footwear is a very simple matter: everyone walks around barefoot, aristocrats as well as the poorest families. However, since people generally have strong feet and women have a gracious and light gait, you notice it much less, despite the contrast it presents with the rest of their outfit.

History reports that Moyobambins are the descendants of an expedition charged with the earliest conquest of the Peruvian Amazon. They were prevented from achieving their goal by the hardships along the way and supposedly decided to settle in these parts. True or false, their complexion has changed so much over time that it is difficult, nay impossible, to recognize their origin, which has also taken on a distinctly Indian character as well.

August 19th, 1853

If, for many days, I have been unfaithful to my diary, it was to allow me to eventually keep my promise of providing a few words on the morale of Moyobamba's inhabitants. I first wanted to study the matter myself and then obtain reliable information from the sub-prefect, as well as from the priest and other locals. Since neither the sub-prefect nor the priest has yet responded to my queries, and since the other people seemed to approach it with their customary scrupulousness and reserve, I feel obliged to pass on my own observations to you.

My impressions could seem artless since in a week or two it is often difficult to get to know one man, let alone a population of eight to ten thousand people. Are my impressions the result of natural inclination towards misanthropy, European prejudice, or the consequences of a sad reality? The fact remains that surely, since the day that I set foot on this vast continent, and the more I learn about the people, their customs, their predilections, and their habits, the more it seems that my appreciation for my fellow countrymen increases in inverse proportion to the lack of esteem I feel for the people of the Americas.

I have often had to clear my mind by refocusing my ideas and thoughts toward the great works of nature this continent has to offer, in order to rid my mind of the disgust that the inhabitants of this land evoke within me. I have been allowed to travel widely and freely through these lands which has given me a broad view of the countries and their people. In all this, my intention is not to judge individuals, but only to comment in generalities.

In many countries, I have been dealt with in bad faith—the United States, Mexico, Panama, and Peru in particular. In truth, my complaint is not solely about their acting in bad faith, but as someone who prides himself on candor and honesty, most of the time I only encountered these qualities as part of a masquerade. It is more in my character and interest to praise, as I do not like to judge because it is easier and less agreeable than the inverse. Despite my good intentions and the favorable preconceptions that I always have, I am obliged—unless I want to forget my quill, ink and paper—to write a great deal about the bad and very little about the good. Before I condemn and judge, I want to plead for the Peruvian people—a defense that seems to me to be of great importance—in an effort to diminish in part the defects and vices of the present generation.

August 20th, 1853

The Peruvians were unfavorably influenced by Spanish despotism whose greater mission had always been to send galleons to the motherland. The Peruvian citizen, a master of his own freedom, has inherited many of his former lords' defects without any of the energy, power, or civic virtues necessary to becoming good and true citizens. One of the character flaws that has passed from Spanish dominance to the Peruvian people was the love of money. The Spaniards told the Peruvians that in order to be happy they had to be rich, and the Peruvians believed them. Heirs of their blood and their tastes, raised in ignorance, they happily made the pursuit of money their primary motivation. There was nothing in this era of transition and tumult that was strong or virtuous enough to restrain them.

Therefore, since the infancy of this republic, there has been a total waste of resources, giving birth to continuous disorder and an even larger passion for money that has continued unhindered. Each individual, charged with the honors of public office, dishonored it through corruption, until other individuals, impatient to enjoy the same advantages, overthrew them in order to enrich themselves. Men quickly succeeded one another. The president, usually a general, was overthrown, either at the beginning or at the middle of his term, by another general who distributed the most important seats to the officers who had shown the most devotion to his ambition. From that moment on, the army became demoralized, and after having fought for liberty, instead of fortifying it, killed it while fighting for money.

Everybody had been very keen to enrich themselves, and you could say it continues today. They have little to no scruples about impoverishing their country. Since then, or rather since the inauguration of the revolution, obstacles and the annihilation of everything good have sprung from this corruption. Education and instruction are not equitable for all classes of the population. Nothing is done to encourage industry and agriculture in this country. Communications, a powerful agent for civilization and commerce, both intellectual as well as material, remain so inadequate that they are made irrelevant. Every province becomes an oasis that has to rely on its own strength, production, and resources, which are insufficient. These resources could be useful and powerful for the whole country's well being, if there was a possibility of trade and commercial relations between the inland and the coast.

You now know in part why Peru is the way it is. It could be one of the richest countries in the world. It benefits from an intelligent race, and Providence seems to have endowed it with all that can encourage industry, empower commerce and above all, nurture agriculture that is vast and fertile. Why then with all of its natural riches is Peru—known in ancient times for its gold—now considered along with its people as the poorest in the whole civilized world?

August 22nd, 1853

Adding to this general unhappiness is the fact that the class of men who could best work against this demoralization is the clergy. In fact, they do exactly the opposite. While they serve many Masses, they preach a poor example, which is unfortunate given their strong influence over the population, all the more so since so many are unlettered. The power of a priest in a place like Moyobamba is greater, even for the most material details of everyday life, than that of the sub-prefect and the local authorities. To follow orders, the priest has to give his signal as well as his approval to obedience. Do not assume that this subordination is the consequence of amoral imperative or Christian lessons. As I said earlier, the priest does not preach by example, and outside the service thinks much less about his parishioners' religious needs than his own interests. Moreover, as his salary comes directly from each individual, it gives his pastoral duties a commercial tinge that is incompatible with the very spiritual respect that they are owed.

Yesterday, I had a long conversation with the local priest, Padre Don Julian del Aguila, whom I questioned for more than an hour about everything of interest regarding Moyobamba and its inhabitants. I told you earlier that I would judge a man's character independently from anyone else's opinion, and I was not mistaken. The Padre confirmed everything that I presumed. The one in charge of healing a population of ten thousands souls spiritually, and therefore the best to describe their character, described them only as *mala gente* or bad people. How could I not be disappointed? He characterized his flock as such, because of their indecision, lack of continuity in opinions and relationships, bad faith, laziness, immorality in family life, and as if that were not enough to diminish all hopes of improvement, an excessive pride.

Besides these great vices, I would have loved to have found some great virtues. I fruitlessly questioned him but there were no redeeming virtues, save one, that of hospitality. While I have seen support for this, their kindness did not exist in its nicest form and best sense: extended to the poor. As for me, I do not accept this completely as I think the benefits of hospitality diminish due to the social position of whoever claims it. I am unsure whether I should analyze these negative qualities and support them with facts. While it is a task that I could dutifully complete, it would surely revolt me. At the same time, not doing so would simply be judging without cause, and for such accusations, I feel that justice demands evidence. I will therefore briefly and shortly present them to you.

A lack of consistency and indecision in opinions and relationships is very clear here. If after criticizing someone—for real misdeeds or imagined ones—you then find yourself face to face with that person, you will invite them to believe that you had just declared your friendship while in fact you just declared your enmity. A change of relationship depending on new interests or circumstances also seems to be made without forethought to the point where you harm the one you just made ardent promises to. This spirit of indecision can also be found at work or in the domestic occupations. You go from task to task, without any order or logic. At some point, for example, you weave your hat, then you go work in your chacra, and in between, you smoke your cigarette, play your viguëla, or rock yourself in your hammock. Bad faith, which already has contributed to what I just described, is in my opinion the main vice of the Moyobambin, and springs from questions of self interest. To gain one real coin, the Moyobambin breaks his promise and sells the work he had promised to deliver to one person to another one, even if he is paid in advance. You can witness this every day, in all kinds of business, especially in the hat business. Furthermore, scruples are absent. The work started by others is often stolen, either to cut down on your costs or expand your business at the expense of someone else.

Moyobambins outshine other Peruvians for promising more and delivering less. Laziness is as common as ambition is rare. You work just enough to live poorly and not more, which leads to more laziness. It is nature that is excessively generous, and since you only need to sow in order to reap, you soon get enough bananas and yuccas to feed yourself and your family.

August 24th, 1853

During my conversation with the priest, I managed to learn many interesting things about Moyobamba's industry, laws, and education. I will describe them as clearly as possible, although they could be more complete.

The main local industry is straw hats, one in which the neighboring villages of Calzada, Habana, and Soritor, to the north, and Lamas and Tarápoto, to the south, participate. I did not manage, despite all the questions I asked of several locals, to determine the true number of hats produced per year, even by Moyobamba alone. The priest told me that the town manufactures twenty thousand at the most per year, the business owners told me some thirty thousand, others claimed sixty thousand, and finally the prefect exaggerates the number even more. Personally, I have settled on the sixty thousand figure, more or less.

The sale of hats takes place at nightfall. All hat sellers bring their wares to the few local business people, enjoying the coolness of the evening as well as the twilight that lends certain brightness to the hats. Joined by a Frenchman, Mr. Charpentier, a local businessman and resident, I decide to investigate the evening sale. Taking into account the actual absence of many natives, we agreed that the number sold in a typical evening was at around two hundred hats. I will therefore not exaggerate and stay with the sixty thousand number. Since a hat costs ten reals on average, sales would bring the city a yearly income of seventy five thousand piasters. Therefore, for each inhabitant, estimating the population at ten thousand seven and a half piasters, that is to say six hats. Since men, women and children participate in the work, you might estimate that half the workers would give you fifteen piasters and twelve hats per individual. Therefore, since it is easy to manufacture four hats per month, if the activity were what it could be, each of these five thousand individuals should make forty eight hats per year. Therefore they waste three-quarters of their time.

Indeed, while walking through town, you see at least ten hats that have been started but that remain unfinished, hanging on the walls for every hat that you see in the hands of a worker. The straw of these hats, very soft, very white, and durable, is extracted from the leaf of the palm tree that is here called bombonaque. The hat is very much sought after, as much in all of Peru and Chile as in a part of Brazil, and there is always some merchant completing his shipment that typically consists of two to three thousand hats.

Another local industry is the lona, a rough cotton fabric, good for making sacks, covers, etc. Fifteen fardos are manufactured yearly, the fardo being two hundred vares (one vare equals nine Spanish pesos) and is worth fifteen piasters, which would represent an income of two hundred and twenty five piasters, that is to say one thousand, one hundred and twenty five francs.

The industry of agriculture does not exist, each individual having his chacra wherever he cultivates the bananas and yuccas that he needs, but nothing more—except perhaps for two or three coffee plants that are most likely located in his yard. The local coffee is excellent and could be an abundant source of income, were there better communication and more local activity. Nevertheless, the town only produces four hundred arrobes of coffee (the arrobe equals twenty-five pounds), or ten thousand pounds per year, which sells for four francs to an arrobe.

Tobacco is also excellent quality, but its cultivation has nonetheless been totally abandoned since the government does not exercise a monopoly in the province, and smuggling does not offer the same advantage anymore as it used to in the time of the Spaniards. Vanilla is another crop that could be very profitable, even if it were only harvested, as it grows abundantly in all neighboring forests. But it is too tiring for the Moyobambin caballero to pursue, and it was only with great difficulty that I was able to buy a pound and a half of it, which cost me a piaster and a half, or seven francs fifty. The best fruits, such as pineapples, cherimoyas, guavas, pitayas, avocados, and lemons, grow wildly in the forests without anyone picking them, and they are cultivated even less. Finally, indigo, sarsaparilla, and a quantity of medicinal herbs could also be cultivated with ease and profit, since the land does not cost anything and the climate is favorable. This occurs to no one.

In summary, it is difficult to be as ungrateful towards nature as the people of this country are, since it could bring them everything in abundance, including well-being and wealth. But they only respond with unlimited laziness and an inexcusable poverty. Their approach to agriculture is to cut down and burn a piece of forest when their old piece of land is worn out. Further, their only farming instrument is a sort of saber with which they cut the wood, and then between the trunks that remain in place, they dig a few holes where they throw their seeds and cover them. With the same saber, they harvest their corn and cut down their banana trees which for the entire time, they abandon to the generous care of Providence, which they barely know how to thank, despite its generosity towards them.

One becomes content rather quickly here, so other, more intellectual demands do not exist. There are twenty carpenters in Moyobamba, so you may imagine that it will be the easiest thing in the world to have a bench made, for example. You will be very fortunate if out of these twenty carpenters, you find one who is inclined to work for you and does not make you wait for two or three months to finish something. It is the same story for everything. There is a complete lack of energy, activity, and ambition.

When somebody is willing to begin work for you, it is almost as if by taking your money, he is doing you a favor and you need to be very grateful for it. This laziness inevitably leads to the lack of skill and advancement in the simplest and most critical professions. I think the provincial cities of Peru could be one of the most, if not the most financially advantageous emigration destination for European craftsmen who cannot earn a living at home, not for lack of skill, but because of the great competition. Material life is so cheap here that their income would almost be net profit.

During the three weeks that I just spent in Moyobamba, I had the misfortune to experience what I described earlier several times. As an example, the cobbler to whom I had given some fabric in order to make three pairs of canvas shoes that are typical here, only made one pair and stole the rest. The cigar maker from whom I had ordered some cigars made of Javeros tobacco did not make them or at least did not deliver them, since he probably sold them to somebody else, etc., etc.

Immorality in family life consists, most of all, in the lack of fidelity. It is rare that after one or two months of marriage, the spouses do not enter into other relationships. Badly raised and abused children soon lose any respect they owe to their parents. Pride comes from ignorance and presumption. Should a Moyobambin have a few drops of white blood, the gives himself the title of caballero and thinks he can excuse himself from constant work or excess servility, by responding, *"somos caballeros"* (we are gentlemen). He despises the cholo (Indian) whom he takes after, walks around with his hands in his pockets more than he works, and smokes a considerable quantity of cigarettes, but does nothing really to deserve the title of caballero through either education or by virtue of his vocation. The only positive aspect of asserting he is a gentleman is that he is very polite, a quality that one must appreciate and feel happy to find, in the absence of others.

August 25th, 1853

The arts and trade professions are in any case, once again, very poorly represented. Besides the twenty carpenters who are also cabinet makers, there are nine blacksmiths who also operate as locksmiths, and four cobblers who also do some saddlery work. On top of being already insufficient in number for a city of ten thousand souls, there is an even smaller number of craftsmen who do their work well.

The quality of doors, windows, locks, and shoes would be pitied by our young European apprentices. Additionally there are no wheelwrights, because nobody in Moyobamba knows what a carriage, a cart, or a wheelbarrow is; everything enters, leaves, and is transported by man or donkey. Everyone sews at home to fulfill their clothing needs, so tailors are not required. Lastly, none of the professions that reveal a certain level of civilization are represented here. In this respect, all our European villages are far more advanced than the capital of the Maynas province.

I forgot to mention that there are five or six masons, if by masonry you mean the poor adobe construction that typifies every Moyobambin house. Despite the ease of adobe construction and the simplicity of the design, both outside and inside, houses are rarely completed in less than one year, more often two.

There is not a single inn in Moyobamba, so the arriving stranger must look for accommodations at a private residence. On a positive note, the accommodations are satisfactory and quite inexpensive, as you can be lodged and fed for only two or three piasters per month. There are no bars either, so whoever wants to drink sugar cane alcohol (a cheap spirit at seventy cents a bottle) or chicha must do so at home.

What is even more surprising still is the total absence of a marketplace. It stems from a certain lack of needs on one hand, and a certain self-sufficiency on the other, given the fact that most Moyobambins are also part-time farmers. I partly regretted it, because the markets in Cajamarca and Chachapoyas had interested me immensely, not only for the number of fruits, vegetables, and produce that were new to me but also for the barter system that took the place of the currency. Few items at the market were worth a *medio* (thirty-five cents), so you were obliged to first buy a dozen eggs for that amount, and then exchange two, three, or four eggs for the fruits and vegetables that you wanted to buy. Here, there is nothing to buy with eggs or with money. This is due to the lack of demand, and also because the Moyobambin does not want to sell his produce, even though he could. I was obliged to send three persons around town in order to procure me a chicken, without much success until the following day. Yet there are thousands of them around; just none is for sale.

The priest places the population at ten thousand. After what I just shared, you will understand when I tell you that there are no poor people in Moyobamba—and yet all here are poor. The greatest fortune amounts to thirty thousand francs. Whoever owns it must be a Moyobambin Rothschild, and more ill at ease than an Englishman to know what to do with his finances. There are four blind people who are the only ones that require public aid. They are allowed to beg, one fixed day a week, Saturday, if I am not mistaken.

Families are usually composed of a father, mother, and on average, five children. The population is growing; according to the latest records, there have been seventy marriages and five hundred births for every three hundred and thirty deaths (a ratio of six to four, which seems a tad extreme to me). The law allows men to marry at the age of fourteen and the women to marry at the age of twelve, but the average age for marriage is sixteen for men and fourteen for women. A father's consent is asked until age twenty one, for fear of losing your share of the inheritance. After that age, you can marry without it, and not lose any of your rights. There is no dowry since from the moment a child knows how to knit, they make a little money to pay their expenses. This way, everyone here, young or old, has their own savings and money is thus generally distributed among the whole population.

Out of four children, there is at least one who is illegitimate. He or she will bear the father's name, should the father not be married, and the mother's name, in case he is. Furthermore, he or she inherits the father's whole fortune, if he is not married, a fifth of it if he is. By law, an illegitimate child can sometimes receive more than a legitimate one. Not so long ago, a father died, leaving ten children, one of them illegitimate. The latter received a fifth of the whole, while the others received approximately one eleventh. Older people generally reach the age of fifty to sixty. However, eighty-year-old people are not uncommon, and there is now one old timer who beat a century by five years.

As far as the country's administration in concerned, the Maynas province does not contribute a dime to the state which bears its administration expenses, and the position of tax collector does not exist. Maynas' expenses are covered by using subsidies obtained from other provinces.

Moyobamba's sub-prefect is the equivalent of the prefect of the Chachapoyas province; he is the executive power appointed and asked by the government to execute the orders and decrees regarding this province. Furthermore, he is the Chief of Police of the whole province and is the head of all the towns' governors. For a long time, the government has appointed a military officer (starting with the rank of major) to this position. His advancement continues during his years as a sub-prefect and he continues to get his salary. As far as a sub-prefect's salary is concerned, he continues to receive his officer's pay. If, for any reason, the sub-prefect does not come from the military, he receives fifty piasters per month.

Justice is administered by three justices of the peace or alcades, appointed for a year by the parish council or second-degree electors. They exercise their functions separately and receive ten per cent of the revenues in return. Two prosecutors or trustees are appointed by the same Electoral College to exercise their functions for two years.

They do not receive any pay. The governor, who is also not paid, exercises the functions of administrative secretary to the sub-prefect for two years. The first-level magistrate resides in Chachapoyas, or to be more precise, fulfills these functions for both provinces. Right now, however, the Moyobamba province is asking the state for one official who would be appointed solely for Moyobamba.

Each village has its own governor and justice of the peace, the former in charge of police, the latter in charge of justice. Two Electoral Colleges, representing the parish and the province, the first one composed of fifteen persons, must elect the justice of the peace, the prosecutors, as well as the governor of the capital. Forty provincial electors join them in appointing the representative to congress. In order to be a second-degree elector, that is, to be part of the Electoral College, a candidate has to be twenty-five years of age, has to know how to read and write, and exercise his civic rights. The representative to congress fulfills his functions under the same conditions as the one in Chachapoyas.

The institutions for education are still relatively undeveloped. Yet two schools for boys and two for girls opened two or three years ago, and they are paid for by the government. Tuition for the boys' school is twenty piasters per month; for girls, it is twelve piasters. At school, you can learn how to read and write and gain the rudiments of arithmetic, but nothing more. The children attend or do not attend, according to their parents' will, and end their studies whenever they please. In the morning, school goes from seven-thirty to nine o'clock and in the afternoon from two-thirty to four.

Education follows a policy of mutual exchange. The student who is taught has to give the teacher an *uovito* (an egg), a *platanito* (a plantain), or anything else edible, in exchange. On Fridays, the teacher receives from each of his students a bunch of bananas and on Easter Sunday, money. This is what the priest told me. He cannot seem to understand the interest I show in such things and finished telling me he did not envy my endeavor. As for me, I envy neither his nonchalance nor his ignorance, and since we were not envious of each other, we parted as good friends.

It has been almost four weeks that I have been stuck in Moyabamba. Wasting my precious time in a town like this is infuriating. It is a consequence of this mess of an expedition, causing a three-week delay until the whole column arrives from Chachapoyas. As of now, there is still a number of effects that have been left behind, most of the boxes cracked open and half emptied. Their owners must resign themselves to never seeing their property again. When we, the vanguard of the column, arrived here, the sub-prefect Mr. Ortiz took measures that in case the expedition had arrived with all its effects, they would have been able, after four days rest, to resume their walk towards Balsapuerto.

But since we all arrived at different times, exhausted by the bad roads and the lack of food, some sick, and most without their effects, the departure could not take place with the dispatch we had hoped for. The porters who had arrived or who were about to arrive were not willing to stay for long, as the authorities were not in charge of feeding nor lodging them, so most of them returned home. After a largely wasted time, the ability, the patience, and the resolve of the sub-prefect were put to the test in order to obtain the right number of pack animals for the expedition (which came to three hundred and eighty)and to resume the march after four weeks. The expedition left in three divisions.

The first one left after ten days, led by Mr. Ijurra; the second one, after fifteen days, led by Dominico (it was supposed to be led by Mr. Lama, but he renounced his charge); and finally the third one, under Mr. de Schütz's command, will wind up leaving tomorrow. When you see how the departure has been planned, you might think that, after the previous disorganization, there would be a chance, however slim, for order to be restored. I do not believe it for a second, because I know the incompetence of our leaders. I feel that after the mess they created, demoralization has taken hold inside the expedition, with no chance of its disappearing, and with a real risk of its becoming more entrenched.

Disgusted by this disorder, and weary of complaints and recriminations I can do nothing about nor have no power to address, I have withdrawn my sympathy for the members of the expedition who have not had the courage to protest Mr. Ijurra's management—as they can and should do. Such protests could have avoided further turmoil which, due to the nature of the road, could again become serious. Eager to regain the freedom that I was starting to lose in this uncertain and disorderly march, I finally made the decision to separate from the expedition once and for all.

Upon arriving here, I learned that there were two roads to Loreto. One road, a good and easy one, which crosses four villages, provides all manner of resources to the voyager. There is also a bad, risky one which offers only tambos for accommodations and has no other resources. The first one embarks at Chasuta, the second at Balsapuerto. The leaders of the expedition chose the second route.

As soon as I arrived, I decided to take the first route and go through Chasuta, not so much as to seek the advantages of a better road but rather to remove myself from this chaos. I decided early on that I would travel this other route with a British gentleman, who also had a deep appreciation of natural sciences. However, I eventually changed my mind due to his propensity to drink and his lack of good faith, and I renounced his company. I later found another companion in Don José Ruiz, the naval architect who also expressed his desire to leave the expedition.

Since I am keeping my servant, and I invited my butterfly catcher to come with us, our caravan will be composed of us four plus the necessary eleven porters. The path will be very muddy, and while Don Ruiz wishes to ride his horse, we have procured three mules: one for him, one for me, and one for either my servant or Hauenstein, the butterfly catcher. We are still delayed by the poor cargadors, who are doing their best to arrive on time. I sincerely hope that we will be able to resume our march before the end of the week.

August 28th, 1853

This is my fourth Sunday in Moyobamba, which has been far too many. Therefore I will be delighted to bid farewell to this town tomorrow, where finding truth is as scarce as pigs are numerous. As far as the abundance of our bristle-snouted friends is concerned, the cities of the United States, famous for such "wealth," pale in comparison to Moyobamba.

There seems to be a linguistic link between the large quantity of pigs here and the natives who must feel some kind of sympathy towards them. Indeed, walk inside a house or a store and ask for anything, you will have the same answer twenty times: "*No hay*" (there is none); likewise, it seems to me that the grunt of the pig is composed of an endless chorus of no hays.

But I digress. I'd like to tell you about the preparations for my departure, as well the Moyobambans I had the opportunity to meet. My traveling plans have been modified in that following an argument that I had yesterday with Don Ruiz in which I was so correct that he apologized today, I let him know that we could no longer travel together. After our quarrel, he agreed with to go through Balsapuerto with Captain Soto, and I consequently find myself traveling through Chasuta alone. I am still accompanied by Auguste Jürgens, my servant, and by Robert Hauenstein, the butterfly catcher. I regret this change in plans since Don Ruiz and

I now get along well again, and since the cause of the argument was totally insignificant.

I leave with two mules, one for me and one for my servant, who will share it with Robert, plus two carrying horses and five cargadors. Having encountered many troubles and not one real friend, that is to say a companion in taste, ideas, and education within the expedition, I feel truly happy about the idea that I severed the chain that bound me to its chaos. I realize that I now have a fresh start that will allow me to travel freely and happily as I have done recently.

TAMBO DE ERA

August 29th, 1853

I want to report that I finally managed to leave the capital of Maynas, but before speaking of my departure and my first day of travel, I would like to keep my word and say something about the planning of my trip and the Moyobambans whom I met, adding a slight description of the house where I resided.

The planning of a trip is totally different in these countries than in civilized Europe. Indeed, in our countries, all you need is a chest with some linen and clothes, together with a well-lined purse in order to travel comfortably from one end of the continent to the other. There, your material needs can be satisfied in the smallest village as well as in the largest cities, if you give your money in exchange. In Peru, it is commonly the exact opposite, which means that you need a wardrobe that is very simple in quality but rather considerable in quantity, for lack of access to easy laundry. Also, the money can be light, compared to the distance that you are about to cover. Finally in these tambos (staging posts) you could very well starve to death while your pockets are full of gold, if you neglect to arm yourself with your fiambre, which is all that you need materially. Let us go over my *petaque*, or my supply box; first, a saw and some sort of a hatchet then, for food supplies, some smoked pork meat, rice, fat, coffee, chocolate, some *chancacas* (blocks of brown sugar), salt, brandy, and finally cornbread; then, in order to prepare all this, a little pot, a drip pan, and a coffee pot.

You can see that it is a whole culinary and domestic arsenal, which first needs a cook. That would be my loyal Auguste, whom I direct with talent. Then for transportation, I need a porter, who only costs me four francs for a four-day route. For other necessary luggage, I have my rifle, my tent, my bed, and a mosquito net. As a natural history amateur, I need a kit for collecting plants, and tin bottles into which I put reptiles and insects, and finally as an artist, my album.

Picture our caravan, composed of myself, my domestic, and the owner of our animals. All three of us mount mules—the first two bearing our rifles and game bags. Then there is Auguste, with an enormous tin box which he wears without complaint, and Robert Hauenstein walking sometimes (when my servant does not lend him his ride) with his rifle slung across the shoulder and the butter-fly net in his hand, plus two beasts of burden and five porters with their canteens.

Imagine that we are on a narrow path, crossing the immense, silent, and magnificent equatorial forests with their gigantic trees, and their long vines which fall from so high in the canopy that it makes it hard for the eye to follow them. Imagine countless orchids and their ferns, graciously shaped and majestic due to their tropical sizes. Imagine an impetuous torrent or a limpid river of distant origin, surrounded by beautiful vegetation. Imagine Indians, barely dressed, with a coppery complexion and fine supple limbs. Imagine the bright colors of the flowers, birds, and butterflies of this country, of the greenery of this vegetation which is as intense as it is grandiose. Arrive with us at a tambo, tie the mules to a long rope which allows them to graze, make a fire to prepare your meal, venture out to collect samples or draw, and you might have some idea of a caravan in the Amazon forest.

Returning to Moyobamba—that I left with equal intellectual and physical relief—I will tell you that Mr. Besséril from

Chachapoyas had given me a letter of recommendation for Mr. Alvarez de Bonfin, a Brazilian businessman, who recently settled in this town, and one for the priest, from Mr. Degola of Cajamarca The former, Mr. de Bonfin, known as the Bahianese, whom I liked immediately, invited me to join him at his table, which I did for some time. But he later used some expressions that were so offensive to me that I regretted having been recommended to him and to have enjoyed his hospitality, which I renounced for the duration of my stay. That is to say that we parted very coldly, without embracing in the least. As far as the priest is concerned, see above what I say about his colleagues, and add to that ignorance and avarice. This is a little severe, but nevertheless true, unfortunately.

As it often happens, the persons who were not recommended and whom I did meet quite by accident throughout my journey, were the ones that I liked best and who suited me the most. In all there were two; one was the sub-prefect, Mr. Ortiz who, thanks to his talents and his spirit of conciliation and firmness, was able to give this uncivilized country a push towards civilization and who furthermore appears to be in his man-to-man relationships a true "caballero," which is rare, especially in this country where there are so many people of little worth. The second person is Mr. Charles Charpentier, a Frenchman who served in the military and who is now in business. I will cherish excellent memories of him, because of the kindness and accommodating attitude of a compatriot which he did not cease to display towards me during my stay.

The first of these gentlemen offered me his table following the coolness between the Bahianese and me, which I accepted for my well-being and contentment. In Moyobamba, I occupied the priest's former apartment, which was part of the building where the expedition was quartered; I was fine there, since I had two well-lit, airy, and modestly furnished bedrooms. But besides this, I would have liked to occupy it by myself, because of the quality and quantity of my roommates; a colony of bats which enjoyed complete liberty since the fabric ceiling had holes everywhere and the windows were naturally without panes. There was an even more considerable quantity of cockroaches, a huge black insect, as innocent as it is disgusting, since it is not harmful and just goes to hide in all your effects and especially where it can find sugar, running over you with its long legs, should the night prevent it from finding its way.

TAMBO DE ROQUE

August 31st, 1853

Until now, our voyage has been very agreeable, and we have enjoyed very nice weather and a beautiful route. Our trip has taken us through forests, picturesque depending on their nature; and gigantic trees followed by palm trees, vines, ferns, or smaller trees that give each area a unique character. I am so far pleased with my muleteers and porters who do a good job, for the simple reason that they are happy with their boss. In getting to know these people better, I try to treat them well and use gentle persuasion, which is at the same time both humane and useful. Humane, because they do not think of abandoning me or my effects en route and useful because they always manage to arrive at the tambo the same time as I do.

As far as quality and location are concerned, the three tambos in Era, Talavera, and Roque look like all the other tambos that I have seen until now, which means that they are always located close to a stream or river which is necessary for watering the horses as well as for cooking. Being near the water, the tambos also find themselves near magnificent and rich vegetation that cast artful shadows. I am still satisfied with Auguste and Hauenstein. Both are helpful and obliging, which enhances the pleasantness of the voyage. During the last three days, nothing worth noting happened except that we collected a considerable quantity of charming butterflies as well as some interesting plants. On the other hand, hunting does not offer us the satisfaction we were expecting. The forests, so gorgeous and so large, are usually silent, especially during the hottest hours of the day, when the animals nap too. When this is the case, they still seem scarcely inhabited, and the silence becomes almost disconcerting. Yet people say the forests are home to deer, tigers, monkeys, wild turkeys, and countless other animals. But despite our desire to use our weapons, all we were able to see were two turkeys, which we could not shoot. We have been dying to eat roasted monkey but we do not see a single one; this will amount to a very sad September 1st.

Needless to say that on September 1st,[55] I thought a lot about my dear cousin Charles de Büren,[56] whose achievements I reflected upon a great deal, and whom I regretted not being able to join, since the distance between us forces us to hunt on very different grounds.

---

[55] *The first day of hunting season.*

[56] *He is referring here to his cousin* **Charles Jules de Büren** *(1808-1879), the Châtelain of Denens castle, near Morges, Switzerland.*

RIO DE SAN MIGUEL

September 3rd, 1853

During the trip from the Roque tambo to the Potrero tambo, my domestic, who has a bad habit of losing things, misplaced a small bag of mine containing my toiletries, which my good mother gave me when I left Europe. He also lost my bottle of alkali, a very useful ingredient in these countries, as well as various other objects I was also very fond of.

Upon our arrival at one o'clock at the tambo of Potrero, my domestic and Hauenstein, who had ridden the mule to the saddle of which said bag had been attached, went back to look for it, but without any luck. Since I really wanted to find those objects, the next morning I sent one of my porters with my servant who came back around noon without any more success; therefore, I had to add to the loss of those things the loss of a whole day spent at the tambo of Potrero which is neither fair nor comfortable.

Yet, since it was September 1st, and I insisted on hunting something, I used my time shooting four wood pigeons which became lunch the next day.

En route from the Roque tambo to the Potrero tambo, you sometimes have to cross or climb slopes covered with grass and pineapples but from which you have magnificent glimpses of the mountains and the valleys you have just crossed. Then, in the great valley, you find Lama and Tarapoto, both of which are stages of our trip. At last, we had reached some elevation.

The heat of the day was tempered by a slight breeze which cooled us down very nicely. The next day, upon arrival of my domestic and the peasant, we started our walk towards the first village we had to pass through on our route, in order to sleep that night in Tabaloso. This time the route was not taking us on any easy paths, but instead on two great descents and two great ascents on steep, rocky paths, interrupted in the middle by a rather difficult walk through the Potrero River. The Potrero turned out to be an impetuous torrent which slices through this road and which we would have to cross more than twelve times.

The difficulties of fording the river did not, however, prevent me from admiring the wild spectacle formed by immense overhanging rocks, with their artistic forms and even more magnificent tropical vegetation. Water churned foam atop huge stones, richly colored soil, and lush vegetation with huge trees and palms casting dramatic shadows. Every bend on our route displayed a new picture as beautiful as the last one.

Finally, after two or three hours of an especially tiring route we had to traverse on foot because of our mules' fatigue, we again enjoyed the pampa, a term that is quite improperly given to those gentle, intertwining paths which take you through immense forests as agreeably as the best paths of an English park would.

It was twelve noon when we arrived in Tabaloso, and since I was told I erred and therefore could not count on the hospitality of the governor or the priest (given that there was neither governor nor priest), I let the light of the *calvilde* (house of commerce) smoothly guide me, which the locals told me had been prepared in advance. Indeed, warned by my porters, the prosecutor (since there was no governor) had the worst one promptly made ready—a house without a fireplace. On the other hand, there was a considerable quantity of bananas for myself and my group.

I found the prosecutor a bit unnerved up by the arrival of a stranger, but I quickly comforted him speedily—by offering him one of my cigars, which he appreciated greatly. He then immediately provided me with some *mescado* and promised me some milk and eggs for the next day.

Mescado is a yucca-based drink made by Indian housewives which is allowed to ferment. Together with a wild turkey which I had shot during the trip, some bananas and chocolate borrowed from my petaque, we had a very respectable dinner which, followed by a good nights' sleep, provided complete rest from the fatigue of the day.

In Tabaloso, I was warned that I would not find the priest, Señor Beategui, upon arriving in Lamas, for whom I had a letter of recommendation, and this because he was supposed to arrive today and stay in Tabaloso for a month in order to participate in the Virgin Mary celebrations. Indeed, having departed this morning after taking my leave from the prosecutor and his servants (who all asked for cigars as I left), I did indeed meet the priest of the Lamas parish, who, having been told of my arrival, was waiting for me. He welcomed me very nicely and offered to spend the afternoon with me, which I did but did not have the occasion to enjoy his company. The meal had been accompanied by some extremely strong brandy and afterward, he and I needed to take a nap. The nap was later interrupted by some Indians celebrating at a neighboring church with a fife, a tambourine, and a shell used to simulate a trumpet.

Once the priest left his hammock, I found him in front of the house and chatted with him briefly, while he fed bananas to his mules and his horse, looking well-fed and flourishing from the priest's care and grooming. During dinner and afterward, a storm developed, accompanied by the unavoidable aguacerras (rain showers). I did not regret having accepted the hospitality of the priest and thought that, with his help, the following day after church I would find the peasants whom I would need to accompany me to Lamas, which is only three leagues away.

There is something peculiar that I observed. The Indians brought their dinner to the church for the priest, which mainly consisted of corn and bananas. Then, when the priest, who was tranquilly feeding his cattle at his doorstep, ran short of bananas, he simply shouted to one of the Indians who was standing by the church to bring him one of these bunches of bananas that was to be blessed at Sunday Mass.

The next day, he had us told that he would be waiting for us at Mass. This placed us in a rather awkward position since I neither could go nor cared to confess my faith in a country where one thinks that Luther and Calvin were atheists or even devils personified. In fact, all Protestants are considered far worse and more perverse than pagans and heretics. Knowing the intolerance of this country in this matter, I was convinced that whoever was known for being a Protestant would not get anything to eat or drink, nor find lodging and would simply be destined to die from deprivation and starvation.

I therefore simply had the priest told that I would not be able to go to church, and he, in return, had the good sense not to ask us any embarrassing questions, possibly because he did not want to receive a contrived response. Our muleteer, who behaved like a good Catholic, had to give him a piaster and a half, or seven francs. This is quite a lot of money, especially for this poor devil, who in Moyobamba already gives his piaster every Sunday, which is a significant sum in these countries.

As we were feeding the mule a day earlier, a little procession arrived, carrying the Virgin Mary's crown. Leading the procession were the violinist and the guitarist, making the usual din, and they were playing for a young Indian who was dancing while shaking a big necklace he was holding, which sounded like castanets. After church and lunch, we started our walk, the priest toward the village of Tabaloso, where he was going to celebrate the day of the Nativity; our group, toward Lamas where we were supposed to lodge. We arrived around three in the afternoon. While the Tabaloso prosecutor had been frightened upon our arrival, the governor of Lamas was napping and did not go to a lot of trouble to welcome us. We found the calvilde (house of commerce) available for us to use. When the governor finally decided to come see us, I made him understand that we were eager to have dinner, which brought us an invitation on his behalf.

The governor is quite a young man who looks like a nice fellow and seems to fulfill this sort of shepherd-dog position rather well, which is the duty of any official who governs Indians in these provinces. Lamas is a big village of between four and five thousand, mostly inhabited by Indians. Although surrounded by a beautiful area, this village is poor and completely deprived of any resources except for plátanos, yuccas, and straw hats.

Its aristocracy is composed of a few whites who do nothing but complain about the Cholos' laziness and, what's more, live almost as miserably as the Cholos do. Then there is the priest, the gobernador, and *basta* (enough), as the Lamistas say. A few members of this aristocracy accompanied us the next day for part of the trip. It is the habit in this country, one I think rather poorly executed, that you scarcely utter one word for the whole duration of journey together. This is somewhat excusable since the narrow, poor paths never allow you to ride next to each other, two of the irreparable qualities of any camino real (royal path) in these Spanish-American countries.

CHASUTA

September 10th, 1853

I am behind in my journal. Therefore I feel obliged to write to you about what Tarapoto and its locals are about and what my stay here has been like. Leaving Lamas, we were, as I said earlier, accompanied by a few members of its aristocracy, which allowed us to drink masato and chicha in the chacras which we encountered along the way. During this part of the trip I shot a very pretty vulture with a white body, black wings and a scarlet red head—very ornate with a beautiful yellow crest. I took it with me, planning to prepare it, but my plan was thwarted by some Indians from Tarapoto who, upon my arrival in that village, stole it from us while we weren't looking so they could keep the feathers.

The road to Lamas is delightful since it takes you through a smooth path and across one of these gorgeous forests I spoke about earlier. Upon our arrival, I headed straight to the priest to whom I was recommended by his brother, the priest of Moyobamba. As I was getting off my horse, his housekeeper told me that the priest had just ridden out to meet us, which meant that we had just missed each other. Indeed, as I recognized my effects, a dashing rider entered the presbytery's courtyard, whom I would have taken for a soldier rather than a priest, had not the housekeeper yelled Don Pablo! and had he not shown me his skullcap when he took his hat off.

After a somewhat premature embrace, we were invited to have some refreshment. During our exchange, I thought of Diogenes and his lantern[57] and was persuaded that this priest was as ignorant and intolerant as his Peruvian colleagues. It was Monday, and since we needed nine porters and three rides, the governor, whom I went to visit, told me that we could not realistically leave before Friday morning–which we actually did.

Being a little indisposed, I lost most of my time during my stay in Tarapoto, that is to say, I did not draw nor collect anything. On the other hand, I made two or three acquaintances, which I enjoyed, and attended a christening as well as a ball at the presbytery, which was also enjoyable. I made the acquaintance of Mr. Moret, his wife, and the governor. Mr. Moret is a native of the island of Majorca, and in my opinion, as far as I was able to learn about him, he must make the Peruvians ashamed, since he is as frank and active as they are dishonest and passive. His business takes place mostly on the Amazon and around Brazil, where he goes to buy goods that he sells here at a big profit.

His wife, who is from Ecuador, has a nice complexion and seems of fine character. They are the ones who, very obligingly, provided me with beans, brandy, coffee, and other items, as well as the canoe which will transport me from here to Yurimaguas.

Purificación Lopez, the governor, is an excellent man, an exception in this country, for the same reasons as Mr. Moret, but with more merit since he is a Peruvian. He is at the same time an elementary school teacher, a task he seems to fulfill with zeal and devotion. Mr. Moret told me that the jealous Tarapotians had tried by any means to prevent him from teaching, but that he had outsmarted them as soon as he realized this. The governor told me that he had not yet been paid for his teaching position, although he had

---

[57] *A reference to Diogenes of Sinope, a Greek philosopher who walked during the day with a lantern, saying he was looking for an honest man, only to find rascals and scoundrels.*

taught for two years. As far as the governor's position is concerned, there is no remuneration for it, as I said earlier. I was in fact visited by some other aristocrats from Tarapoto, but I do not want to waste any more paper speaking about them than I wanted to waste time visiting them.

I am therefore going to tell you somewhat about the christening and the ball. One was the consequence of the other. A Portuguese, who was holding a Tarapotian newborn over the baptismal font, had wanted to celebrate the event by throwing a ball and had asked the priest to give him his premises as well as his assistance. Some time before the baptism, the priest came to ask me if I wanted to attend, which I accepted, I have to admit, out of sheer curiosity. The two judges' assistants had all gathered to pay their respects, and I therefore joined them. I was also given a candle, which, like the others, went out as we left the house.

At the church, everyone was asking for "the creature," which is how you refer to youngsters here. At last he appeared, all made up. He was placed in the arms of his portly godfather after which we began our walk, preceded by a violin player and a guitar player who played something that resembled a litany. The ceremony was very prompt, and the priest seemed to have a great memory and gift for oration. We then went back to the presbytery, this time preceded by the musicians paying a local waltz.

Balls in Peru always feature the same fandango I spoke about earlier and I would not have enjoyed it much without Mr. Moret's vivacious dancing and the priest's terpsichorean efforts. Of course, we drank a rather reasonable quantity of brandy and fermented *guarapo* (sugar cane juice), and we smoked an enormous number of cigars and cigarettes. Then, on the following day, Friday, I took my leave of the priest, which I did without a single regret, since his hospitality had not been outstanding and he had me pay twice as much for the bag of rice that he procured for me. On the other hand, I shook Mr. Moret's and the governor's hands with far more pleasure and not a little regret,

I will not tell you much about Tarapoto itself, except that it is a big village of five to six thousand people, composed of houses and *huertas* (yards) similar to those in Moyobamba, and occupied by even lazier people, if that is possible. A contrast between these countries and ours resides in the fact that here, you have to beg, sometimes insistently, for one of these Indians to come work for you, while at home, it is the worker who comes to you, looking for employment. A few straw hats and some tocuyo[58] are manufactured in Tarapoto, but in such small quantities that you can only count one worker out of a hundred people. Its location is similar to Moyobamba's, since Tarapoto, just like Lamas, is located on some elevated terrain at the center of a beautiful wooded, fertile valley.

Before I left, I bought from the priest a roll of 160 ells or *vares* of tocuyo, since now the currency is going to change, which means that instead of a real, I will be giving a vare of tocuyo, or three needles, or three hooks. This is the actual currency of the country I am about to enter. In terms of other instruments of exchange, I had some pretty glass necklaces and bracelets, but the trouble is that the priest saw them while I was away and found them so much to his liking that he stole most of them, twenty or so, before my servant could prevent him from doing so. I am not going to forgive him as he did not say anything to me about it.

The road from Tarapoto to Chasuta is one of these roads that roll uphill and downhill, with mud, rocks, and tambos, not unlike other roads here. I will therefore not repeat myself and will simply tell you that our trip only took two days, including a night where

---

[58] *Calico*

Robert Hauenstein's mule, which was particularly skilled at sliding downhill, tossed him more than once to the ground.

Upon our arrival, we were very warmly welcomed by the local priest, whom I like because he seems to have a good, serious character that suits his vocation. He promises us that we will leave on Monday with Mr. Moret's canoe and six rowers, and in the meantime is willing to lodge us tomorrow. For a head of bananas (which is 100 bananas), I gave him three needles, and my rowers will cost me four vares of calico each for three days of travel.

September 11th, 1853

I spent the whole day, or at least a great part of it, preparing for my departure tomorrow. After a three-month horseback riding trip, I am going to undertake an equally long one in a canoe. I will let you know later which one is better. For forty needles and two pairs of pendant earrings, I bought the salted fish and bananas that will sustain us and our six rowers. Since the needle is worth a fish and since I received upon my arrival around two dozen as a gift, I am the owner for the time being of sixty fish and four bunches of bananas.

People here remind me of big spoiled children since when you want to pay them with fabric, they want *cuchillos* (knives) and when you have cuchillos, they want fabric. They all asked me for *cintas* (ribbons), probably because I did not have any. The priest obliged me a great deal with all my purchases and preparation, which was as agreeable as useful, since I would have had a lot of trouble dealing with all these Indians. They do not know a single word of Spanish and I do not know any of their Quechua[59] language, which does not sound at all like anything I have heard until now. Yet it will resonate

---

[59] *A Native South American language family spoken primarily in the Andes*

in my ears with all its different dialects during a part of my travel on the Amazon.

Yesterday I already went to inspect the canoe that we will entrust with our fate. It is large, in good condition, and built just like all its fellow canoes—from a single tree trunk that people call here a *cedro*.

BETWEEN LAGUNAS AND NAUTA

September 19th, 1853

Infidelity is in all forms an ugly sin even in the smallest things of life—towards your journal for instance. One that is only pardonable through a sustained effort of recollection and writing. However, one must forgive the voyager more easily than the office man, since the latter can arrange his hours, his time, and his work like music paper, while it is not the same for the voyager in general, and certainly not for the voyager to the Amazon in particular.

If for example, you saw how crouched and hunched over I was writing in my canoe, you would certainly tell me that sometimes you need to sacrifice comfort, and exhibit sincere devotion to your journal, especially when one is surrounded by a cloud of mosquitoes that sing you a very different kind of song.

In Chasuta we danced all day Sunday and long into the night. When it came time on Monday morning to find my six rowers, it was a chore so difficult, I probably could not have found them until Tuesday without the priest's intervention. He was kind enough to lend me both his temporal and spiritual powers so I could finally leave at ten o'clock in the morning, only leaving behind one drunken rower, as well as my gratitude toward the priest.

In my canoe, which was very large compared to most canoes in this country, I had a small tent, very artistically made, thanks to this country's magnificent palm tree leaves. They are so uniform that the leaves can be woven together well and strongly, which produces a roof that defies the most torrential rain showers that you encounter daily in these tropical regions. Furthermore, I had all my effects and supplies in my canoe, plus my two companions, my servant, and his friend Hauenstein.

Once our canoe entered the current, we moved quickly, borne by the waters of the Huallaga which treated us beautifully for the whole week. The conditions allowed us to easily pass through the river's difficult stretches which we encountered on the first day. The banks are most beautiful at the highest part of the river's journey, as the river is still running in the foothills of the Cordilleras. As we moved downstream, this variety of mountainous and rocky landscapes disappeared, only to be replaced by this visual monotonous landscape that will accompany us non-stop through the hundreds of leagues that we have to navigate on the Amazon, banks that I am planning on describing later.

We spent the first night on land. We camped at a sandy beach on a small island that offered a great deal of hospitality during the first part of the night, thanks to the superb moonlight and an abundance of dry wood that enabled us to prepare our dinner. During the second part of the night, and all of the next morning, we experienced a constant deluge that forced us to take shelter under our canoe's tent and then to empty it of all the water it had received, in addition to the water that came on board the day prior.

Subsequent to our departure we were warned of a dangerous location on the river, but the danger seemed so small or at least not apparent that we were still waiting for it when we had already passed it long before. It was a whirlpool that we traversed very easily, thanks to our rowers' skills, without any damage other than two or three waves that swept into our canoe. The following day, after an evening that allowed us to dry off completely, we spent the night in our canoe that we abandoned to the current, like you usually do on such rivers, one of the rowers making sure that the current would not steer us against one of the many tree trunks these rivers are strewn with.

The Huallaga, although a simple and less important tributary of the Amazon, would be considered an imposing river in our countries, since it is at least as wide as the Rhine or the Danube. Having left on Monday, we arrived in Yurimaguas on Wednesday night, where I was supposed to change canoes and personnel and present a letter to the priest to whom I had been recommended. As it turned out, the canoes had been taken away by a previous expedition that was traveling down the Cachyaco. I therefore had to keep the same canoe and would have happily kept my rowers on as well, but neither my good treatment nor the priest's eloquence could persuade them to stay on. They preferred to wait for the canoe to come back from Lagunas than to earn the two ells of fabric that I wanted to give to each of them and that I later gave to each of the six Yurimaguian rowers.

The priest in Yurimaguas is regarded as one of the best. It is true that I found him more honest than I generally found any of his colleagues. He also was very accommodating regarding the preparation for my departure, but less so as far as hospitality was concerned. He neither invited me to dine nor to stay with him, although I was very disposed to accept both invitations. I left him therefore on the one hand grateful, on the other hand aware that he had me sleep under the stars in a tambo, attacked by all the mosquitoes of the shore.

Until now, this plague of these beautiful countries has rarely shown up. If so, the mosquitoes have only been in small contingents, but from now on it will be different. That is because we are leaving the mountains to enter the plains where winds and air streams are more rare, or for some other reason. This means we are going to be assailed from now on by swarms of those damned creatures—especially between Yurimaguas and Lagunas, for three days and for three nights, since in these countries, you always travel at night, whenever possible. I will tell you why later on.

In Europe, people have a terrible idea of the dangers that assail the voyager in these regions; they think mainly about the savages, the tigers, the snakes, and crocodiles. All of this is nothing, absolutely nothing, compared to the little insect that is called the mosquito, although it often differs in shape and aggressiveness. The mosquito can be found in more or less scattered swarms, day or night, on land or on water, and even in hammocks. Nothing can protect you from him. Nothing is sacred. He is relentless, and bites the voyager who wears three layers of clothing as painfully as he bites those who are half dressed due to the immense heat.

When the mosquito bites, he truly attacks your arms and legs, annihilating all the intentions of the voyager, either intellectual or material. You cannot draw nor collect, nor go for a walk pleasantly nor usefully, nor eat, sleep, nor can you barely bathe. As soon as you set foot on the sandy banks of those great rivers intending to prepare a frugal meal, mosquitoes surround you from all sides, not giving you a moment of peace nor rest to the cook and even less to those who would like to enjoy their food. Finally you find yourselves jumping and dancing, shaking your handkerchief, and smoking like a train engine.

You find yourself having to make do with breathing in and observing, then quickly transporting your modest, half-cooked meal to the canal, yelling *vamos* (let's go) to your rowers in order to quickly reach the center of the river where the torments caused by those creatures lose a great part of their intensity. Then, with some of your anguish having gone away, you can have your meal, although this is usually by necessity more than because of your appetite. If you are curious to know what my two morning and evening meals are composed of, I will tell you that until today, bananas are the base of them (since bread is totally gone) along with a few chicken and turtle eggs and coffee.

Finally when the mosquitoes allow, we quickly boil some of the chickens that we brought with us. I would rather go without eating than sleeping in the long term, but here you do not have a choice, you have to go without either one.

If you sleep in the canoe, however, you suffer less and sleep generally a little more than you would in your tent. Although you have your mosquito net with you at all times, you will however rarely use it effectively enough to prevent the mosquitoes that look for even the narrowest opening. This will allow them to invade your tent, wake you up and put you in real despair through their bites and their song that resonates in your ears in the most irritating way.

Finally, the mosquitoes leave you in the position of a weaponless combatant facing thousands of pitiless enemies until you see the day rise and you get up so you can be assailed by an even larger number, once you are out of your net.

Now that I am already a little more used to this kind of torture, I resumed writing in my journal. While slapping my hands, my cheeks, and my forehead once in a while, I will hopefully manage to sum up what happened, whether interesting or not, since our leaving Yurimaguas until today as we sail between Nauta and Loreto.

Before I switch subjects, I still want to mention the social relationships that exist between Indians and mosquitoes. Is it habit or apathy? I think a little of both. The Indian, as bitten as can be, still remains half-naked, barely moving that towel or the jacket he holds in his hand, eating well, sleeping even better and bathing always, in short, totally ignoring mosquitoes. You have to wonder if it is because of a difference in blood or skin, or because of their love of novelty or out of national sympathy that mosquitoes respect the Indians considerably more than whites whom they always bite, especially on their feet and hands.

BETWEEN NAUTA AND LORETO

September 24th, 1853

Our hunt today was not successful. My servant, who is quite clumsy, broke the stick for my rifle and lost all the equipment that I use to remove the filth caused by that poor quality American powder that I bought in Lima. On top of that, the banks of these rivers carry little game. Once in a great while, you may see a heron or a duck. However, we arrived in Lagunas having skinned a heron, a kingfisher, and a grand falcon, all of which I shot in a row. The following day, Hauenstein shot a wild turkey, which was enough for an evening meal of good soup and a passable roast. We arrived midday at the little bridge of Lagunas, and I went at once to the village, half an hour away, leaving Auguste and Hauenstein in charge of the canoe. I did not find the priest for whom I had a letter of recommendation and I was happy for that, since it appears that he is insignificant. However, I was wise to visit the governor with whom I made a fine acquaintance and who provided me very obligingly and without hesitation everything that I needed; a canoe, rowers, salted fish, bananas, chicken, and other items — all paid for with needles, hooks and calico. After having spent a mosquito-filled night, and with my supplies in order, I was able to leave the next morning for Nauta on a voyage that supposed to last four days and three nights, which it indeed did.

The governor, whose name is Don Lorenço, is a young man, but despite his youth, he rules his large village of Lagunas with great skill. It consists of three hundred households, many wicked people among them, but he successfully governs them all. Until now, this village has not strictly speaking had a governor and has only obeyed auracas who are similar, as far as their authority and power are concerned, to those whom the Indians (who are still in a savage state) choose for life.

I was very eager to see the little village of Chamicuros, six leagues away, where on the river's bank they produce a rather large quantity of elastic gum. But the news I received in Yurimaguas about a steamship that was supposed to have arrived in Loreto or Nauta, plus the strength that the mosquitoes had taken from me, forced me to renounce my excursion. I very much regretted not going, not knowing whether I would have a future opportunity to visit such an interesting plant.

We continued our route on Sunday morning after shaking the governor's hand most cordially, and left Lagunas without seeing anything of interest there. The houses, which are quite large, are all built with *caña brava* (wild sugar cane), but still look quite poor. The natives, all fishermen, subsist on fish just like all the inhabitants of the river banks. In addition they only grow the bare minimum which means that they have a small chacra that provides them with plantains, yuccas, and nothing more.

The Lagunas race is tall and strong; the people have large features and high cheekbones. Most of them paint themselves with red and blue lines, going from their ears to the corner of their lips or eyes. Their clothing is very simple. For the women, it is a piece of blue or brown fabric that they tighten around their waist and which hangs to mid-leg, along with a sort of mantilla made of the same fabric, that they wear around their neck in which they place their small children that they carry on their back. They weave their hair in numerous small braids that sometimes tie together on the top of their head.

As for the men, they have a sort of short shirt, and trousers, also in blue or brown fabric and for a third piece of clothing, a loosely woven straw hat. When they go fishing, they carry a lot of equipment with them. First their oar, which is very short and shaped like our cake platters; then harpoons, laced with *barbasco* or *guaca* to poison the fish; a long blowpipe with its quiver full of small arrows; a calabash which is a piece of fine, silky cotton material that surrounds the arrow's extremity so it slides better inside the blowpipe. Those arrows are poisonous so the animal that is stung dies after a minute or two, depending on its size.

Imagine these very long canoes made of a single trunk, with one, two or three rowers who sit at the bow and stir the water more than they row. In the back or the stern the pupero steers, also with an oar. Between them a few bananas and yuccas or their catch are all covered with large palm tree leaves. Have the canoe move briskly or let it quietly follow the current of the river and you might have an idea of the crafts of these countries and of the lives of their natives who spend more time on the river than in their shacks.

It is still the Huallaga, but four leagues after Lagunas, we are leaving it to enter the great Amazon River, the king of all rivers in the world. The night had just fallen and the moon had just risen when we bid farewell to the Huallaga, and started to sail on the Amazon which, although six hundred leagues from its mouth, is already so powerful that human intelligence has a hard time believing that its power can increase ever more. The banks are still flat and planted with these immense, magnificent forests that decorate them during its entire gigantic course. Sometimes you find graceful palm trees, sometimes enormous trees of other species which seem to cover all the trees they dominate with a protective shade. Further away, old and young trees are so covered by climbing vines and plants that they form either immense walls, or high towers. Due to their fantastic forms, they are great colossi of vegetation, one more bizarre than the other. As we are surrounded by plains, the sky is limitless and dotted with immense floating clouds that speak to you from time to time through thunder and lightning, a display as imposing as the rest of the nature that envelops you here.

I say immense, always immense, because in this environment, everything bears the sign of grandeur. The following morning, we stopped in Urarina, a small village with around twenty houses. Right now, it is almost uninhabited since the natives had to help the expedition which is about a week ahead of us. The following night, we stopped in Parinari in order to buy eight bunches of bananas, which I procured but not without difficulty. When the expedition stopped here, they took everything that was available, and further down the river, from Nauta on there has been a sudden rise in the water level, which has caused such damage to its banks that all the chacras have been flooded and have lost their caches of bananas and yuccas.

After half an hour, I was able to get the bananas we needed, as well as a letter of recommendation for the governor of Nauta. I left around ten o'clock at night so I could avoid, at least in part, the thousands of mosquitoes who assailed us on board. Finally, the next evening, which was Wednesday, we arrived in Nauta where we again had to change canoes and rowers. Since it was already eleven o'clock at night, I did not want to bother the governor and I tried to sleep in my canoe, but this turned out to be impossible. The mosquitoes would not leave me alone, stern or bow made no difference. I climbed the staircase that leads to the village and tried to settle under the church porch. Impossible! They are relentless. Finally, as a last resort, I woke up my servant, who sleeps better since his skin is tougher, and with his help, pitched my mosquito net on the bank, and this time, I enjoyed a two- or three-hour sleep.

The next morning, I awoke and went to see the governor. He is old which displeases me, not because I do not respect old age, but rather because I have noticed that all along my voyage, I have been as well assisted by younger governors as I have been poorly served by old ones. Indeed, upon my first request I was treated to a familiar refrain of no hay (there is none). There were no canoes, no people, no salted fish, no bananas, and no eggs. What were we to do?

Over lunch with the Nauta and Lagunas priests I changed the tenor of the conversation by speaking on many subjects and topics, the expedition chiefly among them. I mentioned the warm welcome and the effective help that I had received from priests and governors along our route. This seemed to have won them over. We were still at the table when the governor promised me a canoe, people, fish, and eggs — everything we were in need of except bananas. As a result we were able to leave anew at two o'clock.

As I told you, I met the Lagunas' priest in Nauta, whom I had been lucky enough not to meet in his town. It was actually a blessing, since he is the least agreeable priest one can lay eyes on: no dignity, very presumptuous, and much more inclined to the commerce and the profession of tailor than my servant is. Seeing him cut a pair of trousers, I thought he was one of them and was about to make a fool of myself when I recognized his tonsure.

September 26th, 1853

The priest's tonsure was painted in black or dark blue with a substance that is widely used in this country, supposedly to protect oneself against mosquitoes. A dressed man covers his hands and face with this paint, while Indians of both sexes, who are less covered, are so covered by that blue paint that I first thought that it was the result of their working with color dye. Deeply upset by the torments imposed by the mosquitoes, I was going to cover my hands with this blue product when the governor of Parinari told me all this was *mentiras*, or lies.

Some distance from Nauta, our old canoe started to leak. But after two repairs, we made it waterproof so that now the Amazon just flows around the boat and prevents us from the ongoing worries we have been facing from the start. Close to Nauta, the Marañón welcomes a new, powerful tributary, the Ucayali. It will make the river more imposing and widen its banks even more, banks that still remain flat and densely wooded. We made our next stop at Iquitos after a journey of two days and nights. I would like to find a better canoe and renew my supply of bananas, but in exchange for my canoe, they wanted to give me an old raft that was unacceptable. They didn't want to give me even the smallest bunch of bananas in exchange for my needles and fishhooks. What to do? We embarked with confidence, and hope there are enough supplies to sustain us until Loreto, and without too many mosquitoes. In Iquitos, I heard some sad news: a raft from the first class of the expedition, commanded, not by Ijurra, but actually by Dominico, had an accident and one of the emigrants drowned. No one could give me any more details.

In all of these villages along the river, I am told that the first division is angry at Ijurra, who always walks half a day ahead, for fear of being reached and mistreated. The second division, commanded by Mr. de Schütz, is on time and he is generally praised for it. We arrive tomorrow in Loreto where I will be able to give you more news about the troubles and the goings-on within the expedition. A light wind from the east left behind by the storm and the night is rocking our canoe to the point where writing is difficult, so I leave my journal for now.

LORETO

October 3rd, 1853

Undoubtedly, if my present voyage on water zigzags, my journal does the same, mainly jerkily, since it is only now once a week that I write. Material and intellectual obstacles, laziness, forgetfulness, lack of comfort—everything is at fault.

From Iquitos on, we only stopped to prepare light meals on shore—always with or despite the mosquitoes. However, we also passed by the villages of Pucallpa, Chorococha, Pebas, Corhigunas, Maucamacta, Peruata, Commecheros, Moronorate, before arriving in Caballococha, where I must find new rowers and where we will find most of the emigrants.

I believe that it was in Pucalpa that one evening we found shelter against a terrible *borbonade* (storm) that came at us from the east. Since we had already gone through a few such storms which had not looked too formidable, I told the rowers that traveling toward Pucalpa was unnecessary and that we could face the borbonade. They did not listen and only responded with some vigorous rowing which soon took us to the Pucalpa harbor that one could only see through the lightning, since the night was so pitch black.

I think they had every reason to row, since as soon as we moored our canoe a furious hurricane arrived, complete with considerable thunder and lightning. The rest of the borbonade—torrential rain, thunder and lightning that crisscrossed and cut across the sky in all directions—tore apart huge clouds with dazzling strikes of lightning that illuminated their gigantic forms even better. Although we had found shelter and were moored, our canoe was dancing like a spinning top, whipped by that wind that only lasted twenty to thirty minutes. All my rowers ran away to take refuge in a tambo which, like the village, was located on a hill. My servant did just the same. Since I did not want my canoe and all my effects to be torn apart, I stayed in the canoe as did Hauenstein. Through the opening of my tent, I admired the sky, the water, and those river banks that were merging in one fire that only died down to dazzle us again even more a few seconds later. It was not only one storm, but three that advanced together, seemingly in competition for who had the strongest winds, loudest thunder, brightest lightning, and wettest downpours. It was all so beautiful, the setting so grandiose that I cannot begin to adequately describe it.

Finally, after our canoe had been tossed about by a second gust of wind even more furious than the first one, and after we had emptied it from the showers that filled the canoe halfway, I made my rowers, who were busy installing their mosquito nets in the tambo, understand that I wished to take advantage of the coolness that had followed the storm and set sail again. Thus I hoped to escape the thousands of mosquitoes that would come to assail me after the storm and against which I could not defend myself.

The Indians, led with kindness and firmness, are obedient and therefore, an instant later, they were hitting the waters with their oars, like dignified sons of the great river. To this fast-paced noise they added the sounds of their songs and their melancholic cries which, I think, are in perfect harmony with the solitude of this great river and the thousands of noises you can hear at night in the Amazon forest.

During the day it is indeed quite extraordinary that you see so few animals on the river banks or in the trees, and very seldom do you hear a call or a song announcing one of the animals. At night, however, the calls, hoots, and songs are never ending. One hears the sounds of tigers, snakes, frogs, tortoises, and the great Amazon otters jumping in the water or playing on the beach. The sounds of noisy snoring abound from river dolphins that come noisily to breathe at the surface, as well as the gushing of the water made by thousands of fish hunting each other or wanting to enjoy some of the coolness that the night brings to the air. The singing of countless birds is everywhere; turkeys, toucans, trumpeters, and many more. Some of them have very melodious voices, despite what some voyagers say, who pretend that animals merely call and do not sing in these countries.

Add to these sounds the beautiful moonlight that draws a long channel of fire on the surface of an expansive river, so calm and mirror-like. Imagine the gracious and strange shadows of palms and giant trees with their own crowning vegetation. See those walls and compact towers that the climbing plants form on the river banks, let the vines suspend themselves, and form long teardrops. Picture the reflection of the moon and imagine how artfully it casts shadows on the supple and coppery limbs of our rowers, and you will almost climb aboard our canoe and have an idea of what a nocturnal voyage on the Amazon is like.

October 4th, 1853

———————————————————

Caballococha is not directly located on the bank of the Amazon. In order to reach it, you have to turn down a little river that joins the Amazon and which is the connection that Nature established between the Amazon, and a small lake which is located about one league inland. As soon as we arrived at the small river, the rowers happily beat the water in time to the national fandango, and half an hour later we had reached the harbor of Caballococha.

There, we found all of the expedition rafts, which led me to correctly presume that the emigrants had landed. Since Caballococha is just four leagues away from Loreto, it is if not the titular, at least the primary location of the expedition, primarily because the land is favorable to agriculture. Indeed, after waking up in my tent that I had installed on the beach, I rejoined with my old traveling companions in second class, the first class having directly headed for Loreto, which houses the general governor of the province.

Some of them came to shake my hand, but after reflection and given my experience, I felt that the Germans had fallen in esteem, while I became attached to the few Frenchmen who were part of the expedition and among whom I mention Messrs. Fialon and Dubordieux for the friendship and the respect they showed me. As far as the Germans were concerned, I ended up realizing that their intentions came more from their will to use my wallet, that they supposed was full enough, rather than from my favorable opinions of them. Thus, my domestic Auguste Jürgens, whom I paid the day after my arrival for his service of more than three and a half months, during most of which I had never ceased to treat him with affection, instead of being happy and thanking me for the four piasters (two hundred francs) that I gave him, demanded about twice as much. His behavior towards me took an ugly turn when I refused. He then made accusations that were as absurd as they were untrue, most notably that I had fed him poorly, while in fact, I had always tried to share my meals with him during the various stages of our trip.

I will not say that this ungratefulness, which wounded me, surprised me a great deal. During our trip from Moyobamba to Caballococha, looking at Auguste with fresh eyes, I had learned more about him, as well as his friend Hauenstein. I discovered that my domestic Auguste Jürgens had been implicated in the premeditated murder of General Willisen[60], and that Hauenstein, a former companion of Robert Blum's, had also fled for some wrongdoing. These are not uncommon among the emigrants to the New World and to Loreto in particular, since according to those two, there was at least one rascal for every ten emigrants.

Mr. Fialon is a jeweler, and since he did not have great financial capital, he had not succeeded in Lima where all of his colleagues had. Therefore, since he likes to travel, he decided to come to these parts to see if he could at the same time pan for gold. But he was mistaken, since unless you go to perilous lands belonging to tributaries, there is nothing else for you to do in these countries. I am sad for him because he is a good man, and who deserves more than bananas and mosquitoes. Mr. Dubordieux, who could be his son, does not seem to me like he is cut out to be a farmer, but since he is still young he has more opportunities and time to correct any misstep.

The day after my arrival, as I was about to fall asleep in my tent, I heard the arrival of two gariteas (sort of rowboats) with Mr. Ortiz, the general governor, Mr. de Schütz and two officers onboard. In the morning, I went to pay a visit to the general governor, the Colonel Don Francisco Alvarado Ortiz, who welcomed me very warmly, and with whom I was always on good terms. In my opinion, it is either Providence, or the inhabitants and emigrants who venture here, that under a military administration, you can often find a man who is loyal, of good character, and seeks to develop the material and intellectual interests of the province as well as to destroy the abuses and the nonchalance that the trafficking of the Portuguese and the priests brought over.

---

[60] *I believe this to be a reference to **General Karl Wilhelm von Willisen**, Supreme Commander of the forces of the German Confederation. Most of the men who were on the expedition were former military men and if the story is accurate, Jürgens may have been motivated by the defeat of the Schleswig-Holstein troops under the command of von Willisen at the hands of Denmark during the Battle of Isted in 1850. The defeat was highly demoralizing and effectively broke the back of the Schleswig-Holstein army.*

Furthermore, the general governor is a practical man, both in his observations and his measures, which is essential to leading this development in the right direction. He loves, knows, and has practiced agriculture for many years. Finally, he understands the Indians, and governs them with justice and benevolence, while trying hard to provide the activity and install the ambition that they still lack. I let him know that any industrious, moral man who settles in his province will always find him a friend and a good adviser.

After we had lunch, the governor general convened all the emigrants and told them that since they had arrived at their final destination, they would be given land and the necessary tools. He would not force anyone to stay, and those who would like to register in order to receive land would be supported until the harvest six months hence. Those who wanted to leave would only be supported for one month. To this, Dominico responded, in the name of all, that the emigrants would not deal with this matter until Ijurra, who was in hiding, showed up. They reproached Ijurra for not upholding the promises the government had made, as well as all fostering a culture of lies and exaggerations.

A brief debate followed, during which the governor did his best to make them understand that these matters did not concern him, and that the only purpose of the gathering was to provide land. If any emigrants had any claims, he said, they would have to address them to the government. The emigrants bowed to logic and firmness, and fifty of them registered to receive the twenty fanegas (twenty-five acres) of land that the government promised to each of them, a surface that is approximately a hundred and eighty to two hundred of our pauses.

Such a first encounter, which should have established good relations between the governor and the emigrants, was neither friendly nor favorable, especially for the Germans who acted foolishly. Therefore the governor did not have a problem the following day leaving his young colony, and neither did I. I followed him to Loreto, where I enjoyed simple, kind hospitality, waiting for the right moment to present itself that would allow me to continue my voyage.

Caballococha is, without a doubt, a much more proper location for an agricultural colony than Loreto. The soil is rich and its forests are spread across a very flat, yet somewhat elevated ground, which is important in an area where the water rise is so powerful that it often submerges most of the forests that border the banks. Moreover, in Caballo, the lake is full of fish and surrounded by a good deal of game.

In Loreto, which is subjected to daily rain showers, the terrain is also somewhat elevated, but it is uneven and the soil is partially swampy and rich in clay. It is said that within two leagues or less inland, the ground is more level and favorable to agriculture, but I am only speaking about what I saw.

The town of Caballo is composed of around forty to fifty houses, while Loreto has twenty at the most. These are sad houses, most of them built of caña brava, sometimes adobe, always with thatch roofs. But the area is so rich in fish, tortoises, wood, resins, rubber, honey, among others, that should colonization increase, one can expect that in half a century, voyagers will find a large city where today there is only a poor hamlet.

ABOARD THE MARAJO

October 22nd, 1853

I was continuing to enjoy the quiet and rather monotonous hospitality of Loreto, marked by a few hikes in the neighboring forests, without much success either in hunting or in botany, when, all of a sudden, during the night of October 5th, at one o'clock in the morning, I was awakened by people shouting repeatedly, *el vapor!* or the steamboat had arrived.

The uproar was indeed legitimate, since it was the first steamboat to have sailed the Amazon this far upstream. Until that day, the steamboats were content to limit their itinerary to Barra do Rio Negro,[61] and despite or because of the agreement that had been signed with Brazil, nobody had been waiting for them, since the first run should have taken place in May.

Everybody in Loreto jumped out of their mosquito nets, people started shouting, and church bells were rung. The colonel gave orders that he kept repeating with an ever rising pitch, his commands basically falling on deaf ears, due to the darkness.

The civilized population of the hamlet came out of sheer curiosity to persuade themselves of the reality of something that had become a myth; the natives, meanwhile, were running around with fervent emotion and surprise, reinforced by the suddenness of their awakening, to see what the steamboats were all about. Their

---

[61] *Manaus*

imagination and the rumors had told them for so long that there was no doubt about their existence, but they never allowed themselves to know exactly what they really looked like.

Most of the Indians were flabbergasted. The noise that the steamboat made upon its arrival had already scared them, so when they heard the shriek of steam being released, most of them fled to the forest, I was told.

But you have to give them credit, because the next day, and in subsequent days, they grew familiar with this giant of our times. However, it seemed to me, and I understand this perfectly, that the proud, independent hearts of these children of the river must have bled a little after seeing the boat that would compete and fight with the oar and the canoe that had given them supremacy on the great Amazon until now.

Knowing steamboats well already, I contented myself to only gaze at its silhouette. I made some anthropological observations and reflections, and soon went back to bed, very happy in the knowledge that I would be leaving Loreto shortly and starting my return voyage to Europe by fast and reassuring means.

The next day, a great exchange of civilities took place between the local authority, the governor and his subordinates, and the authorities on board, including the agent, the captain, and the other officers of the steamboat Marajo.

The passengers also came to pay a visit to the governor. There were not a lot of them, actually, only three: Messrs. Carey, a couple of Frenchmen and Mr. *(left blank)*, a Pole, and an engineer major in the Brazilian army.

I am very happy about this circumstance, since I really had the great pleasure of making the acquaintance of the Careys, who are as amicable as they are learned. Meeting them provoked conversations that are unfortunately very rare in these countries. Upon reflection, I realized that I had been deprived of such happiness and pleasure for a long time, and had fallen in some sort of intellectual torpor that felt like a weight that I could not find the strength to vanquish.

I also valued my good luck in meeting these men in the middle of this great continent, on the banks of a river that was barely known before now, on the first steamship that came up river almost six hundred leagues from its mouth. These two men are almost my countrymen, and at the same time they are more than my countrymen. Not only were we from all over Europe, but we also spoke the same language, and shared a commonality of experiences, including having visited the same countries for the most part.

The boat was supposed to go up the river for another eighty leagues, up to Nauta. The colonel wished to go there and was able to take three persons with him. I graciously accepted his invitation to accompany him, since it gave me the opportunity to get better acquainted with the Careys, whom I only just met, since the steamship left the day after its arrival at ten o'clock in the morning.

The boat had taken fourteen days to venture from Barra do Rio Negro to Loreto. From here to Nauta, it took us another seven days. I had settled in on board with good will towards all. It was truly a charming trip, particularly with my two quasi-countrymen, in spite of the mosquitoes and my memories of Nauta where I was refused lodging.

During those seven days, and the two we spent in Nauta, we spoke about travel, business, colonization, and shipping. We also spoke a lot about our good old Europe, which only fellow countrymen can authoritatively speak of and make comparisons about. Finally, these gentlemen, who were just leaving the countries that I am visiting and will visit, gave me a great deal of information and recommendations which can only be invaluable to me.

October 24th, 1853

So I left these European gentlemen in Nauta, after having spent many excellent moments with them—conversing, lingering about, and visiting the city's most famous citizens. This was not too difficult, since there were only one or two local traders who, at least, had the good sense to have decent, room-sized hammocks in which you can relax completely, without missing any of their conversation, simply because there is nothing to be missed.

On the first night, a fight broke out between the colonel and a Portuguese trader over the Indians, or to be more precise, over the way to encourage them to become more active and industrious. After what I said earlier, you will easily understand that the colonel was speaking in their favor. He was angered by the way they are compensated for their work, and the manner in which they are exploited by traders who sell them a used hatchet for three piasters, when it is only worth half a piaster, or giving it to them in exchange for twenty-five pounds of sarsaparilla, which is roughly six months of work.

It is clear that with people who work half the year in order to get a hatchet—their only agricultural tool—and the other half of the year in order to get the necessary fabric to dress themselves, the benefits of work cannot go beyond basic needs. Yet it is an axiom that the level of civilization increases in direct proportion to the needs of the people. Of course, I am excluding from the definition of the word "needs" the speculative demands of life that exist in a people in which civilization leads to laziness.

The Portuguese claim the Indians possess an inborn apathy, the colonel alleges they abuse people due to their ignorance and situation. As far as I am concerned, the first one was somewhat correct, and the second one completely so.

Later on, I had a discussion with the Polish major, who argued that forcing the Indians to take real money would be an excellent way to make him civilized. I maintained that payments in an ell of fabric–the equivalent of a silver real—and the exchange system in general met the needs of the province and the spirit of its natives today. However I admitted that with the progress of civilization, money will triumph over calico when the number of items to trade goes up; consequently, needs will drive trade; it was only a matter of time. It goes without saying, but I hammered my counterpart in our discussion who sometimes managed to do the same.

Finally, Monday, the day of departure, arrived. Messrs. Carey and I shook hands cordially and I was naturally unhappy that they were not accompanying me down the river and that they were indecisive about the route they were going to take. Aware of the fatigue resulting from the trip that I had just made, I did not advise them to head for Lima, even less for Moyobamba. The colonel offered to appoint a detachment to join them, and I suggested that if I were in their place, I would accept his offer and travel up the unknown portions of Marañón River to its source.

This might have seemed a little pretentious on my part, since these gentlemen do not need my advice and know much better than I what they have to do, but I simply told them what I would have done, had I been in their position.

The trip took us seven days going up the river only took two days coming down. The colonel, his secretary Mr. Lamas, and his chief warrant officer, Mr. Bocanegra, were also going back to Loreto, so I was not feeling totally abandoned, despite having lost the Careys.

I had several interesting conversations with the colonel. We talked about the need to establish a route that would traverse the entire country and link the Pacific Coast to the river traffic of these lands. I told him about our St. Claude road engineers and about the advantages such a route would bring Peru. Should the government decide to invite a group of them to Peru, it would be useful—not solely for building roads but also for teaching Peruvians what it takes to build a good road. The colonel believes that the best route would be one that goes across Pasco linking the Ucayali to the Huallaga.

We also spoke about education, that is to say, the imperfection that currently exists in the country's schools and that without providing assistance, a deplorable and ignorant race of disadvantaged men would emerge. We also spoke about the need for proper primary books, and that either due to scarcity, or the lack of will among the priests, such books do not yet exist. Indeed, the children only have a small catechism book to read from, which is acceptable but not enough to give them a true appreciation for reading.

Furthermore, the children should have paper and writing templates, since it is almost impossible to learn how to write while scratching a banana leaf with a piece of wood and copying handwritten models that are, for the most part, nothing more than calligraphy.

We also spoke about the need for priests to have fixed salaries that would be paid directly by the state. This would temper their commercial zeal. The colonel told me that he has sent motions to the government, regarding the schools and the priests, and hopes his efforts are successful. We also spoke about the need to remunerate the governors and vice-governors, who cannot assume their duties in a satisfactory way if, not being paid, they have to take care of other businesses in order to make a living.

October 27th, 1853

We arrived in Loreto on Wednesday, the nineteenth day of this month, after having run onto a sandbank the night before near the island of Cacas. Thanks to a dozen Indians who came to help us, we were able to get out of a tight spot.

Since the boat only stopped for around an hour in Loreto, I barely had time to pack my bags, shake hands with Senor Ortiz, as well as other locals that I knew, and get back on the steamboat. The farewell between the ship's officers and the Peruvian authorities was frosty, despite all the assurance and the usual pleasantries. I will explain why later.

In Loreto, I found several emigrants who had come from Caballococha, among them Messrs. Fialon and Dubordieux, who also bid farewell to the colony with other intentions. Mr. Fialon, who is always sober but does not know the country, wants to partner with an American from the United States, who is always inebriated yet knows the country very well. All this will be in order to negotiate, even settle somewhere on the Ucayali River, whose waters are teeming with fish and whose forests are rich with sarsaparilla and vanilla. This project looks sound to me and would seem to have a future if his partner did not have, in my opinion, two very bad qualities: 1) he is a citizen of the United States, where by nature there are few scruples where business is concerned, and 2) he is regularly inebriated and rarely sober.

It must be said however, when the American starts to drink, he behaves like a good boy, and is exceedingly generous about inviting others to drink with him. He does have some education and a practical knowledge that allows him to conceal his ignorance of the country. He has built towers for churches that did not have any, cast bells, and directed other public works and construction projects. For all of these reasons, he enjoys a good reputation in the Maynas province. As for me, I hope this time that I was mistaken by his American ways and that Mr. Fialon has found a partner who will make him wealthy as soon as possible.

Mr. Dubordieux has spent a great part of his life as a store clerk, dealing with silk and other things that are soft to the touch. He discovered only after a few days that he was totally incompetent when it came to wielding a pioneer's ax. After leaving Caballococha without shedding tears, he came to Loreto to see if in offering his services he could find a way aboard the Marajo. Once he told me what his intentions were and asked me to introduce him to the ship officers, I did so but was not able to have him embark without his paying for his trip, as I would have liked. Those gentlemen did not want to create a precedent, therefore only after the payment of eighteen piasters was he welcomed aboard as a second-class passenger until Barra.

In that respect, I had not been as lucky as the Careys who had succeeded in getting one of their fellow countrymen onboard without a fare. That passenger was also an emigrant and as a professional musician, had been convinced by Ijurra to come to these parts. Ijurra had promised that he would make a small commission that could make him wealthy. When he asked about this commission, Ijurra simply laughed in his face. He has since decided to go back to where music is appreciated. In the meantime, he earns his passage living the sailor's life, which also seems to go against his ideas of harmony.

The reason why I tell you this is because it is the story of three-quarters of the emigrants, who, after living the good life in Lima, gave up what they had for an uncertain alternative. According to what I heard coming from the colony, it appears that some of them took advantage of the possibility of leaving that the colonel had offered them, should they choose to do so. Consequently, from the ninety or more who had arrived, there are only forty to fifty left who, I have heard, work arduously cutting down the forest bordering the village.

My former servant and Hauenstein left with six or seven companions for Lima, after stealing the canoe that they will use to go upstream. It is a fact that those who left just after their arrival did not deserve to be pitied. Apparently, not only did they not like to work, but on top of that they did not make an effort to see if there was anything that could be done. They retreated in the face of hardships that any man who comes to colonize a country as new as this one must initially endure.

The country is so rich and abundant, even more so if you come to know it and work on it. For my part, after a period of one to two years, an intelligent and hard-working man could amass a large number of material resources here. Ijurra treats them haughtily when they come to Loreto individually, but he will certainly avoid going to the colony in Caballococha. It is set against him in such a way that due to all the false promises that he made, he would certainly not make it back to Loreto in one piece.

Therefore, de Schütz is still in charge of most of the work, something that he manages well to everyone's general satisfaction. Without precisely offending me, Mr. Ijurra had vexed me so many times during the trip that I decided to treat him contemptuously at the end of the trip. I did not want to do it earlier because many in the first class wanted him to keep his authority, which is necessary in expeditions such as this, and I found it already so compromised that I did not want to weaken it any more. But I have to admit that when I met him again in Loreto, I found him so low and so changed both from fatigue and drink.

He was stung daily by the colonel's ironic and contemptuous criticism of him and his expedition, and by the disdainful welcome he had received. Seeing him so overwhelmed and so rightfully punished, I did not want to be the latest one to add my blow to so many others. Therefore, I simply kept my feelings to myself, turning my back and completely ignoring him.

When we left for Nauta, the steamboat's headcount was large; now in leaving Loreto, it is but a handful: the officers, the Polish major, and myself. All of them speak Portuguese, and despite its resemblance to Spanish I have yet to grasp it. I have been feeling quite lonely since our departure from Loreto, and I am not on good terms with the Polish major, so my French and German are therefore useless to me.

I cannot quite count as distractions the few conversations that I had with the officers on board, with whom I cannot sympathize much. While knowing how impatient I am, for health and other reasons, to get back to my country, they do not want to grant me the passage to Pará and leave me at Barra. There I will have to wait for twenty-five days until another steamboat arrives, which as a result would waste a very good opportunity to reach Pará, from where I have decided to immediately sail back to France.

The gentlemen pretend that they have a few explorations on their way back that preclude strangers from participating, which seems utterly absurd. I do not believe them and I see other motives for this decision, about which I will divulge later. I will leave that issue and return to my description.

We are traveling a part of the river between Tabatinga and Barra do Rio Negra which is called the Solimões. I will attempt to describe its banks, its villages, and their inhabitants, or at least as much as I can discern when the steamboat passes by, and when both your mind and body are fatigued, as mine are right now, due to my previous long journeys.

The first place we disembarked after just two or three hours was Tabatinga, on Peru's side of the border with Brazil. I had been told that Tabatinga was a fort. All I saw there was kind of dovecote (they say it is a tower), along with two cannons that were cast in Genoa two centuries ago and that have been here for a very long time. The grass has covered the cannon stands so well that you almost have to dig in order to know upon what those innocent guns retained from their voyage. Lastly, there was a poor young officer, I say poor because he was unfortunate enough to lose his mind so completely that those who knew him years ago as being good and friendly do not recognize him anymore.

This dovecote is what defends the Brazilian border. Add to this the officer's house; plus two or three shabby-looking houses belonging to natives; a few stakes that announce the ruins of a stronghold; a garrison of about twelve men with huge holes in the elbows of their shirts, making long faces, because their captain, a lunatic, does not pay them. Finally, visit Mr. Favre from Bordeaux, who will welcome you cordially in his poor shack where he has been living for twenty years, and I expect that you will tell me that you will not go see Tabatinga.

On Friday the 21st, if I am not mistaken, we reached São Paulo de Olivença, where we knocked on all the doors with no answer for good reason—everybody had gone to a nearby beach to make tortoise oil. Almost all houses are made of adobe, and despite their rather miserable appearance, they are fairly well aligned, so you know that the grass you are walking on is also the street. It is so green and dense that you will also easily understand that the cattle you meet here do not need to go far to graze.

The gardens that exist are for the most part found behind the houses, and together with the courtyards, are so dirty and badly maintained that you quickly realize that disorder is not always artistically pleasing.

Finally, upon leaving the first Brazilian village that I encountered, and comparing it with the villages of the Maynas province in Peru, I was thinking that the latter were, if not beautiful, at least far more original than the Brazilian villages—with their Indian reed-and-thatch huts, separated from each other by courtyards and *huertas* (gardens), and planted with an irregularity that grants them some freedom and allow them to partly hide under the shade of their banana trees. The Brazilian villages, whose poor and dilapidated houses with their so-called alignment, looked to me like a savage who was proud to wear European rags.

The only superiority that São Paulo de Olivença appears to have, in my mind, is that it stands on higher ground, compared to the banks of the Amazon in general. Thus, it has magnificent views of the river, which is always beautiful, grand, and vast.

BARRA DO RIO NEGRO

October 28th, 1853

On Saturday the 22nd, we stopped at the lovely village of Fonte Boa. I use the term lovely because, as opposed to the village I described earlier, Fonte Boa is comprised of houses which had to be spread out because of the land and the hills on which the village stands. This encouraged the shadows and greenery that are, in my opinion, the greatest ornament in the village. The insides of the houses are cleaner and tidier than the Peruvian houses. Yet the extreme simplicity you meet makes you realize that you still are in a very new country, far from any civilized location.

Mr. Pinto, the ship's second-in-command and I visited many houses in order to purchase *chimbale*—truly extraordinary jungle animals. Mr. Pinto himself bought two cuilleteros, which are white swamp birds, similar in appearance to small storks, with a flattened beak in the shape of a spoon (in Spanish, *cuchara*) that gave them their name. He also bought a well domesticated toucan and two other birds that could not be separated.

I bought a monkey that people call a macaca, who is supposed to be the most active and mischievous of all the chimbale. They are short rather than tall; the have nice brown-to-gray fur that completely turns to brown on their head, and they have a very intelligent face. After we finished our tour, and after Pinto bought a grinder in order to make manioc wheat—a grinder being composed of a multitude of small parts artistically set on a small plank—we went back to the small river bank where we first arrived. We found a canoe in which we installed all our equipment and then returned, sailing among a crowd of caimans busy loading up wood and heading toward the Marajo, half a league away.

Sometime after we re-embarked, a crowd of female Fontaboasians arrived to pay their respects to the captain. He invited them for lunch, which I can assure you that the ladies obliged. I will not say that the race here is ugly, but it is strongly mingled with some Indian blood that, to my opinion, has not made it more attractive. As far as manners are concerned, however, they are correct and polite which compensates in my opinion for the education they lack.

Once the wood was loaded and our lunch finished, we bid farewell to our party and returned to the great river, which the next day took us to the village of Tefé where we remained all day Sunday, visiting many illustrious locals who seemed in good spirits and joined us for dinner onboard.

The town of Tefé does not look bad at all. Its single-story, very white buildings stand out boldly against the large forest that borders the city and the vast lawn on which it sits. At its feet is one of those small, pretty lakes, like those that you often find on the shore of Solimões. They are always surrounded by a beautiful ribbon of forest, rarely interrupted by some *aloee* (Indian village). Before you get to the lake, you have to go across a beautiful sandy beach where a multitude of canoes is gathered and some small boats or *garites* anchor. The garites are used for business on the Amazon. Despite their heavy appearance and their truncated prow, they nevertheless look quite picturesque.

I will not say that the standards of indoor luxury are high in Tefé, but you will always find the most humble cottage to be clean and tidy. There are not many industries in these Brazilian villages except for tortoise oil, sarsaparilla, and elastic gum, all of which the neighboring Indian tribes collect.

You look for tortoise eggs during the six months when the river level is low; during the other six months, when the river level is high, you rest. If the people here do not demonstrate much learning, you cannot deny that they are polite and affable, which delights foreigners, especially when there is no need to be convinced.

We left Tefé Monday morning after a visit from representatives of the fairer sex, who are more cheerful than gracious. When we weighed anchor, I worked on one last drawing that these good people admired, although they did not know how to use a pencil.

From there, we only stopped once, two days later, to retrieve wood from a beach. We were then supposed to come straight to Barra do Rio Negro, had not fate decided otherwise and had our boat run onto a sandbank rather completely, so we were only able to escape after thirty-two hours with the help of Indians that the captain had sent for.

However, the Marajo had been luckier than its sister ship, the Rio Negro. Upon our arrival here, the first thing we learned was that it had run without mercy onto a reef near the mouth of the Madeira. Fortunately, nobody was lost but what a tragedy for the steamboat that was brand new and apparently very beautiful.

As far as the visual aspects of Solimões are concerned, from Tabatinga to here, they demonstrate a grandeur that is imprinted on this river, yet without any variation. Despite all the islands that one can see, it is monotonous and one eventually becomes bored. You can, however, see elevated banks that protect the villages and their inhabitants from flooding when the river is high. Compared to the banks of the Marañón, the Solimões are considerably less populated. What also struck me is that I have encountered far fewer Indians, which would therefore explain the smaller population.

The government here has made less of an effort to take the Indians out of their forests, given that the Brazilian whites would be less compatible with them.

ABOARD THE MARAJO

October 29th, 1853

The grounding of the Rio Negro, although unfortunate, helped me in one sense: it prevented me from reaching Pará too quickly and from waiting there until the first opportunity for a return voyage arose. Waiting can go on forever in these countries where many things, especially communications, are still uncertain.

Since all correspondence stayed with the grounded steamboat, our ship received the order to fetch it and then go directly to Pará. You will therefore understand that the explorations are reinforced and the passengers are allowed, which is better. I will admit that, after my tour of Barra, I found it to my liking enough to want our ship to stay at least three to four days more. However, as I had the choice between leaving almost immediately or waiting indefinitely, I decided to choose the first option, especially since my money has considerably dwindled given the high cost of the voyage on the Marajo, the trip from Loreto to Pará alone costing one hundred and twelve piasters.

Our ship is moving around so much that I have to delay until tomorrow or another day the little description that I can and wish to give you of the town of Barra. But no, now we are dropping anchor, due to the darkness and our need to be more prudent since the Rio Negro tragedy. This turn of events allows me to tell you what the town of Barra looks like and how I spent two extra hours there.

A name like Barra do Rio Negro will tell you that it is built on the banks of the river that really deserves its name of Rio Negro, or black river, since its waters are indeed very dark. In my opinion, the black color does not spoil the river's appearance. On the contrary, I think that it contrasts nicely with the whiteness of the houses, and the sandy banks at the foot of the city, as well as with the surrounding greenery and the tropical sky. The city itself is consistent in that it is built on three different hills, separated by water in times of floods and linked at all time by bridges that add a touch of originality.

The one- and two-story houses are mostly white, as I said, and are generally clean and well maintained. The streets are a delight for botanists. Grass grows very luxuriously and is only trod upon by cows, not by any wheels, since neither carts, chariots, nor wheelbarrows are things that have ever been seen at Barra since its founding. Ah, I am actually mistaken; two attempts of using wheelbarrows have been made by the Polish major in order to build some sort of fortifications. But these attempts have been unsuccessful. Because of their poor construction, the wheelbarrows broke soon after they were used the first time. It seems that these vehicles will continue to stay off the streets near Barra, unless the major makes a third and more successful attempt.

I passed by two or three shops in the hopes of buying cigars, and could only find loathsome ones, although the shops in question looked clean and orderly enough to inspire admiration as well as confidence.

If you can call an acquaintance someone that you only met for three hours, I will have made two. The first, Mr. Herrion, is a Belgian who makes his living as a tutor and who had been highly recommended by the Careys. In the short amount of time I spent with him, I find him a good man, and I enjoyed his company very much.

The second acquaintance that I made is Father Grégoire, a Capuchin missionary from Piedmont. He is a kind old man with a good face and an enormous white beard, as you would expect a Capuchin to look. He just arrived from inland on a tributary of the Rio Negro, where he says he managed to baptize around thirty individuals in twenty-two tribes. He says baptism is a difficult task, full of sacrifices of all kinds, and not with many spiritual benefits or intellectual resources for Indians. They accept baptism, but without great enthusiasm. They take it as a blessing analogous to the ones they think they receive from their idols whom they continue to respect, along with the new God they have just embraced.

If I left these two gentlemen in friendship, it is exactly the opposite with the Polish major who stayed completely angry at me, due to a slight upbraiding I gave him for his lack of tact. While he is a good man with a fine character, he has strange ideas about manners, which cannot match his strong expectations or bring about the attention he desires.

Speaking of strength, there is supposedly a fort in Barra. Indeed, just before leaving, I noticed something on top of a butte that looked like an old wall, with a flag pole and an unbelievable beam. Perched on top of the beam, I noticed—to my great pleasure—many gallinaceans or domestic vultures that are rumored to be the only creatures to guard the place, since time immemorial.

November 4th, 1853

After more than an hour, you leave the Rio Negro and enter the Amazon region. At this point, you notice that the Rio Negro really deserves its name, for it is that huge basin, the meeting point of these two great rivers, where you can see Negro's distinctly black waters mix with the Amazon's white ones. The river is as large and magnificent, almost as vast as the Great Lakes of the United States, with several large islands whose shapes are in harmony with the rest of the landscape.

Like its banks, the islands of the Amazon are always flat and without the slightest elevation. The islands are so big that you easily confuse them for the banks. What's more, since they have been formed by the river's alluvial deposits, they constantly change form, growing bigger or smaller, even appearing or disappearing.

This is the reason why a large island that appeared on Mr. Mauraval's 1846 map of the Amazon, drawn from the mouth of the river to Óbidos, has completely disappeared. However, in some other spot in the river, another island will have formed. Needless to say, the sandbanks and shores change just as frequently, due to the immense power of the river.

This naturally leads me to the accident of the Rio Negro that we found the next morning, on the rocks where it wrecked. Since no maps or surveying has ever been made of the whole section of the river up to Óbidos—as the government or even the company in charge of navigation should have performed—this accident is even less surprising and cannot be the responsibility of the captain. This is especially true when you consider the following: these stones and rocks that sit in the middle of the river) which is more than half a league wide at this point) are so rarely visible when the waters are low, that only very few people knew of their existence, and even they were unable to tell precisely where they were.

Furthermore, the waters of the Amazon are so naturally troubled that only three inches beneath the surface of the river, it is impossible to distinguish anything. Why would anyone then be surprised if the Rio Negro met its disastrous fate in such waters? I repeat, everything that is related to the laws and modifications of this river is directly related to the mass of its waters and the power resulting from it. Thus, in Loreto, between the low and high levels of the water, there is a thirty- to forty-foot difference. In Santarém, the average hourly speed of ships by month is as follows:

November: 2 knots

December and January: 3 knots

February and March: 4 to 5 knots

April, May and June: 6 to 7 knots

July and August: 6 to 5 knots

September and October: 4 to 3 knots

The overall speed also depends on the volume and the current of the water. In Santarém, the river reaches its greatest heights in June, around the fifteenth, and its lowest level in November; while in Loreto, it is pretty much the other way round. When we came down from Nauta, for example, the river started to rise and would, according to Mr. Ortiz, rise to its highest at the end of November or beginning of December.

This difference which seems surprising at first can be explained by the difference of levels and positions of the tributaries that generally become more powerful, and consequently more influential, as the Amazon gets closer to its mouth.

Thus, the timing of the rise of the water level of the Tapajós, Madeira, Rio Negro, etc. differs from the ones of the Ucuyali, Huallaga, St. Jago, the latter taking place far earlier than the former. Furthermore, as these tributaries grow, they start flooding the low lands around them. This delays the timing of the rise of the water level of the main river which starts to flood the upper parts of its course.

You will understand that navigation, on both the main river and its tributaries, is regulated mostly by the laws that determine the most favorable moment to navigate upstream and downstream. When the level of the river is at its lowest, as it is now, the high tide is felt up to Santarém, that is at [....] leagues from the ocean, and manages to raise the level by half a foot, while at the maximum rise of the water level, it has no effect whatsoever.

Let us go back to the Rio Negro, after this rather long but necessary digression. I will tell you that we found the steamship literally nailed to those rocks, with its stern up in the air and its prow aiming towards the water. The reason is that after hitting the rock in the first place, the strength was great enough to make it rise up, and then down onto the tip of the rock which penetrated its keel. This actually broke the boat's fall and therefore saved it from going further down. It also saved the Rio Negro from an even greater misery since, broken as it was, had it been able to continue its voyage, it would have sunk in the depths around the reef. This way, thanks to Providence, no loss of human life occurred and most of the machinery could be saved as well as much of the cargo. The ship hands were still working on breaking it down when we arrived. It is indeed a great loss for the company, since this steamboat was not only beautiful, but very reliable.

As for me, what disturbed me the most was the misery of the captain who, although innocent of the accident, has found himself for almost a month left alone on the beach, facing his stricken vessel, every day busily removing everything that can still be used. I sympathized even more with his miserable condition, given that he seems to be a very good and dignified man. The accident took place on October 14th, the day when the Marajo arrived in Nauta. It sadly occurred on the captain's birthday, and ironically two days later, the river had sunk low enough for the rocks to be seen above the water's surface.

November 5th, 1853

Monsieur Carey, who spent three months at Barra, had given me a letter of recommendation for Henriquez Anthony, rightfully nicknamed the "Father of Foreigners," for his hospitality toward them has become fairly proverbial. Indeed, as soon as a foreigner arrives in Barra, Henriquez Anthony waits when he disembarks and tells him: "Come to my house, you are a foreigner." Or, if the visitor goes elsewhere, he will ask him, as if it were natural: "Why didn't you come to my house? It is to my house that foreigners go." For more than twenty years, Anthony has called Barra home, and he displays his marvelous hospitality with the same nobility and altruism. This is even more praiseworthy since Brazilians do not like strangers—so foreigners will consequently find themselves alone and deprived of any hospitality. Henriquez Anthony understands that, and as a good European, since he is an Italian from Livorno, he took the noble task of hospitality under his charge. When you hear the residents of the river speak of him, this is supposedly only one of the many qualities that make him so beloved by all.

When Anthony learned about the Rio Negro's tragedy, two big tears ran down his cheeks and he immediately left with his people and one of his *montarias* (river boats) to rescue the survivors. Therefore, I met him in Barra. He had arrived two weeks earlier, leaving his own business behind, and was thinking about staying a few extra days. Had I not been aware of the reputation he enjoys everywhere that people know him, his good, lovely, and loyal face and his benevolent manners would have instinctively produced the same effect upon me.

Although I only spent a little time with him, I will always treasure fond memories of our meeting. Was it because I was both a traveler and a foreigner and I had met people who more or less hate Europeans? I felt and understood everything about this generous man who, through the inclination of his heart, braved public opinion and assumed for himself this noble mantle that so many others refuse. How precious then, under such circumstances, is it for a foreigner to meet such a man on his journey!

Continuing our journey, we went through Serpa, Villa-Bella, Óbidos, Santarém, and Gurupá, which we reached this morning. Serpa is a poor village and there is nothing to miss when you see it in the dark. Its main industries are salted fish and tobacco: shopkeepers get the fish from the Rio Purús, and the tobacco principally from a supplier in Borba, a town that sells superior-quality tobacco for between twenty and thirty thousand reis (between sixty and ninety francs) per thirty-two pounds arrobe. In Peru and this part of Brazil, tobacco is prepared in *masos*, or long rolls carefully wrapped or twisted with reeds.

Villa-Bella is hardly nicer, and nonetheless managed to get its name which means "beautiful village." The main crops here are also tobacco and salty fish, from the species called Pirarucu, as well as some cocoa. Óbidos is undoubtedly, in my opinion, the loveliest place on this part of the river. This little town is located, I will say a bit pedantically, on the continuation of a long sort of cliff that the river forms, approximately a league from its course and on its left bank from the mouth of Rio Trombetas. This continuation forms like a harbor flanked on its left, but mostly on its right, by fast but wooded slopes that nicely surround the few houses that are on the beach, as well as the ones that are on the ridge at top of the hill. From the river, most of the town that sits on a plateau looks shabby. I took advantage of the moment when they were loading up fish to take a walk through the town. I found straightforward streets and some good-looking houses, as well as a church that is one of the most respectable-looking churches that I have encountered on this river.

As in Barra and further away in Santarém, there is a fort, but in all these locations, there are only old ruined walls, protected by one or two defunct canons that you will certainly have trouble discovering if you do not find someone obliging enough to tell you about their existence and location.

It is in Óbidos that the river is at its lowest level, from Barra down to its mouth. Furthermore, there is a very strong current and a great depth of sixty fathoms, so they say. Óbidos could be a very good military position and therefore a stronger fort should be built there. In Óbidos, we took passengers, two ladies and three gentlemen who block the deck with their hammocks, which annoys me since I like to take walks on the deck that seems to be built for that reason. As for this little inconvenience, this added society did not do me the smallest good since these people are quite insignificant, especially for me. I do not understand much Portuguese and do not wish to understand more.

The big industry in Óbidos is cocoa. A large part of the river neighboring it contributes to the cultivation of this plant and its related farms. Cocoa is, so to speak, the only culture of this district that supplies a hundred sixty thousand arrobes per year, that is, five million, one hundred and twenty thousand pounds of cocoa. It sells on location right now for two thousand reis per arrobe. That is seven francs and fifty centimes for thirty-two pounds, which would represent forty centimes per pound, therefore an income of two million francs per year. However, I doubt it when I think of how little wealth is displayed here.

PARÁ

November 7th, 1853

From Óbidos, we arrived the following day, after a stop in Santarém, where we spent a whole day or two loading a good deal of salty fish and sarsaparilla. I was very happy to have received a letter of recommendation from Messrs. Carey for Mr. Gouzenne, the French vice-consul here. He welcomed me very warmly and was very kind and obliging, as was his wife.

Mr. Gouzenne has been doing business in this area for more than ten years. He had the pleasure of also welcoming Mr. de Castelnau and Mr. Mauraval who both praise him in their writings, which does not surprise me since I, a much more insignificant individual, find myself in the same position. He had a few interesting notes to share and accompanied me in order to find a trophy head, smoked by the Mundurucús, as well as a headdress.[62] We managed to find the first one, since I found a head from one of the Maures in rather good condition. As for the headdress that I would have desired (even more so because of the perfection of the artwork), I had to renounce the opportunity, because we were not able to find a single one, or have any of them shown to us by the local Jews, who owned several of them.

Mr. Gouzenne expressed a great deal of regret (sincerely, I felt) for not having been able to give me some local specialties that he

---

[62] *A photo of the Mundurucú headaddress that Henri did in fact bring to Switzerland can be found on page 122.*

was completely deprived of at the moment and that he could not get for me on such short notice. However, since he did not want to let me go empty-handed, he gave me five little budgies which, I hope, will accompany me to Europe in good shape, since they are charming.

Mrs. Gouzenne, although she is from Brazil, (or rather because she is) is an exceptional woman. Not only is she her husband's valiant right hand for all business matters but she also has a great passion and appreciation for music.

Without formal training, she managed to play the piano very nicely, which is extraordinary in Santarém, since she is the only lady in town who has such a talent. Furthermore, she is amicable and her conversation is much more cosmopolitan than that of the women in this country in general, who understand their role so poorly that they contribute very little, if at all, to the entertainment of society. The simple reason is that they are locked up most of the time at home, especially when a gentleman comes to call.

It is said that this is because husbands are excessively jealous, which I find absurd. Most women in this country, without doing them any harm, are not very pretty and are usually poorly dressed and groomed.

The contrast is especially great for those who arrive in Lima where women are generally beautiful, very elegant, and not at all reclusive. As for instruction and education, I however think they are worth it. I was charmed to meet that love of, and that instinct and ability for, music with a woman in this country. I promised Mrs. Gouzenne (and I hope I will not forget to send her) some pieces of good music, since the musical repertoires of these countries are not particularly beautiful nor are they easily understood.

Mr. Gouzenne's business focuses on salted fish, sarsaparilla, cocoa, and lastly shipping cattle, oxen, and horses to Pará. Here are the actual prices for these various items, as indicated by Mr. Gouzenne:

	Santarém	Pará
Oxen	20,000 reis = 62 francs	30 to 35,000 reis
Horses	40 to 50,000	50 to 100,000 reis

(They both come from the Villefranche Lake and from the Lago Grande, fifteen leagues northwest of Santarém).

	Santarém	Pará
Cocoa	2,000 to 2,100 reis	2,500 reis
Elastic gum	15,000 reis	20 to 25,000 reis
Sarsaparilla	20,000 reis	25,000 reis
Salty fish	2,500 to 3,000 reis	5,000 reis
Manioc	3,800 reis, that is 2 piasters for a 1 1/2 arrobe basket	
Guarana	30,000 reis	100,000 reis

Cattle is Santarém's largest industry. A great part of the surrounding land is dedicated to raising cattle, especially after the land has been burned for this purpose. Furthermore, land is so inexpensive that an island of a square league, located across from the town of Santarém, only costs Mr. Gouzenne one hundred thousand reis, which is equivalent to [....] francs. Finally, you only need three men to take care of a thousand head of cattle. Cocoa that has been growing in Óbidos for a long time takes, on a daily basis, more space in the district of Santarém that nowadays supplies a hundred and fifty thousand arrobes, that is four million, eight hundred thousand pounds annually.

The fruit of the Guarana tree is crushed by the Indians, mixed with water, then cooked and turned into paste that is sought after in the Mato Grosso province. This is especially true in Cuiabá where they mix a tablespoon of the paste with a glass of water. It is the most popular drink in these parts and one that many people take for their health.

Manioc wheat is to this part of Brazil what the banana is to the Maynas province. Brazilians always have a plate filled with this wheat, next to them on the table, and they eat it, pinch by pinch, all along their meal. You can make it two different ways: either you first put the root in water, after which you peel it, take it apart, and dry it in the oven. It is the farinha de agua, or water wheat. Or you can simply take it apart, or rather, grate it, then you press it to extract the juice and finally you put it to dry in the oven. That is called farinha seca, or dry wheat. I have heard that sometimes, one mixes it with meat juice or tomato juice to enhance the flavor. Foreigners rarely try it. I however find it good and believe that it is better for you than bananas that are very heavy and give you lots of bile.

Lastly, whatever the Amazon Brazilians say, I believe their food is not much better than their Peruvian river neighbors' food. While it is always turtle in all forms and bananas with the latter, it is always farinha and turtle with the former. I am talking about the food that you encounter in the best houses in the villages and towns that we have just visited. Turtle meat is certainly not a bad meat, but it is so greasy and has such a peculiar taste that it manages to disgust a lot of people, especially when it is eaten every single day for lunch and for dinner.

The turtle eggs that we ate so much of during our canoe journey from Chasuta to Nauta are not, to my opinion, better than meat, and an omelet, made with those eggs, as disguised as can be, totally differs from one you make with hens' eggs. If I give you here a rather long digression about the food habits of the residents of the

Amazon, it is because it is unique, and because I find that the way people feed themselves is important in regards to their physiology.

To get back to Santarém and Mr. Gouzenne, I will tell you that, after having dined and spent a very agreeable and instructive day with him, I left him at night to return to my quarters on the Marajo. We weighed anchor the next day at four in the morning. From there to here, thanks to the adobe coal that we found in Barra, we did not stop until Gurupá. We spent part of the morning chatting without much success, with some local gentlemen who deserve the appellation of Philistines that German students generally use to describe bourgeois in general.

The Gurupá's bourgeois ask with much audacity whether there are any fortresses in Peru. This is because they assume, wrongly and absurdly, that three pieces of old walls on top of which an old canon sit all by itself, looking bored, represent what you call a fortress. I deeply wish that these good people never learn of their profound error, since such a discovery could only be harmful to them.

Shortly after leaving Gurupá, that is to say yesterday afternoon, we left the river of the Amazons to enter a narrow river named Limon that will take us to the Parána River. I have to tell you that it is the best way to move between these two rivers. This kind of natural canal is one of the most interesting sections of my river voyage. It is so narrow that only a few feet separate you from either bank. Both banks have remarkable vegetation giving them beauty and vigor; palms becoming the dominant trees in many places. Palm trees are generally not well represented among the vegetation that forms the immense forests that we encountered earlier on our river journey.

After leaving this canal, interrupted from time to time by a pretty farm set in the shade of palm tree groves, we entered a river as large as the Amazon. It does not differ much from it in its general aspect, except maybe for its islands, which are smaller, less flat, and denser with palms, if I may say.

Finally, after a mild storm, followed by some bad luck that always causes us to arrive at the most interesting locations late at night, we landed here around ten o'clock. From the bridge, I saw a string of large shining lights, but nothing more, which forces me to leave you and defer conclusion of my journal until later.

The end of the journal

The Lost Album

Throughout Henri's correspondence many references are made to his artistic endeavors. In doing research on his voyage I often wondered what had become of all his artwork, since only a handful of drawings remain.

Years ago I found proof that there were far more examples of his artwork than I ever knew existed. Around 1920 (or so the story goes) two of his daughters who were living in St. Blaise near Neuchâtel put an album up for sale that contained 130 original drawings that Henri made on his trip. I was only made aware of this album by virtue of documentation concerning its sale.

That being said, I have no idea whom it was sold to, or if it was ever actually sold. I have included the original information on subsequent pages in hopes of one day finding the album of artwork intact.

What also bears mentioning is that there were a couple of glaring errors in the communication about the album. The first error surrounds the countries he visited; to my understanding he never went to either Bolivia or Venezuela. The second error which is more substantive (or was added simply for drama) concerns why he initiated his voyage to begin with. This synopsis states that he left on his journey to console himself over the death of his young bride. His first wife Madelaine Sillem did die tragically six weeks into their marriage, but it was in 1855, a year after he had returned from the Americas.

For sale: An interesting collection of 134 drawings in pencil and sepia, made in 1852, of many striking scenes in the United States, Mexico and Peru by Mr. de Büren.

Address interest to: Mlles de Büren, St. Blaise, near Neuchâtel

The artwork of Henri de Büren

The Baron Henri de Büren was born in 1825 and to console himself over the death of his young bride undertook a voyage to America. In 1852 and 1853, he traveled through the United States, the Caribbean, Venezuela, Bolivia and Peru; and as he was a talented artist he painted and sketched throughout his journey, 130 of his works are united in one album.

The undersigned has had the opportunity to examine this album and recognizes both its artistic and historic value. The work show many aspects of nature and everyday life that are windows into the past from the new world of last century. The work however more than simply documents a moment in time; it is first and foremost great art, from an artist where talent runs in the family. Henri's ancestor Charles-Philippe (1759-1795); born in The Hague, officer in Holland, Baron of Vaumarcus from 1787 and Member of the Grand Counsel of Bern in 1795, produced countless drawings and engravings, many that are still sought after today.

Henri's technical skill is considerable whether with a pencil, a brush with sepia or charcoal. He shows himself adept at evoking sweeping landscapes, picturesque and well ordered as well as people in all their authenticity. He is an amateur that has taken on the qualities of a dedicated professional. Whomever purchases this one-of-a-kind album will not be disappointed.

Maurice Jeanneret

President of the Neuchâtel History and Archaeology Society
Adjunct Conservator of the Fine Arts Museum of Neuchâtel

Collection of drawings in pencil and sepia by Henri de Büren, 1852-1853

1. Niagara
2. Home of Louis Agassiz in New Cambridge
3. Niagara Falls (Canada Side)
4. Illinois Prairies
5. Niagara rapids
6. Niagara
7. Lake George (New York State)
8. Lake George
9. Niagara Falls (U.S. side)
10. The Mississippi River
11. The Hudson River
12. View of Alpina (New York State)
13. Home of Mr. Warmouth (Prairies)
14. Forest swamps in Louisiana
15. Trees on the property of Dr. Holbrook, near Charleston
16. Rural Cotton gin
17. Cotton shipment
18. Steam powered cotton gin (New Orleans)
19. Aboard the Portermak
20. Caldwell and Lake George
21. Indians near New Orleans
22. Cotton gins on the river bank in Alabama
23. Cotton transport in Alabama
24. Saratoga Springs Lake
25. The Mississippi River near Cairo
26. Farm in United States
27. Tugboat on the Lasalle Canal
28. Chicago

29. Ticonderoga River rapids

30. Plank road near Niagara Falls

31. Cape Vincent

32. Lake Georges

33. Near Matanzas, Cuba with view of the Cumbe

34. Near Matanzas, Cuba

35. Plantation between Havana and Matanzas

36. Pamhaya near Mexico City

37. Elhappi, Mexico

38. Former residence of Cortès in Cuernavaca, Mexico

39. San Nicolás de Los Ranchos. Mexico

40. Las Vigas canal, Mexico City

41. In the vicinity of Atlixco, Mexico

42. Jail of Amecameca, Mexico

43. Cacahuamilpa grotto, Mexico

44. Hacienda resevoir between Atlixco and Matamoros

45. Silver mines of Pachuca, Mexico

46. Garden in Cuernavaca, Mexico

47. Popocatépetl crater, Mexico

48. Bewteen Atlixco and Matamoros, Mexico

49. Church in Tacubaya, Mexico

50. Ordonia falls near Cuautepec, Mexico

51. Popocatépetl crater, Mexico

52. Origata crater, Mexico

53. Main Square, Atlixco, Mexico

54. Tacuha cedar, under which Cortés rested after the battle of the noché triste.

55. Miraflores, Mexico

56. Jalapa, Mexico

57. Catherdral of Mexico City

58. Las Vigas canal, Mexico City

59. Perote's coffer as seen from Jalapa

60. Almanac of famous Mexicans

61. San Francisco church door, Mexico City

62. Cholula pyramid near Puebla

63. Conja garden near Matanzas, Cuba

64. Molingo falls near Jalapa

65. Preira calciente, Mexico

66. Near San Nicolás de Los Ranchos, Mexico

67. Near the Real de Monte mines

68. Regla falls near Real de Monte

69. Franco-Mexican college in San Cosme

70. Chapultepec castle

71. General view of Panama City harbor

72. Cedar

73. Mexican indians in San Nicolás de Los Ranchos

74. Mexican indians

75. Matamoros

76. Arcades of a church destroyed by an earthquake in Cholula, Mexico

77. The main street of Jalapa

78. Morro castle in Havana

79. Loreto, Peru

80. Cloister of the church of San Francisco, Lima, Peru

81. Indian church on the Huallaga river bank, Peru

82. Marañón, Peru

83. Morro mountain near Moyobamba, Peru

84. Church of Chacapoyas, Peru

85. Marañón River, Peru

86. Church in Moyobamba, Peru

87. The Mayo River near Moyobamba, Peru

88. Moyobamba seen from the Mayo River

89. Cordilleras

90. The Amazon River at Petas

91. Callo, Peru

92. Church in Chasuta, Peru

93. Main square in Lima

94. Women of Lima

95. Women of Lima

96. On the Amazon River

97. On the Amazon River

98. Chacapoyas, Peru

99. Indian village bordered by cacti, Mexico

100. Ruins of Xochicalco, Mexico

101. Port of Acapulco, Mexico

102. Cerro Paulino

103. Marching Peruvian soldiers

104. The Amazon – Large format drawing

105. Town of Eja, Brazilian Amazon

106. Hacienda of Miacaltán, Mexico

107. The steamboat Marajo

108. My canoe on the Amazon River

109. My canoe on the Amazon River

110. Island before our arrival in Panama

111. Fort of San Juan de Ulúa, Veracruz, Mexico

112. Brazilian fort in Tabatinga, Brazil

113. Peruvian village between Santiago and the Cordilleras

114. Celendín, Peru
115. Peruvian indians
116. Bull wrangler, Lima
117. Negroes playing with Bull
118. In between Nexim and Acapulco, Mexico
119. Church of Acahuizolta, Mexico
120. Trees on the Amazon river banks near Loreto, Peru
121. The Huallaga river
122. São Paulo de Olivença, Brazil
123. Indian village, Peru
124. Amazon
125. Tambo of Talavera, Peru
126. Small island at the confluence of the Japurus River, Peru
127. Panama
128. On the Ohio River, United States
129. On the Alabama River, United States
130. 14 sketches
131. 8 small drawings
132. Mosquitoes
133. 2 sketches
134. On the road to Acapulco, Mexico

Glossary

Aguaceras—Downpours

Aparejos—Packsaddle

Arrieros—Muleteers

Arrobe—A weight measurement of roughly 25 pounds

Banderilleros—A torero who plants colorful sticks with a barbed point on the top of the bull's shoulder

Barranca—A deep ravine or gorge

Borracho—Drunk

Calvilde—Commerce house

Camino Real—Royal Road

Caña brava—Wild sugar cane

Cañada—Glen, mountain valley

Candlemas—Festival that commemorates the presentation of the Child Jesus to the temple

Chacaros—Indian women

Chacra—Country house

Chicha—Corn beer

Cholos—Mixed-race designation

Cordilleras—An extensive chain of mountains or mountain ranges in the Andes

Creoles—Native born subjects of Spanish colonies or mixed-race designation

Hacienda—Estate

Garapates—Tics

Gobernadors—Governors

Guarapo—Fermented sugar cane juice

Lavaderos—Gold Panners

Leagues—The Spanish league was a measurement of roughly three miles

Malacate—A winch typically used in mining

Masato—Drink made from the root of the cassava plant

Mescado—Drink made from fermented yucca

Mestizo—Someone of mixed-race (European and Amerindian) descent

Piaster—A unit of Latin American currency

Picadors—One of the pair of horsemen in a bullfight that jab the bull with a lance

Poncho—A traditional Peruvian outer woolen garment to keep the wearer dry and warm

Pronunciamento—A declaration of opposition to the government by a group of military officers. A form of military rebellion or coup d'état particular to Spain, Portugal and Latin America in the 19th century.

Putrine—Two-wheeled horse drawn carriage

Semanero—Weekly worker

Tambo—An inn found along Incan roads

Toreador—Bull fighter

Viguëla—Guitar

Volante—Two-wheeled horse drawn carriage

Name Index

A

Agassiz, Louis 11, 14, 17, 30, 40, 41
Almy 130
Anschlitz 95
Ansoatigi 58, 59, 67, 68
Anthony, Henriquez 286
Atahualpa 151

B

Bandelier 26, 27
Barnum, P.T. 34
Béarn (de), Count 72, 74, 77, 81, 82, 83, 84, 86, 88, 95, 165
Beategui 238
Bénéché 58, 59, 60, 73, 74
Berger 95
Bességil 175, 176, 184, 188, 194, 231
Blum, Robert 262
Bocanegra 269
Bofin (de), Alvarez 232
Braillard 24
Brennan 60
Büren (de), Charles Jules 235
Büren (de), Wilhelmine 89

C

Carey 266, 267, 269, 281, 289
Castelnau (de) 289
Ceballos, Juan Bautista 65
Charpentier, Charles 218, 232
Colomb 25
Cortés, Hernán 61, 67, 68, 70, 76, 87

D

Degola 148, 149, 232
Del Aguila, Don Julian 216
Del Barrio 84
Del Barrisa 71
Domingo 151

Dominico 196, 207, 226, 257, 263
Don Ambrosio 182
Don José 168, 196, 227
Don Lorenço 252
Don Lucas 194, 196
Don Luis 144
Don Pablo 241
Don Pedro 135, 153
Don Ruiz 155, 157, 168, 228
Dubordieux 261, 262, 271, 272

F

Falconnet (de), François 59, 60, 63, 65, 70
Father Grégoire 282
Faverger 27
Favre 275
Ferrera, Don Juan 10
Fialon 261, 262, 271
Freudenberger, Sigmund 23, 162
Freudenreich (de) 23, 24

G

Garalli 75
Girard, Stephen 38
Gouzenne 289, 291, 293
Graffenreid (de), François 15, 24, 25, 26, 28, 30
Gray, Asa 15, 16, 30
Guyot 27
Guyot, Arnold 11, 13, 30

H

Hauenstein, Robert 228, 231, 234, 236, 245, 252, 259, 261, 262, 273
Herrion 281
Holbrook, Dr. John Edwards 41, 42
Humboldt (von), Alexander 64

I

Ijurra, Don Manuel 93, 102, 135, 158, 162, 163, 170, 175, 176, 181, 182, 183, 188, 192, 195, 196, 198, 199, 202, 203, 206, 207, 208, 226, 227, 257, 263, 272, 273

J

Jeker 61
Jürgens, Auguste 137, 164, 187, 228, 231, 234, 252, 261

K

Krüger 185

L

Lama 155, 157, 158, 199, 226
Lamas 269
Laval (de) 61, 65
Leisen 76
Lesanna 55
Lesquereux, Leo 16, 30, 31
Lopez, Purificación 242

M

Magherns 55
Mama Ocllo 147
Manco Cápac 147
Mauraval 283, 289
Mazendorf 10
Middleton, Oliver 10
Mildmay 70
Montoya 168, 178, 194, 196
Moret 242, 243, 244, 245
Müller 100
Murillo, Bartolomé Esteban 75

O

Ortiz 155, 157, 168, 196, 208, 226, 232, 262, 271, 284

P

Pahud 23

P

Peabody 10
Penn, William 39
Perret 100
Pillichody, Charles 45, 73
Pinto 277
Pizarro, Francisco 104, 146
Pourtalès (de), Louis François 40

R

Radepont (de), Marquis 56, 61, 64, 72, 74, 75, 77, 78
Rham 45
Robertson 67, 68
Ross 75

S

Sand 95
Sattler, Hubert 36
Schnitzler 44, 48, 52, 129, 131
Schütz (de), Damian 93, 101, 135, 158, 172, 183, 184, 185, 187, 188, 195, 196, 198, 199, 202, 203, 206, 226, 257, 262, 273
Siegnitz 200, 206
Sillem, Wilhelm 58, 59, 63
Smith 98
Sullivant, William Starling 31

T

Turnbull 76

V

Volz 45

W

Wahl 98
Warmouth 27
Wild 60

Z

Zamora (de) 76
Zangroni 65
Zelaeger 101

Made in the USA
Monee, IL
07 July 2026

56544702R00187